TAROT
FOR
YOUR
SELF

A WORKBOOK FOR PERSONAL TRANSFORMATION

BY

MARY K. GREER

NEWCASTLE PUBLISHING CO., INC.
NORTH HOLLYWOOD, CALIFORNIA
1984

Photographs by Ed Buryn

Original illustrations by Susan St. Thomas

Diagrams by Mary Greer

Cover and book design by Riley K. Smith

Edited by Douglas Menville

Grateful acknowledgement is made for permission to print:

"Six of Cups" copyright 1962 by Diane Wakoski from the book *Inside the Blood Factory* by Diane Wakoski. Reprinted by permission of Doubleday and Co., Inc. "The Empress #8" from *Smudging* by Diane Wakoski. Published by Black Sparrow Press, Los Angeles, copyright 1972. Reprinted by permission of the author. Excerpt from "The Queen of Wands" from the book *The Queen of Wands* by Judy Grahn. Published by The Crossing Press, copyright 1982. Reprinted by permission of the author. "The back fence/the ancient Celtic Cross" from *A Passage of Saint Devil* by Duncan McNaughton. Published by Talonbooks, Ltd., copyright 1976. Reprinted by permission of the author. "What Made Tarot Cards and Fleurs de Lis" from *Selected Poems 1943–1966* by Philip Lamantia, copyright 1967. Reprinted by permission of City Lights Books. Excerpt from "Zero: The Fool" in *Pieces* by Robert Creeley, copyright 1969. Reprinted by permission of Charles Scribner's Sons. Excerpt from *The Greater Trumps* by Charles Williams. Copyright 1950 by Pellegrini and Cudahy. Reprinted by permission of Farrar, Straus and Giroux, Inc. "Princess of Disks," a previously unpublished poem by Diane di Prima, copyright 1983 by Diane di Prima. Printed by permission of the author. "A Tarot Story," a previously unpublished short story by LiAnne Graves, copyright 1984 by Lianne Graves. Printed by permission of the author. Tarot processes developed and taught by Angeles Arrien in her classes used by her permission. Adaptation from "Images of Interpersonal Intuition" from the book *Awakening Intuition* by Frances E. Vaughan. Published by Anchor Books, copyright 1979. Used by permission of the author. Reproductions of the Aquarian Tarot deck, copyright 1970, and the Morgan-Greer Tarot deck, copyright 1979. Used by permission of Morgan Press, Inc. Reproductions of the Church of Light Egyptian Tarot deck, copyright 1936, 1964. Used by permission of the Church of Light. Reproductions of the Motherpeace Tarot deck, copyright 1981. Used by permission of Vicki Noble. Reproductions of the Moon and Sybil cards from the Amazon Tarot deck, copyright 1980 by Elf and Dragon Press. Used by permission of the artist, Billie Potts. Reproduction of the Sage card from the Amazon Tarot deck, copyright 1980 by Elf and Dragon Press. Used by permission of the artist, Prairie Jackson. Reproductions of the Voyager Tarot deck, copyright 1984. Used by permission of Jim Wanless. Reproductions of the Xultun Tarot deck, copyright 1976. Used by permission of the artist, Peter Balin. Tarot cards reproduced by permission of U. S. Games Systems, Inc. from the following decks: Aleister Crowley Thoth Tarot deck, copyright 1978 by U. S. Games Systems, Inc. and Samuel Weiser, Inc. Native American Tarot deck, copyright 1982 by U. S. Games Systems, Inc. Rolla Nordic Tarot deck, copyright 1981 by U.S. Games Systems, Inc. Sacred Rose Tarot deck, copyright 1982 by U. S. Games systems, Inc. All rights reserved. Further reproduction prohibited.
Rider-Waite Tarot cards reproduced by permission of U.S. Games Systems, Inc., Stamford, CT 06902 USA. Further reproduction prohibited.

FIRST EDITION

A NEWCASTLE BOOK

First Printing October 1984

8   9   10

Printed in the United States of America

TO MY PARTNER, ED BURYN
AND
OUR DAUGHTER, CASIMIRA GREER BURYN

ACKNOWLEDGEMENTS

I would first like to thank Tristine Rainer for her book, *The New Diary: How to Use a Journal for Self-Guidance and Expanded Creativity*. It was through reading and working with her book that I realized what was to me of most importance in the Tarot: the personal search for self-understanding. Her book was the key that made all the pieces fit, and she demonstrated through her way of writing—as if she were talking to me as a close friend—the way in which I too wanted to reach my readers. Any similarities between her book and mine are due to my admiration for her writing and the inspiration of her ideas.

There are many readers, artists, teachers, counselors, healers, thinkers, magicians and movers of Tarot, especially in the San Francisco Bay area, that I have been privileged to know and study with. I have used what they have taught me, along with my fifteen years of independent study, to the extent that their ideas have blended and merged with mine. I have tried to acknowledge their seed ideas and creations throughout the book, and I want to give special thanks to: Angeles Arrien, Vicky Noble, Suzanne Judith, Diane di Prima, Dori Gombold, Joanne Kowalski, Jim Wanless, Hilary Anderson, Ed Hoscoe, Tracey Hoover, Jean Samiljan, Gail Fairfield and Luna Moth—all practitioners of the art of Tarot. For what I have learned from them in the fields of psychic development, astrology, healing and crystals I would like to thank: Tamara Diagilev, Oh Shinnah, Merlyn, Dale Walker, Aaron Greenberg and Yana Breeze. And to my best teachers all, my students during the last eight years, I offer this book in gratitude.

Special thanks go to four people who were my coaches and midwives as I gave birth to this work: foremost to my partner, Ed Buryn, who inspired, encouraged, edited, cooked and washed dishes and made this whole book possible. To my friends: artist and astrologer Susan St. Thomas, whose illustrations grace these pages; to Tarot and past-life counselor Dori Gombold, whose writing skills and knowledge of Tarot smoothed many an awkward passage; and to Howard Fallon, who introduced me to the wonders of word processing and provided the computer support.

I've dedicated this book to Ed, who knew I could do it and without whom it would have taken many more years, and to our daughter Casimira, born at the time the book was first conceptualized and who has grown with it.

CONTENTS

SUBJECT DIRECTORY

MANDALAS

ACTIVE IMAGINATION AND VISUALIZATIONS

RITUALS

INTERPRETING THE CARDS AND SPECIAL USES

CREATIVE WRITING

FROM THE RIDER-WAITE—
SMITH deck, originally published in
1910: the illustrations were by scene
designer Pamela Colman Smith
under the direction of occultist Arthur Edward Waite. The Major Arcana cards are laid out in three rows
of seven cards each with the Zero
placed above the others. The first
seven cards represent the body; the
second seven, the mind; and the
third, the spirit. If you add a number
from the bottom row to the number
from the top row directly above it,
then divide that number by two, you
have the number of the card between
them. The number 11 is the
arithmetical mean of all the
diametrically opposed cards such as 1
and 21, 8 and 14, etc. According to
Paul Foster Case, the top row refers
to powers and potencies; the middle
row to laws or agencies; and the bottom row to conditions or effects.
Thus you can say that the power of
Card 1 works through the agency of
Card 8 to modify the effects of Card
15, and so on.

INTRODUCTION

*Now we can see the real use of the Tarot pack. It is for
living in and arranging our lives with. The cards are
the exchange-symbols between inner and outer life. . . .
Altogether the Tarots are a most valuable collection of
psycho-physical currency convertible into either dimension.*
Wm. B. Gray, *Magical Ritual Methods*

The traditional focus of Tarot, at all levels of skill, is to read the cards for
others or to meditate upon their symbols. Yet the fact is that nearly every
Tarot practitioner also reads the cards for him or herself. This widespread
practice expresses a basic need for self-understanding that the Tarot is
uniquely well-suited to fulfill. *Tarot for Your Self* is the first book to focus
directly upon this personal use of the Tarot and provides, through the
workbook format, a place for you to keep a record of your process.

Tarot for Your Self is a tool for achieving self-knowledge. It is designed to
actually teach Tarot, rather than merely explain it, and to help you apply
Tarot to your real-life situations as a practical resource.

It is intended to serve both beginning students and advanced practitioners
by introducing a variety of approaches to the Tarot. These include: meditations, rituals, spreads, mandalas, visualizations, dialogues, charts, astrology,
numerology, and affirmations, all directed toward greater self-exploration.
By examining your past, present and future potential, you will learn to deal
more effectively with your problems, recognize your choices and clarify your
goals. To begin this path to self-knowledge all you need are this book, a
Tarot deck of any design and a pencil.

WHAT TAROT IS

The Tarot is an ancient Western occult psychological and philosophical
system consisting of 78 cards divided into the Major and Minor Arcana. The
22 cards of the Major Arcana represent in archetypal symbols wo/man's
journey through life, a journey which Carl Jung envisioned as the process
of individuation.

The remaining 56 cards, which are the forerunners of our contemporary
playing cards, consist of sixteen Court Cards and 40 "pip" or number cards.
They are divided into four suits: Wands (Clubs), Cups (Hearts), Swords
(Spades) and Pentacles (Diamonds). Each suit has a King, Queen, Knight
and Page (or Princess); cards are numbered from Ace through Ten.

Because the Tarot relies on the universal language of symbolism, its influence has, over several centuries, spread throughout the world unrestricted by language barriers or semantics. And, since symbolism is also the language of the unconscious, the use of the Tarot tends to activate the intuitive mind, or right-brain center. Because of this, the cards have been most commonly used for "psychic" divination based on a variety of layouts, one of the oldest being the Celtic Cross.

A reading consists of shuffling the deck, selecting the cards, arranging them in a particular pattern or layout and interpreting the meaning of the entire symbolic picture in relation to your question, or the current influences in your life.

But working with the Tarot should not be confined merely to random choices of cards. Each card, especially among the 22 Major Arcana, embodies an entire philosophical and psychological text, and any one of them can be selected as a subject for meditation or visualization.

TAROT FOR YOURSELF

Because it is difficult to be objective about your own problems, most books on Tarot suggest ways of reading for others, but discourage reading for yourself. They point out the tendency to read your own desires and fears into the cards; and since most spreads are not designed to offer new options or choices for action, the reader is left with a sense of helplessness.

The Tarot should be approached, not merely as a means for divination, but as a potentially dynamic tool for personal growth and transformation. I have written this book to share with you methods that grew out of my own personal experiences and those of my students. It is dedicated to making the use of Tarot for yourself a powerful and enlightening adventure.

Before you begin, here are several ways to avoid the usual difficulties and confusions of reading for yourself:

1) You don't have to interpret the cards! Do a reading as part of a journal entry and simply observe how the cards relate to what you have written.

2) Tape-record your self-readings and explain everything aloud, just as though you were reading for someone else.

3) Spend time with one reading. Look at it from several different points of view. Leave it out on your dresser to look at.

4) If there is a card that is particularly confusing or upsetting, get to know it through meditation or visualization.

5) Have a friend assist you. Exchange readings in which each of you reads your own cards, but offers commentary and feedback to the other.

6) Use the Tarot for other purposes than readings, such as creating mandalas or stories, or simply describing situations through the symbolism of the cards.

WHICH DECK TO CHOOSE

Since working with Tarot involves relating to symbols, it is important to choose a deck with which you can feel comfortable and familiar. To get the most from the exercises in this book, you will need pictures on all the cards, whereas many decks, mostly European, use abstract designs (similar to modern playing cards) on the Minor Arcana. Any of the following Tarot decks would be suitable for use here, although they only begin to suggest the variety available. You can write for an extensive catalog of decks from U.S. Games Systems, whose address is given in the Bibliography.

DECK	COMMENTS
Rider-Waite-Smith	Published in 1910. The first deck in which the Minor Arcana concepts were illustrated. Pamela Colman Smith was an artist of the "Stieglitz Circle" and set designer for the London and Irish stage. She was also an accomplished storyteller. When someone is in doubt about which deck to buy, I usually recommend this one.
Aquarian	Variation on the Waite-Smith deck. Designed by graphic designer David Palladini in an art deco style.
Morgan-Greer	Variation on the Waite-Smith deck. Bright colors, close-up design, so that the people are emphasized, and background and symbology minimized.
Sacred Rose	Designed by Johanna Sherman. Inspired by the artistry of medieval stained-glass windows and Byzantine icons. Vibrant colors.
Royal Fez Moroccan	Variation on the Waite-Smith deck. Designed by Berrill and Hobdell and based on 12th-century Fez design style. Partially colored, detailed line drawings with the scenes pictured through an arc border.
Thoth	Conceptualized by Aleister Crowley and strikingly illustrated by Lady Frieda Harris. The Minor Arcana do not have scenes pictured, but they do express definite moods and subtle indicators of meaning.
Motherpeace	Designed by Vicki Noble and Karen Vogel to express matriarchal history and reclaim the Great Goddess. This deck is round. Male imagery is minimal. Address: P.O. Box 1511, Cave Creek, Arizona 85331.
Amazon	Originally designed by the Elf and Dragons collective, and now in a revised edition. A combination of line drawings and photographs—some cards having several variations to choose from. No male images. Address: Hecuba's Daughters, Inc., P.O. Box 488, Bearsville, NY 12409.

The New Tarot　Designed by William Hurley and J.A. Horler. Black and white illustrations. Contemporary psychological interpretations with a sense of humor.

Voyager Tarot　Created by Jim Wanless and Ken Knutson as a mirror expression of yourself. It is a universal deck expressing cross-cultural archetypes that are ancient as well as futuristic. Done in striking colorful collage, they feature suits of crystals, cups, wands and worlds. Deck and Voyager Guidebook available from: Voyager Tarot, P.O. Box 1227, Carmel, CA 93921.

Xultun　Designed by Peter Balin. Based on Mayan and Aztec art and mythology. The Major Arcana placed together in order form a Mayan pyramid.

Native American　Designed by Magda and J.A. Gonzalez. Based on lore from all the North American nations.

I have used the Waite-Smith and Crowley-Harris decks as my basic referents in writing the text and in all correspondences between the Tarot, astrology, numerology, Hebrew letters, etc., as summarized in Appendix C.

RATIONAL AND INTUITIVE THINKING

All of us are familiar with the rational-logical way of thinking. It is the way we were taught in school, and it is the way society encourages us to operate throughout our lives. Intuitive thinking is based on "in-sight," the acceptance of an innate harmony in the universe and a meaningful connection between the past, present and future, between ourselves and everything that exists.

The exercises in this book will encourage the use of your intuitive abilities in a systematic way. The workbook format provides a place to record your progress on the path of self-evaluation, a process which can then be continued in a creative and spontaneous manner throughout your life. Your tools are the visual symbols of the Tarot, which transcend the limitations of verbal thinking. Together, they will facilitate the use of both intuitive and analytical thinking in a balanced and harmonious way.

HOW TO USE THIS BOOK

Whether you are a beginner or a more advanced practitioner, it will be to your advantage to work your way through the book chapter by chapter. In this way you will experience the cumulative effects of the way the exercises have been arranged to build the confidence and expertise needed to use the Tarot for yourself as well as for others.

Always remember that this is a workbook: don't just read the exercises, *do them*, and write down your results. It is especially important that you do the beginning exercises spontaneously, not looking up the meanings of the cards, but discovering the unique significance they have for you and trusting your choices. After you've established your own rapport with the symbols, you can begin using the interpretations in Appendix A to expand your knowledge of the symbols. There you will find key questions to pinpoint the specific purposes of the cards in your layouts, and affirmations to program the highest qualities of each card into your thought patterns.

Use this book as a journal, a place to record not only the results of the exercises, but your own personal growth: the insights, thoughts and experiences that occur as a result of your work and meditations. As in any journal, be sure to date your exercises and entries: month, day and year.

It is important at all times to be uninhibited and spontaneous in your writing. You do not have to show your work to anyone else unless you wish to.

The exercise worksheets can be photocopied for your personal use. See the section "Charts" in the Subject Directory for those which would be most useful. However, the formats of these worksheets are meant to be suggestive, not prescriptive, and you should feel free to write in them any way you wish, or on other sheets.

DEVELOPING INTUITION

Since one of the main purposes of this book is to help you develop an awareness of your intuition and how it works, here are a few suggestions with which to approach the exercises:

1) Always write down your impressions and images spontaneously. Write down even those ideas you started to reject; don't censor your thoughts!

2) Be free, open and expressive. Don't worry about spelling and punctuation. Criticism and editing have their place in formal writing, but not in this book.

3) If you write something that seems to be wrong at the time, put a single line through it, so it can still be read. You may see that comment in a different light in retrospect.

4) If you are right-handed, try writing with your left (or vice versa). Although it seems awkward at first, it may free you from rigid patterns of expression.

5) If you get stuck, write the last word over and over until a new thought presents itself—and it will.

6) Fantasize. Lie. Reach for the incredible, the unusual. Into what uncharted realms and surprises can your mind take you?

If writing is not enjoyable or appropriate for you, try taping your impressions, using the same ground rules as above; or verbalize your impressions to a partner. You can even act out the majority of these exercises, or find some other artistic means of expression. The important thing is to express and objectify your intuitive awareness so that by becoming conscious of your behavior patterns you will be free to change them.

THE PHOTOGRAPHS

At the beginning of each chapter is a photograph of Tarot cards laid out in a pattern that can help you understand the relationships, interconnections and deeper meanings of the cards. Their teachings are unlocked primarily by intuitive insight through contemplation of the patterns.

You can learn about the structure of the Tarot and about your own psychic structure from meditating on the visual interrelationships of the cards as explained in the notes accompanying them. Some authors have discussed insights they have had through particular patterns, and I have tried to refer you to those sources in the suggested readings. But, as indicated by the term "meditation," the significance of each pattern is personally and individually divulged, never fully apprehended through verbal means. I have included them here in this book as an indication of a possible further direction for your studies.

SAMPLE EXERCISE

Stop right now and get a pen or pencil and write "Rose" in the space following this paragraph. For five minutes write down every thought that enters your head as you contemplate roses. Use word association, memories, your sense impressions. Write as quickly as possible. Include such thoughts as, "This is silly—I hate roses anyway—what good will this do?" All thoughts are important and must be captured. If images come to mind, capture them in short word pictures; for example:

"Rose red, red rose. Thorns hurt. Scent overwhelms. Blood red and fingers torn but I can't stop myself from stealing the neighbor's rose. Watch the petals blow full, then fall—pool like dried blood."

This example would never win a writing contest, but that is not the point. Humor is a good way to get you started. Think of the most absurd associations you can, be scarcastic or nutty; after all, you are The Fool beginning a new journey. . . .

Roses appear frequently in the majority of Tarot decks. When you have completed your intuitive writing exercise, *but not before*, look through your cards at the way the rose has been used in your deck. Do any of the thoughts you've written give you insights as to why the rose might have appeared in a particular card?

FROM THE SACRED ROSE
TAROT, designed by Johanna Sher-
man and first published in 1982 by
U.S. Games Systems, Inc. The Major Arcana are here arranged in
three horizontal rows by nines. Any
card below will reduce, through add-
ing the digits, to the number in the
top row directly above it; for example,
16 = 1 + 6 = 7. The difference between the higher and the lower
number is always nine, as in
7 + 9 = 16. According to Richard
Roberts, the archetype of each
number is thus raised to another
level by the addition of nine (The
Hermit or Seeker). In his book,
Tarot Revelations, Roberts explores
common motifs in each vertical
series, such as the judging motif in
cards two, eleven and twenty, and
what happens when you add each
card to the succeeding ones.

CHAPTER ONE

GETTING ACQUAINTED WITH THE CARDS

ROTA TARO ORAT TORA ATOR
The wheel of Tarot speaks the law of Hathor.

Deciding to work with Tarot is like embarking on a long journey, an inward journey which cannot be taken lightly. It is a discipline, the origins of which are ancient and obscure. The word "Tarot" has been associated with the Egyptian "royal road of life"; and the anagram "rota," which is Latin for wheel, suggests the means of progressing along that road.

It has also been referred to as a map, or a key. The Major and Minor Arcana into which the deck is divided are "arks," or containers that, according to the *American Heritage Dictionary*, "hold the great secret of nature that alchemists sought to find," the concealed knowledge of the self. Yet at the same time these arcana are the keys that open the container of the self.

Paul Foster Case envisioned the keys of the Major Arcana as making up the structural dimensions of a cube of space—the foundations of our universe. At the heart of this cube is a cross, similar to the rosy cross pictured on the back of the Crowley-Harris Thoth deck.

The Rosy Cross

The French occultists Eliphas Levi and Gerard Encausée (Papus) saw the Tree of Life as a living Tarot landscape, a detailed map of which may be found in Gareth Knight's *A Practical Guide to Qabalistic Symbolism*.

As in the quotation at the beginning of this chapter, "rota" gives the Tarot its definition of "wheel," a spinning center of energy which Charles Williams, in his novel *The Greater Trumps*, described as dancing the dance of life: if you could follow the intricacies of this dance you would be at one with the Fool—the still center of the dance.

The Wheel of Fortune

The Tarot also represents "torah," which translates from Hebrew as "the law." The first five books of the Jewish Testament are also called the *Tora*. The Tarot as a book of "tora" is the law book held in the lap of the High Priestess, representing the law which can only be known by intuition—by personal experience. She is the oracle or sybil, a priestess of Hathor, the

The Fool

The High Priestess

Egyptian earth goddess who predates Isis. The horned headdress of this cow-headed goddess marks the waxing, full and waning moons; the cycle or wheel of creation, the basic measure of time used in all civilizations.

In this chapter you will learn to explore the cards intuitively, opening yourself to your own impressions of the cards—learning what they mean to you. You will learn what you *already* know about them. Expect to surprise yourself with your perceptions. You know more than you think you do!

Several years from now, the things you write in this book will be an important reminder of who you were when you began your journey of self-discovery; so always keep a pen or pencil immediately available to record the thoughts and insights that emerge as you work with the various layouts and exercises. As you read the questions that follow, note your first response; capture it and write it down, spontaneously and without judgment.

What is Tarot? (Write your own definition as if you were explaining it to a friend.) *78 Cards - major + minor arcana - depicting values, forces, directions, encouragement traits, states, obstacles, problems, solutions through a variety of layouts + subject to the interpretation of the reader.*

What do you feel is the purpose of the Tarot Cards?
Expansion of self-awareness; contemplation

What do you want to learn from the Tarot?
More about myself; my place

What are you hoping to gain from this workbook?
Background info on cards, readings; enough to design my own deck.

Date: *3/21/90*

TAROT PROFILE

Personal Tarot Symbols for Guidance and Inspiration

Basque anthropologist and Tarot teacher Angeles Arrien teaches a method of determining which of the Major Arcana cards can be used as your individual lifetime cards. In a way, they are similar to astrological sun signs. It is an ideal way to establish your own personal relationship to these ancient archetypal symbols: a way to discover how the Tarot can help you gain personal insight into the significance and purpose of your individual journey.

Your Personality and Soul Cards

Using your birth date you can numerologically calculate your Personality and Soul Numbers. The corresponding Personality Card indicates what you have come into this particular lifetime to learn. The corresponding Soul Card shows your soul purpose through all your lifetimes.

To determine these two cards you add together your month, day and year of birth like this:

Example:
October 14, 1947 =

$$\begin{array}{r} 10 \\ 14 \\ +1947 \\ \hline 1971 \end{array}$$

The Moon

Then you add each digit in the resulting number: $1 + 9 + 7 + 1 = 18$. Keep any number from 22 to 1. The resulting number is the Personality Number, which in this case corresponds with the eighteenth Major Arcana card: The Moon.

You then add together $1 + 8 = 9$. This is your Soul Number, which in this case corresponds with the ninth Major Arcana card: The Hermit.

In some cases the number will add up to more than 22. Since there are only 22 Major Arcana cards, reduce the number down to 22 or less; for example:

May 29, 1934 =

$$\begin{array}{r} 5 \\ 29 \\ +1934 \\ \hline 1968 \end{array}$$

The Sage/Hermit

$1 + 9 + 6 + 8 = 24$. $2 + 4 = 6$. In this case the number six (The Lovers) is *both* your Personality and Soul Card. In this lifetime you are specifically working on your soul purpose. It makes you more focused and directed.

There is one case in which more than two cards can appear. If your first number is 19 you will have three cards.

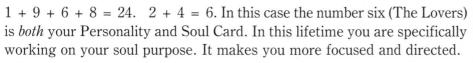
The Lovers

Example:

November 16, 1954 =

$$
\begin{array}{r}
11 \\
16 \\
+\,1954 \\
\hline
1981
\end{array}
\quad = 19 = 1 + 9 = 10 = 1 + 0 = 1
$$

The Sun

The Wheel of Fortune

The Magician

This is an especially creative path in which all three cards operate as *both* Personality *and* Soul Cards. People with this sequence *must* learn to communicate their individual creative expressions. Their personal identity and sense of self will be inextricably combined with their life and soul purpose. Their ability to relate to others will depend on a harmony of vision and purpose with them.

If your birthdate adds up to 22, you have a number of great impulsiveness and great mystery, a fine line to balance. 22 represents 0 (The Fool) and reduces to 4 (The Emperor). But in this case the 4 (The Emperor) is the Personality Card and the 0 (The Fool) is the Soul Card.

The Emperor

Figure your own Personality and Soul Cards as indicated below:

ADD

The month I was born: ___11___
The day I was born: ___20___
The year I was born: ___1956___
                 Equals: ___1987___
Add each digit: __1__ + __9__ + __8__ + __7__ = ___25___
If you have a double-digit answer, add again:
__2__ + __5__ = __7__

My Personality Number is ___7___ (the higher of the two numbers you received, but 22 or less). The Major Arcana card corresponding to this number is *The Chariot* ___.

The Fool

My Soul Number is ___7___ (the single-digit number in your final reduction). The Major Arcana card corresponding to this number is ___*Same*___.

(Note exceptions as explained above.)

Once you have determined these cards, it is important to find out what they mean to you. You can look up meanings of the cards in appendix A and in other books, but the best way to get in touch with their personal significance is to live with them. Take your Personality and Soul Cards from your Tarot deck and put them up on the wall in your room. Identify with the images and visualize them in meditation.

7 Self-control, discipline - harnessing desires, strengths to achieve some goal —

Another method is to ask one of the images in your Personality or Soul Card what you need to learn from it in this lifetime. Write down *the first answer you can think of.* Ask some more questions and write down your impulsive, uncensored responses. You will get different answers at different periods in your life, so go through this process again at another time. Gradually you will come to understand who The Hermit or The Empress or The Moon are to you.

Do this right now in the space provided before you go any further. Spend seven minutes writing steadily every thought which goes through your head while focusing on the images in your card. You can expect to experience some blocks or resistance to continuing past the first comment or so. It is important to go on writing. Remember that humor often helps break through these blocks and perseverance is rewarded with unexpected and more interesting material. Use extra paper if necessary.

My Personality ☑ or Soul ☑ Card is 7 - Chariot. (Check one)
Today's date 3/21/90.
Pick a specific figure in the card to address your question to.
I picked driver.
Ask this figure, "What can you teach me about what I need to learn in this lifetime?"

#1 Movement - transition - enjoyment of the journey - change - non-arrival - restlessness - strength, accomplishment - different scenery - departures - changes in companions - gathering knowledge - travel - drive, achievement motion - doing different things - ability to go places.

7 Know limits - when to stop + rest. What roads to take - the best path is most important part of journey - care for those who travel with you - (horses? people?) Be aware of surroundings. Enjoy the ride.

Hierophant - wisdom, balance, learning, mercy, teaching, care balance, spirituality, wisdom of experience, contemplation

Temper your impatience with the wisdom taught by time. Don't be distracted by the rush of your passage. Learn by looking inward as well as outward. Keep to the still center also. Commit to authority only in accordance w/teachings of inner self.

You can keep track of the Personality and Soul Cards of your relatives and friends here:

Name	Birth date	Personality # and card	Soul # and card

Your Year Card

You also have a personal Year Card representing the tests, lessons and experiences you will go through this year.

Add the month and date of your birth to the current year:

Example:
October 14, 1984 =

$$
\begin{array}{r}
10 \\
14 \\
+\,1984 \\
\hline
2008 = 10 \text{ (The Wheel of Fortune)}
\end{array}
$$

In determining the Year Card, you always keep the highest number under 23. (Remember 22 = The Fool.) The resulting number corresponds with your Year Card.

Native American

MEDICINE WHEEL

The Wheel of Fortune

     ADD

The month of my birth: _____*11*_____
The day of my birth: _____*20*_____
The current year: _____*1990*_____
       Equals: _____*2021*_____

for the year 19_*90*_____ my Year Number is _*5*_____, which corresponds with the Major Arcana card _*The Hierophant*_____.

There are two ways to establish when this "year" begins: 1) January 1 of this year; or 2) on your birthday in this year. In either case, you are dealing with a twelve-month period. I find that both systems work and I use them simultaneously. For example, the person born on October 14 would only be in a purely ten (Wheel of Fortune) year for two and a half months during the overlap from the birthday to the end of the year. During the majority of 1984 The Hermit will be in effect simultaneously with The Wheel of Fortune. From January 1985 to October 14, 1985, The Wheel of Fortune will be interacting with Justice. Each person, by having a birthday at a certain time of the yearly cycle, establishes his or her own rhythm. Personally, in my life I have found the January-to-January time to be of greatest outer significance in helping me to understand the events in my life. The cycle from birthday to birthday seems to be a time of integration during which the new lessons become a part of me. So January to January I experience circumstances which demand that I learn new reactions or directions. Around my birthday I begin integrating my learning, and during the birthday-to-birthday cycle these new awarenesses, which yield new actions, are tried and tested and thus become a natural part of me.

Other cards which are of significance to you are given in the charts below. Fill them in on your Tarot Profile on page 18. Work with each one in meditation and through intuitive writing.

The Hermit

The Wheel of Fortune

Your Zodiac Card

To determine which card corresponds with your astrological sun sign, check the chart below. (All astrological correspondences follow those of the Order of the Golden Dawn, Crowley, Waite, Paul Foster Case, etc. Substitute your own if they are different.)

ARIES—The Emperor (4)   LIBRA—Justice/Adjustment (8/11)
TAURUS—The Hierophant (5)   SCORPIO—Death (13)
GEMINI—The Lovers (6)   SAGITTARIUS—Temperance/Art (14)
CANCER—The Chariot (7)   CAPRICORN—The Devil (15)
LEO—Strength/Lust (11/8)   AQUARIUS—The Star (17)
VIRGO—The Hermit (9)   PISCES—The Moon (18)

Justice

My sun sign is ___Scorpio___. My Zodiac Card is ___13 - Death___

Your Numerological Lessons and Opportunities Cards

These are the four Minor Arcana cards (one in each suit), which have the same number as your Soul Number. For instance, if your Soul Number is three, then your Lessons and Opportunities Cards are the Three of Wands, the Three of Cups, the Three of Swords and the Three of Pentacles.

My Soul Number is ___7___. My four Numerological Lessons and Opportunities Cards are: the ___7___ of Wands, the ___7___ of Cups, the ___7___ of Swords and the ___7___ of Pentacles.

Your Zodiac Lessons and Opportunities Cards

These are three Minor Arcana cards which correspond with your astrological sun sign. Find your sun sign on the chart below. The three corresponding Tarot cards represent your zodiac lessons and opportunities.

ARIES	March 21 to 30	Two of Wands
	March 31 to April 10	Three of Wands
	April 11 to 20	Four of Wands
TAURUS	April 21 to 30	Five of Pentacles
	May 1 to 10	Six of Pentacles
	May 11 to 31	Seven of Pentacles
GEMINI	May 21 to 31	Eight of Swords
	June 1 to 10	Nine of Swords
	June 11 to 20	Ten of Swords
CANCER	June 21 to July 1	Two of Cups
	July 2 to 11	Three of Cups
	July 12 to 21	Four of Cups
LEO	July 22 to Aug. 1	Five of Wands
	Aug. 2 to 11	Six of Wands
	Aug. 12 to 22	Seven of Wands
VIRGO	Aug. 23 to Sept. 1	Eight of Pentacles
	Sept. 2 to 11	Nine of Pentacles
	Sept. 12 to 22	Ten of Pentacles
LIBRA	Sept. 23 to Oct. 2	Two of Swords
	Oct. 3 to 12	Three of Swords
	Oct. 13 to 22	Four of Swords
SCORPIO	Oct. 23 to Nov. 1	Five of Cups
	Nov. 2 to 12	Six of Cups
	Nov. 13 to 22	Seven of Cups
SAGITTARIUS	Nov. 23 to Dec. 2	Eight of Wands
	Dec. 3 to 12	Nine of Wands
	Dec. 13 to 21	Ten of Wands
CAPRICORN	Dec. 22 to 30	Two of Pentacles
	Dec. 31 to Jan. 9	Three of Pentacles
	Jan. 10 to 19	Four of Pentacles
AQUARIUS	Jan. 20 to 29	Five of Swords
	Jan. 30 to Feb. 8	Six of Swords
	Feb. 9 to 18	Seven of Swords
PISCES	Feb. 19 to 28	Eight of Cups
	March 1 to 10	Nine of Cups
	March 11 to 20	Ten of Cups

My sun sign is ___*Scorpio*___. My Zodiac Lessons and Opportunities Cards are ___*5 of Cups*___, ___*6 of Cups*___ and ___*7 of Cups*___.

Your Destiny Card

Your Destiny Card is the Minor Arcana card which corresponds with your actual birthdate. It is taken from the list above and will be one of your Zodiac Lessons and Opportunities Cards. From this card you can find indications of your fundamental impulses, desires and reactions as an individual. (See *The Pursuit of Destiny* in this chapter's booklist.)

My birthdate is ___*November 20*___. My Destiny Card is ___*7 of cups*___.

Your Persona Cards

The Persona Cards are three cards based on correspondences between the Court Cards and your natal horoscope chart. You need to know your sun, moon and rising signs to determine these cards (except for the Personal Potential Card, for which you only need your sun sign). If you do not have a natal chart, consult an astrologer, or you can write to the horoscope chart service listed in the Bibliography. The astrological signs are given with their corresponding Court Cards. (If you use a different system of correspondences, change the ones below to be in accord with your own system.)

		Insert your own Correspondences
ARIES	Queen of Wands	_____
TAURUS	King of Pentacles	_____
GEMINI	Knight of Swords	_____
CANCER	Queen of Cups	_____
LEO	King of Wands	_____
VIRGO	Knight of Pentacles	_____
LIBRA	Queen of Swords	_____
SCORPIO	King of Cups	_____
SAGITTARIUS	Knight of Wands	_____
CAPRICORN	Queen of Pentacles	_____
AQUARIUS	King of Swords	_____
PISCES	Knight of Cups	_____

Your Personal Potential Card is the Court Card corresponding to your sun sign. My sun sign is ___*Scorpio*___, so my Personal Potential Card is ___*King of Cups*___.

Your Inner Teacher card is the Court Card corresponding to the sign your moon is in. My moon is in _____, so my Inner Teacher Card is _____.

Your Mode of Expression in the World is indicated by the Court Card corresponding to your rising sign (ascendant). My rising sign is _____, so my Mode of Expression in the World can be described by _____.

TAROT PROFILE

Personal Tarot Symbols for Guidance and Inspiration

NAME _____   DATE _____

The following cards, used in meditation and visualizations, can help you find significance, purpose and direction in your life.

PERSONALITY CARD _THE CHARIOT (7)_____
Indicates my life purposes, aspirations and lessons to be learned.

SOUL CARD _THE CHARIOT_____
Indicates my soul purpose and qualities that will assist me.

ZODIAC OR SUN SIGN CARD _SCORPIO - DEATH (13)_
Indicates what I need for self-expression.

CURRENT YEAR CARD _5 - HIEROPHANT_____ for 19_90_
Indicates qualities I need to develop this year.

PREVIOUS YEAR CARDS   UPCOMING YEAR CARDS

19_87_ = _2; HIGH PRIESTESS_   19_91_ = _6; THE LOVERS_
19_88_ = _3; EMPRESS_   * 19_92_ = _7; THE CHARIOT_ *
19_89_ = _4; EMPEROR_   19_93_ = _8; STRENGTH_

Put a star next to any Year Card which is the same as your Personality, Soul or Zodiac Card. These years are significant as indicators of how you will express your life purpose.

NUMEROLOGICAL LESSONS AND OPPORTUNITIES CARDS
The four Minor Arcana cards corresponding to my Soul Number:
_7_ of Wands, _7_ of Cups, _7_ of Swords, _7_ of Pentacles.

ZODIAC LESSONS AND OPPORTUNITIES CARDS
The three Minor Arcana cards corresponding to my sun sign:
_5 OF CUPS_____   _6 OF CUPS_____   _7 OF CUPS_____

DESTINY CARD _7 OF CUPS_____
The Minor Arcana card indicating the fundamental impulses, desires and reactions of myself as an individual.

PERSONA CARDS:

PERSONAL POTENTIAL CARD _KING OF CUPS_____
The Court Card corresponding to my sun sign.

INNER TEACHER CARD _____
The Court Card corresponding to my moon sign.

MODE OF EXPRESSION IN THE WORLD _____
The Court Card corresponding to my rising sign.

RITUALS

Rituals are very important in establishing rapport with your cards, but need not be formalized. Through time and practice, you'll naturally find yourself developing personal rituals through such actions as how you shuffle, where and how you keep the cards and at which times you use them. Such repetitions of action will help prepare you for a reading by relaxing you and taking you out of the ordinary stream of things. Do not hesitate to experiment; create your own rituals. But remember that to empower the ritual and the symbolic objects you choose to use, you must have faith in them; you must also feel confident that the act will have significant results spiritually, psychologically and/or physically. It is through observing the results over a period of time that you validate your rituals.

Suggested Rituals

When you first get your deck of cards, try sleeping with them under your pillow, or at least put them with your very personal possessions, to begin creating a special link between you.

Wrap your cards in a cloth, or keep them in a bag that "feels" good to you—something that you find beautiful and are pleased to look at and touch. Many Tarot readers use finely embroidered satin or velvet bags. Other interesting wraps are Chinese bags, second-hand or antique evening bags, leather pouches with bead work, hand-carved imported boxes and ceramic or enamelled containers.

Black silk is a traditional wrap because silk is an especially good psychic insulator. Fabrics such as cotton and wool are also quite suitable. White pine is the preferred wood for boxes, although that's never kept me from a box I find beautiful.

PURIFYING YOUR TAROT CARDS

Purify your cards when you get a new deck. Also purify them between readings and before reading for yourself or meditating on them, especially if you last used them on someone else.

There are several methods of purifying your cards:

1) *REPEATED, RYTHMICAL SHUFFLING OF THE CARDS.* This is the most basic form of purification, an essential part of any reading, which does not make it any less evocative of focused consciousness—one of the results of purification. Purification means cleansing. Shuffling not only puts in new energies but takes out old ones. It is good to shuffle at the end of a reading as well as at the beginning.

2) *SMOKING THE CARDS* with cedar, sage, pinon or sweet grass. It is especially efficacious to burn such dried herbs in an abalone or similar shell, for it represents the element of water; the plant represents the element earth;

the smoke the element air; and the fire is its own element. This bringing together of the four elements is an important part of ritual. But don't hesitate to use whatever you have at hand. Pass the deck of cards through the smoke several times and be sure to waft the smoke upon yourself and anyone else present. This is known as "smudging" and can be done with a large feather to distribute the smoke.

3) *FILLING THE DECK WITH LIGHT.* To do this, first close your eyes. At a position about eighteen inches above your deck, picture a tiny seed of pure radiant white light, or the color of your choice (gold is also recommended). Imagine the seed of light growing into a crown which then pours a stream of light into your cards. Know that this stream of light is purifying your deck for your use. Use this technique in conjunction with the others.

4) *RUBBING WITH A SILK OR COTTON CLOTH*—perhaps the one they are wrapped in.

5) *CLEANSING WITH SEA-SALT AND WATER* (for plastic-coated cards). Wipe each card with a sponge lightly dampened with sea-salt and fresh water.

6) *BURYING IN EARTH.* An especially strong unpleasant energy may require burying the deck in earth for seven days or for the period from full moon to the first sliver of the new moon. Visualize Mother Earth absorbing all negative energies. Rarely is it necessary to burn a Tarot deck, though I have known people to do so.

7) *ORDERING THE DECK AFTER USING IT* is an excellent way to know the cards in their archetypal order; it purifies them. A Tarot deck in its archetypal order is symbolic of the path to self-knowledge. You can place a card on which you have been working on top of the deck so it will be the first thing you see when returning to your deck. The order I use is: Major Arcana, Fool through Universe; then each suit in order (Ace through Ten) followed by the King, Queen, Knight and Page. The suits are ordered: Wands, Cups, Swords and Pentacles.

The atmosphere when working with your cards should be pleasant and relaxed. It is preferable not to drink coffee, black tea, alcohol or take drugs. Herbal teas which traditionally benefit psychic development, visioning, clarity of mind, joy and well-being are: vervain, mugwort, anise, lemon verbena, chamomile, cinnamon, bay laurel, hyssop, pennyroyal (don't use if you're pregnant), plantain, rosemary, uva ursi and yerba santa. You might want to try one or more of these instead of a caffeine drink.

Energy is traditionally considered to flow from east to west and from north to south. You can take advantage of these earth energy currents by facing the direction from which the energy comes—usually east or north.

Another matter is whether anyone else should touch your cards. This is completely personal. The fear of someone else "desecrating" your cards can be disturbing and actually cause adverse reactions if it happens. I fill my cards with love and invite my friends to partake freely of that. Occasionally I do not feel comfortable with a particular person touching my cards. I find that purification restores good feelings and well-being.

Experiment with the above rituals and others of your own making. Remember that repetition and belief are what give power to your rituals. There is a theatrical element to ritual, involving a willing suspension of disbelief, which creates its own magic and defines a special time and place.

Note here your own ideas for rituals:

ACTIVE IMAGINATION

In reading Tarot you can look up the meanings of the cards in Appendix A or in other books, or you can look at the images and symbols on the cards themselves and imagine your own meanings for these pictures. Much the same method of actively imagining is used in interpreting dreams and in psychoanalytic processes such as gestalt or psychosynthesis. Other names for active imagination are directed reverie, creative visualization, symbolic manipulation and imaginative play; even self-hypnosis uses these principles.

To activate your ability to use your imagination productively, it is important to be relaxed yet alert, with your mind clear of mundane concerns. Use the following relaxation exercise before all your work with the Tarot.

RELAXATION AND GROUNDING EXERCISE

First, read through the directions that follow. You may then want to record them on a cassette tape or have a friend read them to you. After doing the exercise several times, you will no longer need the tape; upon taking the initial three breaths, the process will become almost automatic. Eventually you will be able to clear your energy field quickly and achieve a deep, relaxed state in only a minute or two; but at the beginning, take your time.

The exercise is also called a "grounding" exercise. In any psychic work, the goal is to make yourself a clear channel so that you do not hold any of the work inside your body, where it can create blockage and possibly be experienced as tension or even illness. By grounding your energy, you note but do not hold onto your experiences, allowing them to pass through you and into Mother Earth or out into Father Sky.

It is best to sit upright on an ordinary chair, with spine straight, feet flat on the floor and shoes off. Place your hands on your legs, palms down.

Do This Exercise Before Beginning Any Tarot Work:

Take three deep breaths: pull the air first into the bottom of your lungs and slowly fill them to the top. Your stomach should expand. Hold for three counts. Exhale by pushing the air from the top of your lungs, expelling until the bottom is completely empty and your stomach pulled in. Hold for a count of three before inhaling again.

Continue to breathe in the same slow and careful way. On every exhalation, visualize all your cares and tensions leaving through the soles of your feet. On every inhalation, draw up revitalized energy through the soles of your feet. Picture yourself as a tree drawing up life and nourishment from Mother Earth and releasing the waste matter of your life. Continue to do this until you have established a regular, even rythmn to your breathing. Try to maintain this even breath for the rest of the exercise.

Next, as you inhale, visualize bringing the vital energy or sap from Mother Earth all the way up through your body and out through the crown of your head, releasing it into the atmosphere around you as sparkling golden dust, creating an oval cloud around you. Feel the sensation of well-being and health that this energy brings.

On your next inhalation, connect with a point of light about eighteen inches above your head and draw down a ray of gold into your heart. When you exhale, this ray of gold radiates out from your heart in all directions.

Variations

After you are completely comfortable with the above exercise and have practiced it many times, you may want to try one of the following variations or create your own.

1) Exhale pink-colored light (the color of rose quartz) from your heart. Envision it as the color of Universal Love.

2) Exchange energy from above and below by inhaling golden light energy from Mother Earth and Father Sun simultaneously, meeting in your heart center as you suspend your breath. When you exhale, send the nourishment and life of Mother Earth up to Father Sun and send the enlightening ray of Father Sun to quicken Mother Earth. This generates clean, free energy for all.

3) When you inhale and exhale, learn to keep your throat open. To do this allow a slight sound to emerge from your throat with your breath. Once you know what it feels like to keep your throat open, you can breathe that way without making any noise.

4) Add your own variation here:

ENTERING A CARD

Lay your Major Arcana cards out in front of you in three rows of seven cards with the Fool above. (See the illustration opposite page 1.) Pick out the card which most attracts you: _17 - The Star_

1) Describe what you see, allowing your eyes to move freely over the card and recording the symbols as you focus on them. Note which symbols seem to command your attention. *A star - large, centered; a young woman pouring 2 pitchers of water into a stream; 7 flowers, 3 ℞, 3 ℓ; one over her head, a bush - + 1 large flower - in 2 bushes; 1 with a bird in it. The stream itself. Green hills behind. She's nude; has a band or circlet on her head. Stream may be a lake or pond.*
Noticed 1st - the water, I think.

2) List any images or objects in the card which you didn't mention above.
She's on 1 knee w/ the other leg bent. The star & flowers are yellow. Bird is black; bush 1 is green + red; bush 2 red (bloom), grn stem.
(bloom)

3) What colors predominate? *↑*
green, blue, white (sky)

Close your eyes and see if you can recreate the card in your imagination. Then open your eyes and see if you left anything out.

Read through the following directions completely before beginning this exercise. Use the same card as in the previous exercise. You may want to tape the instructions or have a friend read them to you.

Close your eyes and take three slow, deep breaths to center yourself. Imagine the card you have chosen becoming larger and larger until the figures in it are life size. . . . Step over the border of the card and enter it. The landscape now extends as far as you can see in all directions. Look around you. What do you see? . . . Do you hear any noises? . . . What can you smell? . . . What is the temperature? . . . What time of day is it? . . . Examine more closely anything that interests you. . . . Touch it if it's appropriate; what does it feel like? . . . Who else is there in this Tarot landscape with you? . . . Approach the figure who most attracts you. He or she has a gift for you, something which you can take back into your life to help you on your path to self-knowledge. Accept the gift and look at it carefully. . . . Thank the giver. Ask what it is to be used for. . . . Take one last look around and then imagine that the border of the card is behind you. Turn around and step over it and watch the card instantly shrink back down to its normal size. Open your eyes.

As in dreams, your experience will quickly lose details if you don't write them down. While writing, you may become aware of more details than you thought you had seen; record those impressions and feelings too.

Card Entered ___THE STAR___ Date _3/21/90_
Reason for picking this card _Just appealed to me._
What did I see? Describe in as much detail as possible.
Pretty much what was on the card, only "real-life". Also saw a cabin-ish structure + some woods behind her off to the right.

What smells were there? Water, green stuff, fresh air.

What did I hear? Birds singing, water running (being poured? A stream?)

What were the temperature and weather? Summery, a slight breeze. Nice.

What time of day was it? Mid-afternoon.

What did I touch and what was its texture? Trees-leaves - just "leaf-ish" - But the grass was strange. dry + woody, like I was rubbing a woodcut.
Did I taste anything? No

Colors I didn't mention in my description: Blue sky, forest colors

What figures were there (animal/human/spirit)? Describe them.
The girl - young, blonde, pretty; looked a lot like my Galadriel.

What gift did I receive? From which figure? *From the girl - a bathing suit, my mask, + snorkel. (!)*

Were there any messages or instructions for me? *She said I knew what to do - just jump in.*

What positive qualities does my gift represent to me? *I get to go swimming - self-exploration?*

Write a statement affirming that you already have those qualities within yourself. *I am involved in exploring + enjoying my deeper, hidden self.*

Variations

It is possible to enter any of the Tarot cards and explore them or meet the figures in them. You can also have sustained dialogues and ask for information about the cards themselves or for advice in your life. Some other possibilities are:

1) Entering your Personality, Soul or Year Cards.

2) Entering a card you dislike or which disturbs you to see if you can learn more about it. Remember that you can leave whenever you wish.

3) Entering two cards at once simply by placing them next to each other and imagining their landscapes connecting. You can then observe a meeting between the figures in the two cards and listen to their dialogue or initiate a three-way conversation. This will help you understand interrelating cards in a reading.

4) By entering a card you can ask an image or symbol directly what its meaning is. Some of the answers will be surprisingly enlightening and appropriate for you.

Be sure to write your answers down immediately after leaving the Tarot card, or you can try writing *while* you are imagining the experience.

SUGGESTED READING FOR CHAPTER ONE

Numerology and the Divine Triangle. Faith Javane and Dusty Bunker. Rockport, MA: Para Research, 1979.

The Pursuit of Destiny. Muriel Bruce Hasbrouck. New York: Warner Destiny Books, 1976.

Mind Games. Robert Masters and Jean Houston. New York: Dell, 1972.

FROM THE TAROT DE MARSEILLES, originally published in 18th century France and still one of the most influential and popular Tarot decks. The Major Arcana are here arranged in three vertical rows of seven cards each. John D. Blakeley, in The Mystical Tower of the Tarot, *describes his search for the possible Sufi origin of the Tarot. He found a book written in 1899 called* The Mystic Rose from the Garden of the King *by Sir Fairfax L. Cartwright. It is a tale told by a mystic dervish in which a wanderer approaches a tower "impelled by a desire to learn." In answer to the question, "What seekest thou?" he answers, "Knowledge," and affirms that with guidance he has the "strength and determination to climb to the topmost chamber of the tower." There are three chambers on each floor, each containing a living Tarot archetype, and each floor presents "another plane of thought . . .another aspect of things." The strange land in which this Temple of Knowledge is to be found, he finds, is the human heart.*

CHAPTER TWO

THE TAROT JOURNAL

The best way to acquaint yourself with the Tarot is to find out how the cards function in your own life. Recognize the ups and downs of fortune by watching the daily patterns of the cards. Watch how certain cards, say The Sun, The World and the Two of Cups, or perhaps The Devil, The Tower and the Nine of Swords, appear and disappear in an ever-changing rhythm; discover what these cards signify for you. For example, in daily life The Tower can often indicate losing your temper, or scratching or cutting yourself, or getting the sudden impulse to clean out your refrigerator—a quick burst of energy. If The Tower occurs frequently, you are probably going through a period of change that involves a breakdown of old patterns. Sometimes it can mean a shattering of all that is familar and "safe" in your life, or the destruction of your security structures, such as suddenly losing your job. In the case of The Tower, you are being asked to break through old structures in your life that no longer benefit your growth but are causing you to become rigid in your beliefs and values. It is an opportunity for you to open yourself to new freedom and to awaken to new knowledge. All of your old defenses are shown to be antiquated, allowing you now to move beyond them. In this way the cards point out the lessons and opportunities being presented to you. How well you handle life's situations depends much on how quickly you learn your lessons.

Write down *all* your readings and date them with notes on the significance of the cards to you at the time. Append copies of significant readings to your journal if you have one, or note on the reading itself what is generally happening in your life right now—quick thumbnail sketches. Four to eight weeks later, go back to these significant readings. Note the progress of events. Can you now identify persons more specifically? Who was the mysterious Knight of Wands? How were you actually manifesting this masculine Knight energy? What was that argument about (Five of Wands)—or was it something other than an argument? What did you have to let go of (Death)? What was the final impetus that made you let go? Can it be identified by another card in the reading?

When I go back over an old reading I use different colored pens, writing my new comments next to the old. I date these comments and then come back six months or a year later and add a third series of notes in a third color of ink.

By the third overview you can begin to see your own personal patterns evolving. Moving through the layers of self-deception, you begin to recognize the games you play with yourself—your inability or unwillingness to "see the facts." Look for evidence of your own intuitive insights, inherent wisdom and words of advice coming back to you at the most appropriate times. Note also particular themes which keep reappearing. And ask yourself what aspects of your life never seem to appear in your readings. Why not?

It is not necessary to reflect in depth on every Tarot layout you do for yourself over the next several years; but set aside particular readings to represent milestones and turning points in your life, such as the commencement of anything: new job, new home, new relationship, your birthday; also the ending of anything, or readings for the new and full moons. For women, during the first day of your moon (menstrual period) is an excellent time to focus on yourself and your own needs. Men might want to ritualize their own cycles in a similar way: try that day every month when the moon returns to its natal position in your astrological chart. You can thus observe your emotional rhythms.

THE THREE-CARD SPREAD

Now we've come to the first spread you will learn, which is used by almost all practitioners of the art. Although basic, the Three-Card Spread is profoundly useful, especially for keeping a Tarot journal. The Three-Card Spread is a powerful tool for feeding back information about your own processes of making decisions and dealing with situations. It can help you to clarify options before acting and to understand the dynamics that take place afterwards. You will also learn to perceive in which directions you are being urged by the three levels of self: body, mind and spirit.

Every question can be examined from three aspects. Every action, for example, usually involves three choices: your current position, a new possibility or opposite action, and the integration of these two in a new way. Problem-solving can be approached from your experience in the *past*, how you feel in the *present*, and expectations of the *future*. And involved in every choice are your *body* with its urges and habits, your *mind* with its thoughts and reasoning and your *spirit* with its ideals and goals. The three cards of the spread may then be read as three choices, three aspects of time and/or three levels of the self.

The number three is also the basis of creativity. Creativity has been defined as combining at least two things in a new way, forming a third. This is exemplified in Tarot Card Three, The Empress, who carries in her womb the new child . . . of her body and man's seed, and yet a new and wholly different being.

Preparing to Read the Three-Card Spread

To use the Three-Card Spread as a Tarot journal, set aside a particular time and place for each day's reading. It helps to do the spread as part of your daily meditation or centering practice, assuring a calm state of mind.

Record the cards you draw; then throughout the day observe how they manifest. Later, write down what you've observed or simply describe the events of the day. Keep a daily chart (shown on the next page).

Color-code your chart by lightly shading each suit with different colored pencils: Wands, Cups, Swords, Pentacles and Major Arcana. Note which cards or suits keep reappearing. Is the King of Pentacles a particular person in your life? Who is the Queen of Cups? Are there certain cards that represent an experience of anxiety and tension and others that represent creativity and passion in your life? What cards seem to represent you when you are in a particulary "high" space—when everything is going perfectly?

If you miss a day, you can always choose cards at a later date for the missed day by making it clear before shuffling that you *intend* the reading for the day you missed.

But to understand, it is best to do. Now you will want to lay out your Tarot cards.

The Shuffle

Using any deck you prefer, shuffle your cards to release any energy from previous readings. Pause and breathe deeply in and out three times, bringing the energy up through your feet with every inhalation and releasing it back into the earth as you exhale. Shuffle the cards again until you feel they are well mixed. Cut the cards into three stacks with your left hand.

Choosing the Cards

Rub your hands together rapidly until they generate heat and feel tingly. With palm down, move your left hand over the three stacks and intuitively decide which one is your body, which is your mind and which is your spirit. The body stack is usually the easiest to find. It tends to have a "magnetic" pull, is warmer or more "tingly," and somewhat denser. Then decide which stack is your mind and which is your spirit. I find the spirit stack to be the easier to determine. It tends to be the lightest and most "ephemeral." Your hand may seem to float above it. The feeling is extremely subtle and expansive. The mind stack may be electric and cool. Observe what you feel, try to describe it, and most of all, trust that whatever you do is appropriate! Place your stacks in the following order, left to right: body, mind, spirit. The simplest and most direct methods are to either cut the deck three times and turn over the top card in each stack, or to restack the cards after the cut, fan them out and choose three cards from anywhere in the deck.

Before you turn the cards over, note any impressions that come to mind regarding suit, color or image. The cards whose emanations are so strong that you feel them might be especially significant to you. You should also note any cards that fall from the deck while you shuffle. If Tarot reappear during the reading, give them extra consideration in your interpretation. Accidents count.

DAILY READING CHART

DATE	BODY	MIND	SPIRIT	EVENTS OF THE DAY

Interpreting the Cards

Do one three-card reading thoroughly, following this format. After that im-
provise and use those steps that work best for you. Turn over the top card
in each stack. The cards you have picked are:

BODY: _EMPRESS_   MIND: _PAGE OF WANDS_   SPIRIT: _QUEEN OF WANDS_

Note your first impressions:

What do you see? *2 dark-haired women / foolish looking Page*

What colors? *Empress – red / Wands – green + gold*

What does the number on each card mean to you? *Empress – 3 – Unity; triple-phased - varying aspect - Body/mind/spirit?*

What human figures or animals do you see?

What is the environment of each card?

·What symbols are there?

Can you describe the cards in terms of an emotion? How do you feel when
you look at each of them: Apprehensive? Expectant? Glad? Sad? Angry?

Note which way figures in the cards face: toward or away from each other,
moving in the direction of body or spirit, focusing on the center, etc. Write
down the relationships you see:

Now relate each card to its position meaning. Work with the pictures on
the cards as if they were dream images. Or create a story by role-playing.
Become the various persons and things in the cards. Dialogue orally or on
paper to find out what the images have to say to you and each other. If you
don't know the card meanings, look them up in Appendix A.

BODY: The state of your physical body and the environment. Habits and automatic responses. How you ground yourself. How you've been manifesting yourself and things you have produced. Often the origin or source of the situation. Feelings.

My Body Card is telling me:

MIND: What you are thinking about and are consciously aware of dealing with. The way you reason and rationalize things; your attitudes. The state of mind in which you approach the reading.

My Mind Card is telling me:

SPIRIT: Your ideals, goals and aspirations. The spirit is like your higher self offering new possibilities and advice on how you can work through your problems. You tend to be drawn toward manifesting what the card indicates. If the card is negative, you might be blocking or resisting the things spirit wants you to see.

My Spirit Card is telling me:

For example, in the following reading The Hermit appeared in the body position, the Three of Swords in the mind and The World in the spirit position. (The Waite-Smith deck was used for this reading.)

My body wants me to withdraw and be alone, to heal myself of the mental pain and sorrow that my mind is telling me I am experiencing, while my spirit is urging me to overcome my feelings of limitation and experience the sense of freedom that comes once I accept the pain and loss.

Connect the three cards you drew into one statement. Can you weave a story, or tell a tale using what you see in the cards? Write down your own message using the following format:

While my body wants   _____,
my mind is telling me   _____,
yet my spirit is urging me to   _____
_____ .

At this point you can end the reading or you can continue for more depth and understanding. The rest of this section tells how to gain more insight using these same three cards.

Reading for Depth

The next step is to go back and look at your reading from a "time" perspective: past, present, future, for instance:

I have been a loner, turning my back on entanglement because I fear being hurt. And now I am having to face and deal with that pain in a relationship. My spirit is asking me to be much freer and more open to life opportunities in the near future. In other words, to remove this cloak with which I have been protecting myself. I must allow the falling rain in the Three of Swords to wash me clean in order to use the insight of my inner Hermit journeys despite my fears.

What does your reading tell you about your past, present and future?
PAST: _____
_____
PRESENT: _____
_____
FUTURE: _____
_____

It is time to be daring. Take your life into your own hands: move the cards around in any way you wish. For instance, to continue the example:

Now the Hermit is looking for The World—my own inner soul, my self, which is not afraid to confront those in my life who bring me sorrow and pain. I can now see that the painful situation will serve to lead me back to my own sense of self and integrity. (Note how the direction in which the figures are looking or moving becomes important to interpretation.)

Put your cards in a new and different order. Do you like this order better? What new perspectives do you see?

You can move the cards again; for instance:

I have overcome my hurt, rising above it by relying on my Hermit—my own wise self—to understand what happened, and utilize what I learned from the experience. I look back, shedding light on the path I took out of that stormy scene. I am setting out on a new path, alone, yet taking with me wisdom and confidence in my ability to function in the world.

Note down any further insights you have by moving your cards around:

After you have looked at your own three cards from these different perspectives, put them back in their original positions. Notice how much information you have gained about this original layout and the possibilities it presents. The emphasis has been on Time—whether something has happened in the past or will happen in the future. The past was at one time your future. The future will someday be the now. By switching your perspective you gain understanding as to what "now" means, and you begin experiencing it in a cyclic way.

You can continue moving the cards into a variety of positions and orders. Each one will add to the depth of your understanding. Some possibilities are:

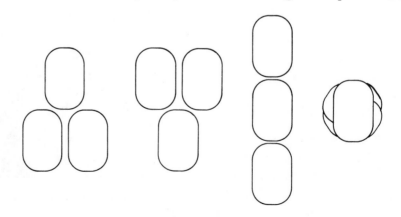

The three positions of this spread can also take on a variety of meanings. The following are some of my favorite variations, but add your own as you find what works for you.

BODY	MIND	SPIRIT
PAST	PRESENT	FUTURE
SUBCONSCIOUS	CONSCIOUS	SUPERCONSCIOUS
CHILD	PARENT	ADULT
MAYA/ILLUSION	KNOWLEDGE	MAGIC
THESIS	ANTITHESIS	SYNTHESIS
COMMENCEMENT	OPPOSITION	INTEGRATION
AN IDEA OR PLAN	CRITICISM OF IT	HOW TO MAKE THE MOST OF YOUR LIMITATIONS

Reviewing Your Daily Readings

One of my students, Linda Tigges, recorded one month of daily three-card readings and then selected out all the cards appearing three times or more for further insight into her development throughout the month. She also looked at the numbers she drew most often, for instance, Aces. She then looked at all the Aces and at the Major Arcana card numbered One, The Magician, as keys to the meaning of her month's experiences.

SELECTING CARDS BY PERSONAL CHOICE

In many of the following exercises you will be using a new method of working with the Tarot. You will select cards from the deck while looking at them face up. In some cases you will be picking a card based on your personal reaction to the pictures and images on it, in other cases I will give you a list of "uses" of each card and you will select a "use" and the card that goes with it. Working with the images on the cards is especially important in both these cases.

The extent of the imagery on your working deck will make a big difference in your choices and in your interpretations. The cards you have chosen to work with must be meaningful to you personally and, unless you are especially adept in numerology and working with abstract imagery, should have pictures and symbolic images on both the Major and Minor Arcana. (The Introduction has a list of many decks that are currently available.)

As you work with the exercises that follow, you may, for example, be instructed to "pick one to three cards which represent your best abilities." To do this, go quickly through the entire deck with the cards face up. Pull out all cards that could possibly fill the description. It is usually better if you don't try to predetermine your response, but rather ask each card, "Do you represent an ability of mine?" If you hesitate over a card (should I pull it or not?), then place it in your "possible" pile. You will probably pull from five to 25 cards. Spread these cards out and eliminate those which you now see don't belong or don't express your theme question as well as some of the others. You should now have about five to seven cards, more or less. Compare each card with one of the others in turn by asking yourself, "If I had to eliminate one of these two, which could I do without?" In this way, you gradually reduce your pile to the one to three cards which most succinctly and aptly express your best abilities. You will usually have the option of choosing more than one card, especially when one card's energies must be modified by another. Although sometimes it may be difficult to eliminate cards, you will find it much easier to work with fewer cards.

Now do the following exercise in the way described here: My best abilities can be described by: (Pick one to three cards.)

_____   _____   _____

These cards describe the following abilities:

LIFETIME YEAR-CARD GRAPH

In the first chapter you learned how to find your Year Card for the current year. You can also calculate Year Cards for your entire life and plot them on a graph. In this way you have the opportunity to see the pattern of your lifetime lessons unfold before you. Some cards will appear over and over throughout your life. Other cards will appear once or twice and never again. Some never appear at all. Because our mathematical system is decimally based, you will find that the numbers run in ten-year cycles, and that certain numbers or cycles will predominate, depending on when you were born. For instance, after January 1, 1988, there will be no more 19–10–1 personalities born for a long time although they have been relatively abundant in the recent past.

Using the graph form provided (or any graph paper), designate a Major Arcana card for each horizontal line. Each vertical line represents a year in your life. Beginning with your year of birth, write each consecutive year across the top of the page, and as an easy reference, write below each year your age on your birthday that year.

After determining a Year Card for each year of your life (following the instructions in Chapter One), plot them on the graph with a series of dots. Connect the dots with lines to see the patterns that form, as in the example that follows.

Examine your graph. Look for the ten-year cycles. The end of each cycle indicates an important turning point in your life.

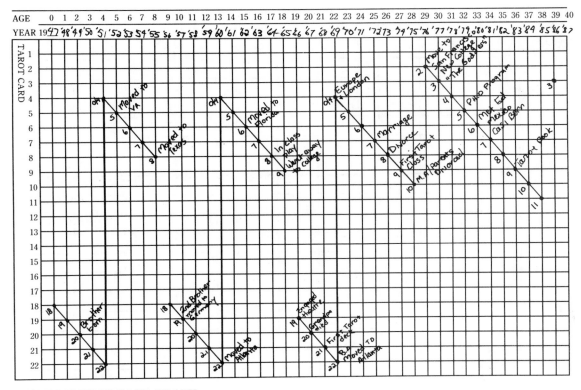

LIFETIME YEAR-CARD GRAPH

In which years did you end a ten-year cycle? What personal cycle were you completing in each of those years?

YEAR   AGE   COMPLETED
_____   _____   _____
_____   _____   _____
_____   _____   _____
_____   _____   _____
_____   _____   _____

In which years did you begin a ten-year cycle? What personal cycle did you begin in each of those years?

YEAR   AGE   BEGAN
_____   _____   _____
_____   _____   _____
_____   _____   _____
_____   _____   _____
_____   _____   _____

Circle on your graph the years in which you have cards that are the same as your Personality and Soul Cards. These are especially significant. In your Personality and Soul Years you were probably drawn to and involved in things that are especially important to your soul purpose in this lifetime. In other words, you were probably doing something that could potentially utilize your highest qualities. You were doing things that could teach what you need

LIFETIME
YEAR-CARD
GRAPH

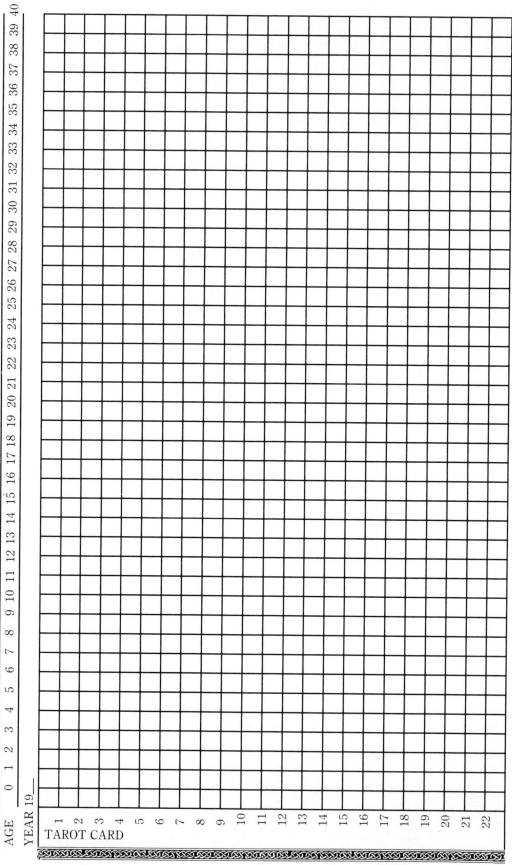

AGE 0 1 2 3 4 5 6 7 8 9 10 11 12 13 14 15 16 17 18 19 20 21 22 23 24 25 26 27 28 29 30 31 32 33 34 35 36 37 38 39 40

YEAR 19___

TAROT CARD 1 2 3 4 5 6 7 8 9 10 11 12 13 14 15 16 17 18 19 20 21 22

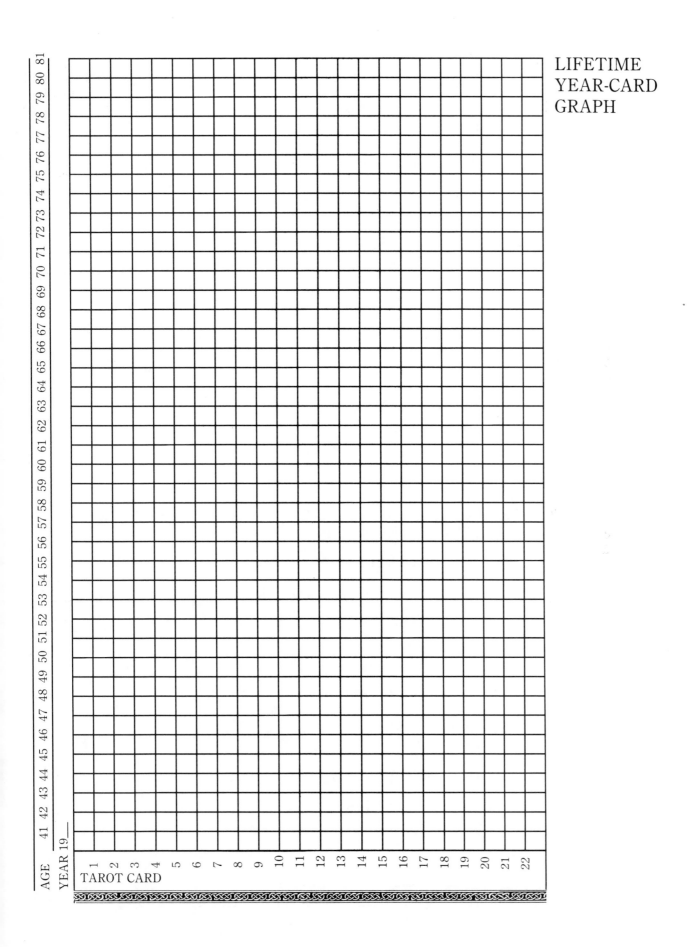

LIFETIME
YEAR-CARD
GRAPH

to learn in order to bring out your fullest potential. As they come up in your life, each of these years offers you the opportunity to reaffirm your direction and get in touch with your life goals. Note below some of the outstanding events of your Personality- and Soul-Numbered Years in order to gain more insight into your lifetime lessons:

PERSONALITY- AND SOUL-NUMBERED YEARS:

YEAR	AGE	CARD	SIGNIFICANT EVENTS
___	___	___	_____
___	___	___	_____
___	___	___	_____
___	___	___	_____
___	___	___	_____
___	___	___	_____

Also look for the appearance of new numbers. These are new experiences and lessons that you must now integrate. Note below the years in which new numbers first appear (especially after the first ten-year cycle):

FIRST APPEARANCE OF NUMBER/CARDS:

YEAR	AGE	CARD	YEAR	AGE	CARD	YEAR	AGE	CARD
___	___	___	___	___	___	___	___	___
___	___	___	___	___	___	___	___	___
___	___	___	___	___	___	___	___	___

When do numbers drop out, not to reappear? These are lessons learned. Note below the last appearance of a number:

LAST APPEARANCE OF A NUMBER:

YEAR	AGE	CARD	YEAR	AGE	CARD	YEAR	AGE	CARD
___	___	___	___	___	___	___	___	___
___	___	___	___	___	___	___	___	___
___	___	___	___	___	___	___	___	___

What cards appear the most? These are the areas of greatest testing and strengthening. You won't be able to learn it all the first time, so you'll get many more chances. Note below the cards that appear most frequently in your life—six or more times—and what you have noted about their significance in your life.

MOST FREQUENTLY APPEARING NUMBERS:

CARD	# OF TIMES	SIGNIFICANCE TO YOU
___	___	_____
___	___	_____
___	___	_____
___	___	_____
___	___	_____
___	___	_____
___	___	_____

I have found it helpful to write key events on the graph next to each year. Thus I found that twice in a Fool/Emperor (22/4) year I moved to Atlanta—ten years apart. My grandfather died in a Judgment (20) year, which corresponds with the planet of death and rebirth—Pluto. I sought out important teachers in three different Hierophant (5) years and taught my first Tarot class in a Hermit (9) year (which is my Soul Card, indicating my soul purpose). I also spent a ten-month honeymoon in Mexico during my Lovers (6) year. As I write this book I am in another Hermit (9) year, which seems auspicious for its completion.

Although I have found similar examples of outstanding congruence in other people's Year-Card graphs and their accounts of events in their lives, I feel it is important to stress that you should focus on *observing* what the Year Cards mean for *you*. For instance, the Lovers card could be experienced during a year of celibacy in which you are questioning yourself deeply about what you really want in a relationship—thus emphasizing that you can choose a relationship that will be meaningful and worthwhile.

Year-Card Lessons

The following listing suggests a few of the possible lessons you might learn from your Year Card:

THE MAGICIAN: Focusing your attention, writing, communicating, magic, the use of mind over matter, all mental endeavors.

THE HIGH PRIESTESS: Independence, intuitive or psychic development, your ability to relate to women, self-nurturing.

THE EMPRESS: Creativity, pregnancy, nurturing others, relating to women, love of pleasure and beautiful things, being magnetic and attractive.

THE EMPEROR: Beginning new things, pioneering, building, structuring, being assertive and authoritative, establishing a groundwork or secure base. Relating to men.

THE HIEROPHANT: Learning and teaching, listening and speaking, working within social structures and hierarchies—understanding "the system."

THE LOVERS: Relating, major choices having to do with relationships, making decisions and accepting responsibility for them.

THE CHARIOT: Proving yourself out in the world, moving, travel, learning to protect—taking care of yourself and others.

STRENGTH/LUST: Desire for creativity, strong passions and desires, a challenge calling for great strength and endurance.

THE HERMIT: Solitude, introspection, learning by experience or through a role-model, perfecting, seeking, completing a project.

THE WHEEL OF FORTUNE: Major change—of residence, job, outlook; completion of one cycle and beginning of another, luck and fate, fame and fortune.

JUSTICE/ADJUSTMENT: Legal and financial considerations, balance and harmony, learning to get along with others yet be true to yourself, partnerships, contracts.

THE HANGED MAN: Handling your hang-ups, self-sacrifice, martyrdom, alcoholism and addictions, surrendering your fixed ideas, attitudes and beliefs.

DEATH: Letting go of something, cutting through outworn forms to allow for new growth, rebirth and regeneration, pain, examining things to their full depth, research.

TEMPERANCE/ART: Developing health and healing practices, testing and trying out your beliefs and philosophy, creative combinations.

THE DEVIL: Power struggles, manipulation, keeping a sense of humor, stirring up unrest, questioning authority, strong sexuality.

THE TOWER: Cleansing—bodywork, diet, fasting, housecleaning; anger and pain, tearing down or burning out old structures no longer necessary.

THE STAR: Recognition for your achievements, idealism and humanism, with the need to act on them; consciousness of the earth as a living entity, with the desire to heal her.

THE MOON: Imagination and dream work very strong, sense of being drawn by an unknown desire, karmic relationships.

THE SUN: Recognition, achievement of a major goal, marriage and/or birth, sense of self-worth.

JUDGMENT/AEON: Dealing with judgment, criticism, evaluation from yourself and others; breakthrough to new beliefs, world view, understanding; born again, dealing with death and transitions.

THE WORLD/UNIVERSE: Learning to dance on your own limitations, working within limitations or structure, sense of endless potential.

THE FOOL: Adventure, travel, daring, openness to new experience.

VISUALIZING THE TAROT

The following narrative was written as an assignment by LiAnne Graves, a student in one of my Tarot classes. It grew out of a meditation on The Fool, The Magician and The High Priestess cards and had such universal appeal that I adapted it as a guided visualization and read it to my students using a musical background. By using music with a slow, soothing rhythm, you will find it easier to relax and let the words enter without the usual judgments and barriers. I have found some sections of Vivaldi's "Four Seasons" to work especially well with visualization, as do many of Steven Halpern's recordings.

Record the story on a cassette or have someone read it to you, preferably with musical accompaniment, allowing the music to carry the rhythm of the words.

As with all visualizations, you should first take three breaths and ground your energy. Reread the instructions in Chapter One if you don't remember them.

A Tarot Story

The garden surrounding the temple is one beyond description. You have been led there by a colorful character with a carefree way about him. His absorption with the world around him makes you feel a bit uneasy. If it weren't for you and this little white dog, he would have fallen into many mishaps. You have to be very aware of where you are in order to follow him; his seeming lack of reality leads you to believe he is out of it. As you climb and jump from cliff to gully, you begin to become light-headed. Stopping to catch your breath, you see him disappear into a rose garden. When you return to your senses, a new awareness comes over you. You feel as though a transformation has taken place. An incredible energy force is beckoning through the rosebush.

You move through the hanging vines. On the other side is the garden; in the distance, the temple. Entering this wondrous oasis, you are struck by the intensity around you. On your left is a square wooden table. In front of the table stands a man whose beauty takes your breath. He seems to be leading an invisible symphony as he raises the baton in his right hand and directs the energy in his left hand. Electricity shoots from every inch of his being. On the table before him is a cup, a rod, a sword and what seems to be a giant coin with a star in the middle. He seems somehow familiar to you, as if in a dream you had followed him there. You ask him his name. He looks at you and winks. It seems he is playing tricks with your mind. Visions and fantasies dance between you, and yet, each one is beyond mere hallucination. With each new thought-picture presented to you comes a clarity and awareness that you've never known before.

It is all you can do to keep up with him. On top of that, he is so attractive in his white shirt dress and red cape. What is really too much is this lazy eight that hovers over his head, turning, twisting, emanating light and energy. It is hypnotic. Only his eyes keep you centered. They look deep within your soul as none other have ever done. Standing in the garden, surrounded by hanging vines, roses, plants and flowers too numerous to mention, you feel unified with this being and the garden around you. Your souls are one. You want to merge with him, enter his channel and become one with the source that surges through him.

Before you can finish your thought, a voice enters your brain. "You must first complete your journey. You must leave the garden and enter the temple. There, if you are accepted, you will be given futher information and set upon the path." Your heart feels a loss, with which the reply comes, "We are one; our souls are from the same Father. Before I can return and take you with me, you must go through the initiation. Many such as you have stood before me, and none have been able to remain as long as you have. I have deceived, dazzled, amazed beings greater than you, and yet, in your beauty and wonderment I find myself beginning to feel an excitement. It's as if all that I have created to fill this loss of true enchantment stands before me in its own perfect creation. I am the Magician, and yet your innocence and faith has me dazzled. Before we can truly become one again, you must leave the garden and me. If you are who I believe you to be, we shall be one again as in the beginning. The path is hard; the journey is long. The end, eternity, as one. Your search has led you to the garden once again. You have found me and have seen yourself within me. I can give you nothing material to take—not nourishment, not shelter, neither talisman nor potion. I am allowed to give you one bit of inspiration—a word, a vision, to remember who I am. Think well upon this. This and this alone shall lead you back to me. Here I'll remain, forever to be the illusionist until a force outside myself can show me vistas beyond my own. I see the horizons in your soul. I feel the presence of a spirit within you as great as the one I channel. You are my soul, you are my mate, you are the part of me that left my side when we tumbled from grace. Eternity has been but one night's dream. I have watched you sleep and now you have awakened. Choose well, my love, for this alone shall be your memory of me until we both can lift our hearts to God to be taken back once again.''

It is as if you've been here before and before and before. His eyes never leave yours, his mouth never once moves. You know where you are and who he is. A chill of electricity passes through every atom of your being. You lower your head and thank Source for this blessing. You look again and see he is pleased. The time has finally come. You have crossed the threshold, you have moved through the maya, your destiny is before you. You ask him for a song. A song that will weave itself through all the songs you will ever hear. His eyes glow with inspiration. He nods his head and adds, ''To such a simple request another shall be added. You will know me when I'm there. This shall be your greatest test. I am the breath of life, the brook which flows through all. And yet, illusionist that I am, my essence cannot be mistaken. I am one; there are none before and none after. You will know me without knowing why. Do not seek me, I am always there. Have faith in my presence and listen to my song. If you pass the initiation and complete the journey, we shall be united and leave the garden as one. If at any point you fail, you will once again find yourself before the rose garden—only each time the veil will be harder to push aside, the innocence less, the hope of renewal a little farther from your reach. All of this shall fade from you, as well as from me. All that will remain shall be the song and a certain look that shall pass between us before I leave. Go with a pure heart and an open mind. I am with you, as before, as forever more.''

The sound of his last words echo throughout the garden. The light around him becomes brilliant. You are unable to keep your eyes on him. As you venture one last look through the glow, you are struck with a gaze that reaches into your being and strikes a chord, creating a sound within. As the sound grows, the light dims until both sound and light merge into one thin distancing tone. You could follow this note, yet something inside keeps you grounded and you find yourself before a tall white temple. Taking no thought of how you got there, or even what passed before you entered the open portals, you see at the end of a long hall a woman dressed in blue flowing veils. You feel the presence of a being filled with knowledge. A cup to quench your inner thirst—the journey has begun.

High Priestess Guided Visualization

Take a short break, then continue the story by approaching the High Priestess in her temple. This should also be recorded or read to you. Make sure to pause for several breaths where indicated by the #s. More #s mean longer pauses—about one long inhalation/exhalation each.

Close your eyes, relax, and take three deep breaths. # # #
Now imagine yourself before a tall white temple.

Accept whatever image comes to mind. # # #
Approach the temple and enter it.
A long hallway stretches out in front of you.
Look around. Imagine what the interior of this temple looks like.
You might find yourself in a very unusual place—that's okay.
This is the temple in your mind
and it can be anything you want. # # # #

Walk down the long hallway,
deeper and deeper into the heart of the temple. #
You now stand before the High Priestess of the temple.
Look at her carefully, notice what she is wearing,
where she is standing or sitting
and what she is doing.
She might change appearance as you watch her—
becoming slowly more clear. # # # #

Take a moment to breathe deeply.
Breathe in the scents of the temple. # # #

Listen—
Do you hear any sounds? #
If so, what do you hear? # # #

The Priestess is also known as the Oracle.
She stares deep into your soul with the look of inner knowing
and from her place of ancient memories and deep mysteries,
summons you. #
From her you will receive assistance in your quest.
In one hand she holds a book in which is recorded
your beginnings and your previous lives.
In her other hand she holds an object that you cannot see.
She motions you to come forward—
she wishes to give you something
to help you on your path.
In your left hand she places the object she has been holding.
What is it? examine it closely. # # # #

What are you to do with this object?
Ask her how it is to be used in your life. # # # #

Then thank her for her help. # #
Turn and walk back down the hallway
and out through the portal.

Take a few moments to come back to the here and now.
Feel the chair or the floor beneath you.
Stretch your body and open your eyes when you are ready.

Immediately answer the following questions:
What did your High Priestess look like?

What did you see and feel in the temple?

How did it smell?

What did you hear?

Wht object did you receive from your High Priestess?

What did she tell you to do with it?

SUGGESTED READING FOR CHAPTER TWO

The New Diary: How to Use a Journal for Self-Guidance and Expanded Creativity. Tristine Rainer. Los Angeles: J.P. Tarcher, 1978.

The position and phases of the moon can be found in astrological calendars and almanacs such as the *Celestial Influences Calendar* and the *Daily Planet* and *Witches' Almanacs*.

Music for guided visualizations, relaxation and meditation: Halpern Sounds, 1775 Old Country Rd. #9, Belmont, CA 94002.

FROM THE MORGAN-GREER TAROT, illustrated by William Greer under the direction of Lloyd Morgan and published in 1979. These Major Arcana cards are laid out in the pattern of the Rose from the Hermetic and Rosicrucian Rose Cross. This Rose contains 22 petals representing the Hebrew letters, the corresponding Tarot Keys, and the astrological signs and planets. In the center are the three mother letters of the Hebrew alphabet: Shin, Aleph, Mem, corresponding astrologically to Fire, Air and Water. Around them are the seven double letters: Beth, Gimel, Daleth, Kaph, Peh, Resh and Tav, corresponding to the seven traditional planets. The outer circle of petals are the twelve single letters: *Heh, Vav, Zin, Cheth, Teth, Yod, Lamed, Nun, Samekh, Ayin, Tzaddi and Qoph, corresponding in order from Aries to Pisces with the signs of the zodiac. This combination of the letters and the sounds for which they stand are the key to the Name or Source, which is the object of mystic contemplation.*

CHAPTER THREE

READING THE CARDS

*The Tarot need not imply that our fate is bound to
overtake us, but rather it indicates how we may best go
forth to meet our destiny—that we have a choice.*
Suzanne Judith

We all seek quick solutions to our problems. We look for someone or
something that will resolve our conflicts, give us security, fulfill our hopes,
allay our anxieties. Out of this human desire have sprung the oracular
methods common to all cultures—a means of predicting the future, a way
to divine what the gods and goddesses have in store for us. Oracular
knowledge represents a way to escape the anxiety of risk. However, there
is danger of delusion here, because it is only through your own individual
encounters with life and chance that you evolve.

It is the clarity and perceptiveness with which you view the events around
you that heightens self-awareness and personal growth, and this is where
oracular information will help you. Specifically it answers such questions as:
How do you use the circumstances that come your way? Do you value your
own strengths and use them effectively? Do you live in a way that is beneficial to yourself, planet earth, and all living beings? What options have you
to express your individual free will in any given event?

UNLOCKING THE DOORS OF OPPORTUNITY

The Tarot encourages you to look at life symbolically—to look deeply into
its simultaneous levels of meaning. It urges you to go beyond the chaos that
appears on the surface and seek for deeper, universal truths that lie buried
in the unconscious mind in order to understand, thus, the true meaning of
cause and effect. When you take responsibility for what you have drawn into
your life, only then can you find the power to bring order out of chaos.

For example, The Devil card represents symbolically our bondage to ignorance. In a reading it may denote a power struggle in your job or personal
relationships, but also suggests that you recognize that the wheel has turned
and the struggle itself now controls you. Your obsession with the problem
is the real devil, limiting your freedom of choice. A bleak interpretation

perhaps, but it also suggests an option, another mode of perceiving the situation. The Devil card advises "mirth," that is, learning to laugh at yourself, seeing the humor and absurdity in a fixed and stubborn view of reality. It is harder to get pompously embroiled in a battle for power and control when you see the absurdity of the whole structure. The Devil card thus urges you to see the existing situation as an inversion of reality. Rather than giving in to guilt and anxiety, The Devil reminds you that this can be an opportunity to create new order out of chaos. Will you choose to see and act on your opportunity? Your rewards are commensurate with the level of chaos into which you have plunged and the energy you exert in creating a new understanding. It is the way to the top via the bottom. It may mean the reversal of all your values. And for the obsessed struggler, bound by the lust for control and power, it points the way to freedom from a self-created bondage. The Devil offers opportunity!

It is only by carefully arranging and rearranging the cards and studying their subtle interrelationships that you can begin to understand how the various aspects of your life interrelate. You can then see how the different events in your life are interconnected, how your actions in one aspect of your life are manifestations of concerns in another; for instance a backache can stem from resentment at the heavy responsibilities you've undertaken.

In order to do a reading either for yourself or for another person, there are several steps which are necessary before you actually lay out the cards. These include:

1) Deciding on the purpose of the reading: Are you, for example, asking a specific question, or doing a daily journal spread?

2) Deciding on the most appropriate spread for your reading.

3) Having paper and pen or a cassette recorder handy to record the reading.

4) Dating the reading.

5) Purifying your cards. See page 19 for suggested purification techniques.

6) Centering and grounding yourself. See page 21.

7) Shuffling, cutting and then laying out the cards.

HOW TO ASK QUESTIONS

First, it is not always necessary to ask specific questions in a Tarot reading. I usually ask for general guidance, using a question such as, "What do I need to examine or look at right now?" trusting my Higher Self to focus the reading on the most appropriate issue. In the reading, emphasis on a particular suit often points out the area of life being dealt with. In general Wands represent creativity and enterprise; Cups are emotions and the psychic realm; Swords are intellect or struggle; and Pentacles are work, money and security. Court Cards focus on people, including the different roles you play in your life; and the Major Arcana speak of your processes and methods.

In an "open" reading you look first for the issue being presented, and then for the advice concerning that issue. Sometimes there is no "advice," but simply a specific and clear description of the situation. If this is the case, the message is often about the relationship between factors.

For instance, a reading for a man that was clearly about his work (many Pentacles) also emphasized a feminine Court Card that seemed to him to describe his mother and ultimately her influence upon his choice of work, but also how he was perceived on the job. By acknowledging that through his desire to gratify her he was trying to live out her projected fantasies, he was able to see more clearly the dynamics that had been created on the job. It also released some of the resentment he had often felt toward his mother, through the realization that his choices had often been based on a misplaced, though unconscious, anticipation of what she expected of him, rather than what was appropriate to the situation. He also became more conscious of the appearance of the feminine cards in his self-readings, representing the transformation of his inner female, as he dealt with this issue.

You may wish to state that your intention is to be guided by advice from your Highest Self, the Universe, Source, the Great Goddess, or a particular angel or guide. Asking for an entity to protect and guide the reading is called an "invocation." You might want to add to your request that the advice be for the "greatest good of my spirit and the planet (or all others concerned)."

Write in your own words one or more invocations or statements of intention that you can use for your general readings:

However, most of the time you will have a more specific purpose in petitioning the archetypal energies of Tarot. Besides asking for general guidance and direction, some things you may want to ask are:

1) Questions about the most appropriate action you can take.

2) Questions of choice; that is, which option among several is best, or what would be the consequences of various choices.

3) Questions asking "Why?" These are best expressed in the form, "What is the lesson I need to learn?" or "What is this situation trying to teach me?"

4) Questions that can be answered yes or no.

It is worth spending as much time as necessary to clarify your question, looking at its different aspects and deciding what you really need to know to resolve it. The form the question takes will ultimately determine the kind of spread you use, including whether to create a spread to get exactly the information needed. For example, one man wanted to know if he and his wife should have a second child, a major point of dispute between them. Through analyzing the question, we discovered that he needed to know three things: Was it in his best interest to have another child? Was it in his wife's best interest to have another child? Was having another child in their best interest as a couple?

We decided to use a simple three-card Yes-No Spread, with each question assigned to one of the three positions. (The Yes-No Spread is discussed in Chapter Five.) The results were "yes" for him, thus strengthening a link with his own inner child; "no" for them as a couple; and "no" for his wife, as it would be both physically and mentally detrimental to her. With the clue that more children would allow him to express his frustrated inner child, we discussed alternative ways to bring more children and play into his life.

How to get answers to your questions will be explored as you are introduced to the various spreads in this book.

INTERPRETING THE SUITS

If this is your first experience in interpreting your own cards, you may feel the need to look up all the meanings in this or other books. Although this is one way to familiarize yourself with the cards, you may also notice that interpretations vary from one author to another. Keep in mind that there is no definitive set of meanings. The way you read a card in a particular position in a particular layout may alter from one reading to another. If at the start you develop your own personal interaction with your cards, you'll soon discover that they are trying to communicate with you in a way as unique as your dream symbols.

Begin by looking at them in a relaxed, receptive way, allowing them to tell you about themselves. In the case of the Major Arcana, the symbols are ancient and archetypal and basically similar from one deck to another. In approaching the Minor Arcana, it is best to begin with a deck that has pictorial rather than abstract symbols.

You can, of course, memorize each card in its upright and reversed state (156 meanings altogether), or you can choose to learn a system for understanding not only the meanings of each card but its relationship to the card before and after it, and to the same-numbered card in the other suits.

In this section the suits and the elements are introduced. In Appendix A the Minor Arcana "pip" cards are listed by number and preceded by a general explanation of the symbolic significance of each number. By putting together the concepts of each number as it would act in each suit (or element), you will have a good working knowledge of any card.

Although what is given below is neither the only way to conceptualize the suits, nor the only possible association of element to suit, this is the system I have used with confidence for fifteen years. It is also the system that Crowley, Waite, Case and their followers had in mind when they designed their decks, and so it is in complete harmony with most British-American designs. If you use a different system, be sure you understand it thoroughly and use a deck compatible with your system. Please add your own ideas to these pages, with explanatory drawings and variations from other texts.

WANDS
(Rods, Staffs, Batons, Scepters, Clubs)

Wands are associated with Fire and are usually represented either as fiery brands or as cut branches with new green leaves sprouting from them (indicating new life).

Wands represent growth, virility, creativity, self-development, inspiration, enterprise, energy, clear perception, enlightenment, passion and desire. Wands are future-oriented, entrepreneurial and inventive; they initiate action. They light up dark spaces and get things moving.

When you get a Wand in a reading, ask yourself, "What do I desire? How can I creatively express myself and my ideas? What options for self-growth are present? What first step can I take?"

VIRTUES: Creativity, enterprise, drive
VICES: Pride, restlessness, willfulness
ELEMENT: Fire
STYLE: Exploding, activating, inspiring
JUNGIAN FUNCTION: Intuition
DIRECTION: South
SEASON: Spring
IMAGES: Candles, flames, matches, volcanos, sunflowers, phallic objects, salamanders, lions and all cats, rams, all forms of new growing life: babies, spring plants, etc.

CUPS
(Vessels, Cauldrons, Hearts)

Cups are associated with Water and are usually seen as full or empty goblets; sometimes as flowers, especially lotuses.

Cups represent emotions, relationships, the subconscious, dream and astral worlds, psychic and intuitive arts, fantasy, illusion, fertility, grace and serenity. Cups are pleasure-loving, with an aesthetic orientation, and sociable.

When you get a Cup in a reading, ask yourself, "What or whom do I love? What am I dreaming or fantasizing about? What am I feeling?"

VIRTUES: Serenity, love, creative visualization, imagination
VICES: Moodiness, excesses and addiction, psychic drains
ELEMENT: Water
STYLE: Flowing, expanding, diffusing, loving
JUNGIAN FUNCTION: Feeling
DIRECTION: West
SEASON: Summer
IMAGES: Cups, goblets, containers, bodies of water, wombs, flowers (especially lotuses), the phoenix, undines, dolphins and all water creatures.

SWORDS
(Blades, Spades)

Swords are associated with Air. Notice that in the Waite/Smith deck the clouds and sky are often indicative of the "atmosphere" of the card.

Swords represent your mental, rational, logical functions—also communication and thoughts. Swords are also indicative of a struggle or conflict and point to a need for decisions about or separation from past attachments. Desire for truth and a need for discrimination are often indicated.

When you get Swords in a reading, ask yourself, "Where are my thoughts focused? What decision am I facing? What tension or conflict do I need to deal with? What changes have to be made?"

VIRTUES: Penetration, courage, strength, truth and justice, organization
VICES: Thoughtlessness, judgmentalism, sharp-tonguedness, fear or confusion
ELEMENT: Air
STYLE: Storming, freezing, striving, conceptualizing, communicating, confronting, cutting through
JUNGIAN FUNCTION: Thinking
DIRECTION: East
SEASON: Fall
IMAGES: Clouds, wind, sky, all sharp objects: razors, knives, glass; sylphs, four winds, birds

PENTACLES
(Deniers, Disks, Coins, Stars, Diamonds)

Pentacles are associated with Earth and are often represented as money, crafts made by hand or fruit (of plants or of your labors).

Pentacles indicate a concern with money, the result of labor, the accumulation of knowledge and development of skills. Pentacles represent what grounds and stabilizes you. Also traditions, foundations and inheritances. Since they question your sense of self-worth and what you value, Pentacles can represent money, work, or your home—depending on where your sense of security lies. Drawing from the assumptions of its own culture, the Waite/Smith deck depicts Pentacles within a capitalist framework and often shows the disparity between the haves and the have-nots.

When you get Pentacles in a reading, ask yourself, "What do I value? Where do I find my greatest sense of security? What do I feel insecure about? What goals are being materialized? What messages am I getting from my physical body and from my environment?"

VIRTUES: Knowledge and ability, endurance, stability
VICES: Stress and anxiety, stubbornness, inability to change, possessiveness, greed
ELEMENT: Earth
STYLE: Drying, cracking, materializing, solidifying, crystalizing
JUNGIAN FUNCTION: Sensation

DIRECTION: North
SEASON: Winter
IMAGES: Money, platters, stones, fruits of the earth, crafts, machinery, Mother Earth, gnomes, bulls, cows, goats

PURIFICATION WITH EARTH, WATER, AIR AND FIRE

In this exercise you actually experience the energies of each of the four elements corresponding to the four suits. As with the creative visualizations, you'll need to record the exercise on your cassette recorder or have a friend read it to you. The exercise was inspired by one I experienced at a Sufi meditation retreat with Pir Valayat Khan which can be found in his book, *Toward the One*. I borrowed ideas from Charles Williams' *The Greater Trumps* for the purification with Earth.

Basic Preparation

Sort your Tarot deck into four piles by suit, Aces through Pages. Place them in front of you on a table. You may also wish to place a ritual object for each element; for example, a candle or a wand for Fire; a cup of water; a stick of incense or knife for Air; and a coin, small pot of earth, or herbs for Earth.

Begin by taking off your shoes and standing with your hands held out in front of you, palms up. Breathe slowly and evenly through your nose.

As you inhale, visualize that you are drawing energy in through the solar plexus (a point two inches above your navel), through the soles of your feet and through the cavity at the top of your head.

As you exhale, radiate energy from your heart-center and simultaneously from your shoulders and the palms of your hands.

Continue to do the above.

Thus we have three *inlets* for energy: 1) Earth energy from the magnetic field of the earth, entering through the soles of the feet; 2) Prana, or cosmic energy, entering through the solar plexus; and 3) Celestial energy entering through the crown.

Inhale energy through these centers.

We also have three *outlets* for energy: 1) Love radiating from the heart-center; 2) The aura, or personal magnetic field, radiating from the shoulders; and 3) Healing energy radiating from the palms of the hands.

PURIFICATION WITH EARTH (Breathe IN and OUT through the NOSE.)

Take the suit of Pentacles in your hands and think of Earth: garden-mold, the stuff of the fields and the dry dust of the roads; the earth your flowers grow in, the earth to which our bodies are given, the earth which in one shape or another makes the land as parted from the waters. Earth, earth of growing and decaying things—fill your mind with the image of it. Let your hands be ready to shuffle the cards. Hold them securely but lightly, and if they seem to move, let them have their way. Help them; help them to slide and shuffle.

Feel gravity pull—grounding you. You are sending out roots deep into the earth, pushing their way into the moist, dark earth, seeking nourishment.

Exhale all the toxins and denser aspects of yourself into the earth where this stale energy is renewed. Inhale the filtered energy, nourished and recharged by Mother Earth.

When you exhale, feel how the magnetic field of the earth draws the magnetic field of your body toward it.

As you inhale, feel how the magnetic field of your body draws the magnetic field of the earth into itself, just like the plant draws the earth and water into itself.

Shuffle the Pentacles. Feel the cards sliding over one another like earth crumbling between your fingers. You are breaking and rubbing a lump of earth between your hands. They are full and heaped with earth. A card of earth wants to fall from between your fingers. Let it. Let one card fall to the floor at your feet.

Now press the cards back firmly into a stack, thinking of them as only cards—drawings: line and color. Place them on the table before you. Pick up the card you dropped and lay it aside for later.

PURIFICATION WITH WATER (Breathe IN through the NOSE, OUT through the MOUTH.)

Take the suit of Cups and think of Water: a clear, blue lake, a silver stream running through a forest, the salty ocean waves engulfing you, the pouring rain refreshing the earth, cleansing and making things green, renewing. Feel the Cups in your hands flow from hand to hand as ripples in a pond, the current in a stream. Let the water flow through your fingertips; let your hands, like the banks of a river, guide the flow.

Imagine that your own magnetic field is a fluid lake with a clear stream running through it. It washes you clean, cleansing you with its flow.

As you exhale, the impurities in your magnetic field are drawn into the stream. You feel porous as a sieve, with lots of little holes in your solidity.

As you inhale, the cosmic fluid pours into every cell.

Let the energy flow through you. Stand on your toes under a waterfall. Let the water flow through you, through your hands. Feel completely relaxed. You are wet, soaking wet.

Shuffle your Cups. Feel the water flowing through your hands: you are still under the waterfall, the water is flowing through the open spaces in your body—between each cell, cleansing, purifying. You feel it in your hair and on your skin and between your fingers, wet and flowing. The waves wash a card into your fingers. Take this card and put it aside.

Now become aware of the cards again as cards—as cardboard drawings. They are stiff and unyielding in your hands. Restack them firmly and place them on the table before you. Place the Cup you received with the Pentacle.

PURIFICATION WITH AIR (Breathe IN and OUT through the MOUTH, with the lips almost closed, so that a refined and gentle stream moves in and out.)

Take the suit of Swords: think of Air. Imagine you are outdoors in the wind. It rushes past, lifting your hair, blowing at your clothes. Breathe in through your mouth and out through your mouth, spreading your fingers and toes wide and your arms out from the shoulders.

As you breathe in, feel like an eagle ruffling its feathers.

Breathe out, letting the air flow through your wings.

Breathe in through the pores of your skin, feel the wind blow through you, through the spaces between your cells, the atoms of your body. As you breathe out, you dissolve in the air currents, become one with the breath of the world.

Feel the Swords in your hands, suspended in the space between your breaths, poised. Now they are moving into action. Shuffle them. Allow the fluid motion of the wind to take them where it will—just as it takes you, moves you. You may feel the wind sway you, spin you, lift you like a bird, on the tips of your toes. Between breaths you hang, balanced on sword-point. Then the wind picks you up again—you are flying. All density, all gravity is left behind you. You are totally receptive to the ever-flowing currents of the breath of light, the Holy Spirit. Hu-u-u-u-u. As you breathe out, you are blown apart by the winds of destruction, then drawn back together and bound by a breath. Suspended.

The winds lift a card into your hand. You accept it. Now the wind dies down.

Push the cards gently back into place. They are cardboard paintings. Solid against your fingers. You stack them neatly in a pile and place them on the table, putting the Sword card given you by the Air with the Pentacle of Earth and the Cup of Water.

PURIFICATION WITH FIRE (Breathe IN through the MOUTH, OUT through the NOSE; on the inhale, the lips should be almost closed—a fine stream of air enters.)

Take the suit of Wands: think of Fire. The glowing end of a stick of incense, a candle flame dancing in a dark room—red, orange, yellow, blue. Oak logs burning in a fireplace, warm, engulfing. A dark volcano against the night sky suddenly erupting in brilliant sparks, golden molten lava moving down through the black rocks. Feel your own internal process of combustion— the food in your body being burned as fuel. Feel yourself burning with desire for your ideals—and one by one, as you manifest them they turn into light: pure white light which illuminates everything around you. Feel the Wands in your hands. Cards of light—they are flowing, have become transparent to the light. As you shuffle the Wands, they illuminate everything around you.

With your mouth almost closed, breathe flame in through your solar plexus and light in through the Crown Chakra, drawing the flame and the light to the heart-center, where they meet and explode into pure radiant light.

As you breathe out through the nose, the heart-center opens up and radiates like the sun, while the light also rises through the crown in the top of your head like a fountain. The light breaks up into all the colors of the spectrum and falls as a mantle around you in colored sparks. Inhale fire. Exhale light. Breathe in through the solar plexus and from the fountain of light above your head. When the light meets and explodes in your heart-center, breathe out and feel the light radiate from your heart, filling the room, while from your crown a rainbow fountain enshrouds you. You feel luminous, you begin to experience yourself as a being of light. The rainbow lights are flickering in your hands. Shuffle them. They are dancing balls of light. Pick a fiery Wand from the stack to light your way and place it with the other three cards.

Restack the cards. They become two-dimensional and opaque. They are simply cards. Just pictures with the colors painted on. The light has dimmed, though you now know where to find it.

Write here the cards that were given you from each stack.
I received the

_____ of Pentacles   _____ of Cups
_____ of Swords   _____ of Wands

These cards indicate where you can find the actions and energies of that suit/element in your life right now. Write down here where and how you feel they are currently manifesting, as indicated by the cards you drew:

REVERSED CARDS

Another issue that must be resolved before a reading is how to interpret "reversed cards," or cards that, when turned over right to left, appear upside-down.

When I first began to read the Tarot, I disliked interpreting "reversed" cards. I dreaded their appearance and always had to look up the meanings because I could never remember them. I finally decided not to read the reversed cards differently, which freed me to trust them at a much deeper level. I saw each card as a spiral or diagonal containing a spectrum of meaning. At one end of the scale were the negative interpretations of the card, and at the other end were the most positive and beneficial meanings of the card. When I drew a card, I tuned in to its energy in general, but I could usually tell which end of the spectrum was manifesting (as in the *I-Ching*, when it refers to the "superior man," and you must ask yourself if you are the "superior man"). I also found that once I acknowledged my ability to choose, I could slide back and forth along that spectrum, thus manifesting by choice the more positive or negative aspects of any card. From this I confirmed that the Tarot is not "predicting" a fixed and fated future, but is actually a tool for determining the type of energies I can draw on, allowing me to step back and look at them and to accept personal responsibility for the actions taken. I could also see directions to take to use my own highest potential.

Several years ago I began reconsidering reversed cards. After all, if there is a significance in the cards that drop from the deck as I shuffle, or in the positions they occupy in a particular layout, then there must be a significance to a card turning up in a reversed position in a reading. I have also come to realized that *my intention* plays a major role in intuitive and psychic work. This is why so many vastly different interpretations and techniques will "work" for different people.

Here are two approaches that I have combined in my personal interpretations with satisfying results:

One approach (suggested by Tarot teacher Suzanne Judith and by author Rachel Pollack) treats reversed cards as signs of energy that is blocked or closed off, resisting or denying its clear flow. The potential is present but not used or released. Judith sees the reversed card as an opportunity to take action and bring that quality into conscious expression.

The other approach (suggested by Gail Fairfield in her book, *Choice-Centered Tarot*) treats reversed cards as particular expressions of the inner, private and personal self. The qualities of the card are sometimes subconscious, sometimes known; but always internal and probably not known to others. For example, a reversed King card could mean that although others see you as quiet and unassuming, inside you have the determination and capability to carry out the action you propose.

The appearance of reversed cards gives you the opportunity to acknowledge what's going on beneath the surface of things and perhaps, if appropriate, take some kind of externalizing action.

Now, with some knowledge of the suits of the Minor Arcana, experience with the basic Three-Card Spread, and an understanding of the possibilities of reversed cards, you are ready to explore the possibilities of one of the most versatile spreads that Tarot has to offer.

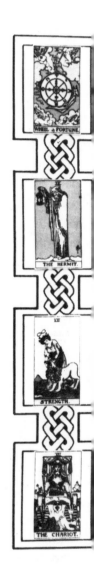

*THE FIRST TEN MAJOR AR-
CANA cards from the Rider-Waite-
Smith deck are laid out in order on
the Celtic Cross pattern drawn by
Susan St. Thomas. The Magician
and The High Priestess represent
basic duality or opposition—directive
will versus receptivity. The Empress
is the fertile unconscious in which
you plant your seed ideas. The
Emperor is established form and
structure: your past. The Hierophant
is your highest aspirations. At The
Lovers you choose the direction of
your future. The Chariot is your personal vehicle, while Strength is your
ability to handle your environment.
The Hermit seeks the lesson in it all,
and at The Wheel of Fortune you
find that the end is only a new
beginning.*

CHAPTER FOUR

THE CELTIC CROSS SPREAD

Although the earliest mention of the use of cards in Europe dates back to the 14th century, with specific references to their use in Switzerland, France, Germany and Italy (where they are supposed to have originated), the oldest known method for reading the Tarot is Irish, known as the Celtic Cross or Ten-Card Spread. With occasional minor variations, it continues to this day to be the single most popular method of "spreading" the cards. First referred to by A.E. Waite in 1910 as an "ancient Celtic method," not much is known about its origins. This lack of information makes it all the more extraordinary that the Celtic Cross Spread has maintained essentially the same form and significance, while the Tarot cards themselves have evolved, been reinterpreted, and occasionally radically changed.

There are many styles and ways of reading the Tarot. The fact that both amateur and professional Tarot readers still rely on the Celtic Cross Spread after years of experience testifies to its broad applicability, practicality and meaningfulness. This section will demonstrate what makes this spread so versatile and archetypal and also present new ways to expand upon its capabilities for personal and spiritual growth.

THE HISTORICAL AND SYMBOLIC BACKGROUND OF THE CELTIC CROSS

The Celtic Cross is a form of cross found throughout Ireland, many of which, like the famous Muireadach's Cross at Monasterboice, Ireland, served in the 10th century A.D. as visual aids during open-air sermons. These stone crosses, up to 21½ feet tall, are typically carved with spiral motifs and scenes from the Bible and the life of Jesus. "The deep relief scenes fitted into panels all over them were used for teaching the scriptures to peasants."[1] Muireadach's Cross is covered with scenes from the Old and New Testaments that culminate in the center with Christ at the Last Judgment. These crosses are unusual in Christianity in that the four arms are linked in a large wheel, representing the unity of Spirit with Matter.

Never far from these Christian structures are found the Celtic and pre-Celtic monoliths of the Old Religion. Variously known as cairns, megaliths or omphalos (navels), these upright stones seem to connect the sky and earth, often actually pointing out particular stars, as the earth turns in its yearly cycles. In the ancient pre-Druidic fertility religions, the monolith represents the

The Celtic Cross

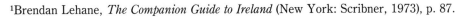

[1]Brendan Lehane, *The Companion Guide to Ireland* (New York: Scribner, 1973), p. 87.

generative creative phallus. It also stands for a single unified vision like the wands of The Magician. As monolith, it is a pathway or ladder through which we can aspire to the spiritual heavens above—wo/man's eternal attempt to attain god(dess)hood. As omphalos or navel, it is the connecting link with Mother Earth and the way to eternal protection and nurturing. Either way it points toward unity with the Whole. It is interesting that the ladder motif is also found as Monasterboice in a legend about its founder, St. Buite, who is said at his death to have climbed his way to heaven on a ladder provided by the angels.[2]

It is possible that these joint Christian/Celtic objects inspired the Celtic Cross Spread, for the cards here are laid out in the form of the archetypal cross, together with an adjacent ladder monolith of cards, usually to the right of the cross. Symbolically, the horizontal bar of the cross represents the positive/negative duality of the material plane, the earthly self. The vertical bar represents the spiritual impulse descending into matter (involution) and ascending out of matter (evolution), impregnating the earth, creating consciousness in physical form. It is the world axis forever pointing to its own center, wherein lies the sense of self. Here, all dualities meet: light/dark, above/below, spirit/matter, conscious/unconscious, logic/intuition, masculine/feminine. J.E. Cirlot in his indispensable book *A Dictionary of Symbols*, identifies the cross as "a magic knot binding together some particular combination of elements to form one individual."[3] That individual is most often identified as the Christ, but is also an apt description of the Celtic Cross layout in which we seek our own highest selves, the Christ within us. As a sign of crucifixion, the cross represents suffering, conflict, agony, pain, death; and contrariwise, rebirth, hope, love, unity, forgiveness. You can recognize yourself in either or both perspectives. The cross represents the way in which you deal with a problem (the cross you have to bear). The ladder is a way in which you can surmount barriers and overcome limitations.

THE SPREAD AND THE SIGNIFICANCE OF TEN

The basic Celtic Cross Spread is made up of ten cards, which represent totality, perfection and completion. Ten, a symbol for the end of a cycle or decade, returns us again to one, but now having experienced all other numbers, conscious of itself. The ten is sometimes pictured as a dot or a line within a circle. The masculine and feminine duality (or left and right brain)

merge into consciousness of the whole. We begin with a one and end with a one which has become more conscious and aware of itself. The cycle of events is complete, now to start on another, higher cycle. It reminds us that

[2]Lehane, p. 86.

[3]J.E. Cirlot, *A Dictionary of Symbols* (Philosophical Library, 1962), p. 68.

every point on The Wheel of Fortune (Arcanum Ten) is a starting and an ending point. So each spread is, therefore, a total picture, complete unto itself. Although other cards, such as significators and "wish cards," may be added, I personally do not find it necessary to use any other cards in the Celtic Cross Spread and will not refer to them. If they work for you, however, feel free to use them.

The first six cards form a cross consisting of the four directions: North, South, East and West, with which we are familiar, and the two additional directions represented by the center cards of sky and earth, the above and below which are found esoterically within our heart-centers, known by the Native Americans as Father Sky and Mother Earth. Therefore, there are actually six directions. These six cards form the basic cross of the spread.

NORTH
Up, Above
The Head or Crown
Astrological Midheaven
Consciousness, Aspiration

WEST	SKY/EARTH	EAST
The Left Hand	The Heart	The Right Hand
The Setting Sun	Center, Duality	The Rising Sun
The Descendent	Life Energy	The Ascendent
Passive, Receptive and Past-Oriented	Dynamic Tension	Agressive, Active and Future-Oriented

SOUTH
Down, Below
The Feet or Base of the Spine
The Nadir
The Basis or Subconscious

EXPERIENCING THE CELTIC CROSS SPREAD

Before doing an actual layout, you may wish to personally experience the dynamics of an internalized Celtic Cross Spread. Begin by sitting crosslegged on the floor, or upright in a chair. With your elbows hanging relaxed, extend your hands out to either side, palms up. Imagine a Tarot card in the center of your head, one in each hand, and a fourth at the base of your spine.

Spend a little time sensing each of these parts of your body and each Tarot card you find there. How do you feel toward each card? Can you see them clearly? As you picture them in their respective positions in your body, do specific cards from the deck come to mind? Write down any characteristics of the cards which you can discover:

In my head: _____

In my left hand: _____

In my right hand: _____

At the base of my spine: _____

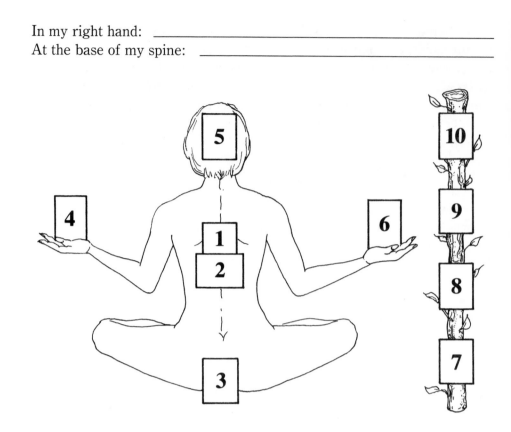

Now add two cards crossing at the center of your being, over your heart and just above your solar plexus. Feel the tension and the balance of these two cards.

What characteristics do these heart cards have?

Uncross them, putting one directly on top of the other. Now put the bottom one on top. Do you feel the shifting, gliding energies as first one then the other predominates, as they mesh and merge and cross? These two center "heart" cards are truly the heart of the reading—often you need go no further, and ultimately you must return to them. The other cards are only a further elaboration on this central theme. Gather these six imaginary cards together and put them back in their deck.

The cards which you visualized in this exercise have demonstrated that you can work with the archetypal energies for which the cards stand whether you actually have a physical deck or not. The ability to see a card clearly and feel its significance within yourself is important when you select cards later for inspiration and meditation.

Besides the six cards making up the basic central cross, four more cards form a vertical line to the right. These four cards represent the way, path or ladder on which you travel, the direction you *might* take. It is a probability line: the action you will probably take, based on who you are, what you have learned, your past and your expectations at the moment of the reading.

Paradoxically, because you are doing this reading, becoming conscious of the energies at work in your life, you now have the option of changing this probability line. These four cards represent the four elements and the four suits of the Minor Arcana: the perceptual (Wands), emotional (Cups), mental (Swords) and physical (Pentacles) aspects of yourself. Occasionally you will find them placed at the four open angles of the cross, much like the symbols of the four fixed signs of the zodiac: the Lion (Leo), the Eagle (Scorpio), the Angel (Aquarius) and the Bull (Taurus), which also appear on many versions of The Wheel of Fortune and The World cards.

READING THE CELTIC CROSS SPREAD

Everyone reads the Celtic Cross Spread slightly differently, and the order in which the cards are laid out varies somewhat. These ambiguities can actually become a strength. Test your sense of ambiguity and read the same cards using *all* the various methods.

As you read each card, try to understand it from many perspectives at once. This helps to prevent being fixed and dogmatic about what you see. For instance, the left-hand card (#4) traditionally represents what influence is passing away, but it can also be seen as the creative talents and natural abilities that you bring to the situation. Thus, it acknowledges that your present abilities come from past experiences, possibly even past lives. Whatever strengths you are developing now (mostly cards five, six and ten) will serve you in the future, and eventually, in some future reading, become cards of the past. (This concept is developed further in Chapter Six.)

The Meaning of the Positions

The following is a selection of variations in the meanings of the Celtic Cross positions adapted from books on the Tarot and friends who have helped me to see the Tarot in many different and simultaneous ways. The sources of the meanings are identified by the originator's initials (wherever possible). They are:

TRAD: Traditional, mostly Waite
JUNG: Jungian style developed from several sources
A.A.: Angeles Arrien
J.K. Joanne Kowalski
OTHR: A conglomeration of sources, including the author

Before reading the following section, take out your cards and shuffle them in any way that feels comfortable, making sure you've mixed them thoroughly. Don't forget to breathe deeply and evenly, to ground and center yourself. You many now either take the first ten cards from the top of the deck and lay them face down in the order of the layout, or you may fan out the deck and draw the cards at random. As you study the meaning of each position, turn over the card you received and consider what it means to you.

CARDS ONE AND TWO

The first two cards actually give the essence of the whole reading. They express the dynamic tension of your present situation, created by your past actions, which is the impetus for future actions. As your heart/core/center, these cards tell you what your inner (true) self wants you to know. The rest of the cards will give you the opportunity to explore this basic energy tension and to understand your personal responsibility for the events that are occurring in your life. Only then can you control them.

CARD ONE

TRAD: The general environment or atmosphere. That which covers you.
JUNG: Same as traditional.
AA: Your heart in the past. Karmic relationships.
J.K. The way to self-development. What you must work on. Strengths you can use, trust, count on.
OTHR: Where you put your energies previously, your habits, past lives. What is developed and manifested. The focus of your energies. What you are aware of. Commencement. What you want to create. Inner Self.

CARD TWO

TRAD: Conflicts and obstacles. That which crosses you.
JUNG: Same as traditional.
A.A.: Your heart in the present. Visionary in outlook.
J.K.: Impediments that prevent your self-development.
OTHR: What is developing and manifesting. That which either deflects or augments the focus of your energies. An imbalance, causing the potential for change, growth. Reaction. What you want to preserve. Outer Self.

CARD THREE

TRAD: The foundation or basis for the situation. Something which is already part of your experience. That which is below you.
JUNG: Your shadow. What you cannot or do not want to look at in yourself. The collective unconscious.
A.A. The subconscious mind. The legs and feet. The ability to ground and express your natural energy.
J.K. Internalization of past attributes.
OTHR: The base of the spine. First and second chakra energy. Your subconscious desires and physical and emotional needs. What you are not yet consciously aware of. Roots. Unconscious habits. Balance. Subconsciously known integration of cards one and two. Motivating force. Intuitive abilities.

CARD FOUR

TRAD: The past. What is passing out of influence. What is behind you.
JUNG: The anima. Your receptive, feminine nature.
A.A.: The left arm (or side of the body). Ability to receive and structure situations and opportunities. What you attract toward yourself or receive. Creative talents, skills and abilities.
J.K. Same as traditional.
OTHR: Opportunities presented, which you may or may not take. The aesthetic, visual, image-producing part of yourself. Things that you "know" without knowing how; your intuition. Your ability to relate to others. What you have realized or accomplished through experience. Past resolutions. What you already possess.

CARD FIVE

TRAD: Your goals. What is above. The best that can be accomplished. Purpose. Aim. Ideals.
JUNG: Your Higher Self or Guide.
A.A.: The conscious mind. The head or center of human awareness. Awareness of your own power.
J.K.: What you should strive to incorporate within your self.
OTHR: What you are consciously aware of. What you strive for or aspire to. The Freudian super-ego: what you think you "should" or "ought" to do. Recognition: how or for what you will be recognized. That which you are guided by or in which you place authority. A new direction or new talents that you need to develop (in contrast to what you have already developed [card four]) and which will help you resolve the tension between cards one and two. Key to the conflict.

CARD SIX

TRAD: That which is before you. The future. The next turn of events.
JUNG: The animus. Masculine, directive, outgoing energy.
A.A.: The right arm (or side of the body). The ability to give and execute situations and opportunities. What you cause. Your ability to make decisions.

J.K.: Same as traditional.

OTHR: Your ability to take action. What you put out into the world. The outer expressions of your self and needs, especially through action. How you will use your abilities.

CARD SEVEN

TRAD: Yourself as you see yourself.

JUNG: The persona or mask.

A.A.: Status, work, creative possibilities.

J.K.: Your source and level of energy, motivating forces, individual perspective.

OTHR: Your condition and attitudes at the time of the reading. Personal strengths and weaknesses. Self-concept.

CARD EIGHT

TRAD: Your environment. Your home, work, family, friends, lovers. That which surrounds you.

JUNG: Same as traditional.

A.A.: Same as traditional.

J.K.: Same as traditional.

OTHR: What is not you. Influences, attitudes, emotions of those near to you. The world. Others' attitudes toward you, or their influence on you. How other people see you (which you tend to "project" back on your experience of them).

CARD NINE

TRAD: Both your hopes and fears of attaining the goal.

JUNG: Same as traditional.

A.A.: How you confront and handle the polarities within your being.

J.K.: Something unresolved which is creating an energy block. That which must be resolved for further development to take place.

OTHR: The way to integrate yourself with the environment. Inner emotions and secret desires. Anxieties. Secrets kept from other people. The lesson to be learned.

CARD TEN

TRAD: The outcome.

JUNG: Same as traditional.

A.A.: Your individual expression in the future, based on your thoughts and energy expression in the present. Blocks or obstacles you are determined to release.

J.K.: Same as traditional.

OTHR: Culmination. Resolution. The result of the path taken. The quality or tool that will help you achieve a breakthrough. The end of one cycle and beginning of another. An additional element you may or may not have considered. The reward. What you will gain from this experience.

Sample Reading—Celtic Cross Spread and Permutations

The question is, "What lesson do I need to learn now in my relationship with Casi?" Ed is out of town for a month, I am working full time at New College and trying to complete this book. My 2½-year-old daughter, Casi, is in daycare, but from the time I pick her up in the evenings and on weekends, I find it impossible to do anything which requires concentration or focus because of her need for my constant attention. I am frustrated in my need to work on this book and angry at myself for sitting with her in front of the TV rather than spending quality time relating to her, yet I feel so exhausted that I fall asleep soon after getting her to bed. I am overwhelmed with feelings of guilt, resentment, frustration and anger at myself.

I've decided to use the Motherpeace deck since I find in it a lot of support and sensitivity to these inner conflicts of personal growth versus relationship. I've drawn the following cards:

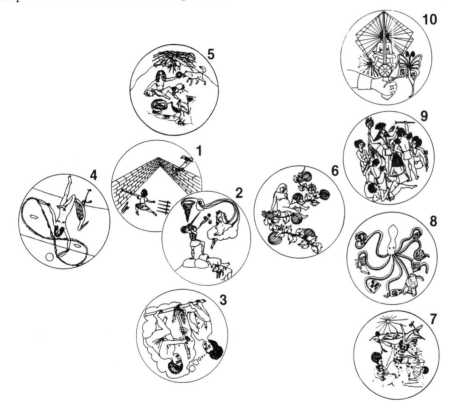

The first two cards are the Eight of Swords and the Daughter of Swords. As always, these aptly describe the situation and even help me to redefine my question. I see in the Eight of Swords my sense of futility at feeling fenced in by responsibilities with no way out and waiting to be rescued when Ed returns. The Daughter of Swords makes me think immediately of Casi as communicator, always talking, always jabbing at me; thus I'm fenced in by her communication needs. But I too am the Daughter bravely trying to cut through my own depression.

The third card—the unconscious—the Two of Wands reversed, indicates my sense of being out of control. It shows how I am blocking my realization that

CELTIC
CROSS
READING
PAGE ONE

```
        5                    10    Date: _____
                                   Reading for: _____
                                   Birthdate: _____
   4        1        6         9   Read by: _____
                                   Deck used: _____
            2                      Question asked: _____
                               8   _____
            3                      _____
                               7   Personality #_____ Soul #_____
                                   Year # _____
```

CARDS

1 & 2 What is the inner (1) and outer (2) focus of your energies? What conflict or tension is in your heart?

3 What are your subconscious needs and desires that form the basis of the situation?

4 What talent or ability that you bring with you from the past will assist or hinder you? What opportunities are you most receptive to?

5 What are you thinking about? What are your ideas and amibitions in the situation?

6 How will you act and use your abilities in the near future? What decisions will you make?

7 How do you see yourself in the situation?

8 How do others see you in this situation? What is the environment in which this takes place?

9 What lesson do you need to learn? What must you resolve for further development to take place? What do you hope for and fear?

10 What is your individual expression in the future, based on your thoughts and energy expression in the present?

Note that card two links cards four and six, and card one links cards five and three.
What numbers appeared most often?

DATE AND PUT NOTES HERE WHEN REVIEWING THIS READING:

I have control and denying my ability to make choices. And with the Two of Swords reversed (card four) behind me as the skills and abilities I've brought with me from the past, I realize that I have been compromising my needs. I need to make peace with both Casi and myself.

The card above (five), indicating what I am consciously aware of and my ideals in the matter, is the Strength card. I know I need to express my love and be in affinity with my instincts. This card also represents my desire for my creativity. How can I be in affinity with Casi and still be able to work on my own projects?

In the future (card six) I have the Seven of Disks—evaluating my efforts and examining my values. Seeing the results (or fruit) of my work and hopefully learning from my mistakes. I need to see clearly what I value so I can know more precisely where to direct my energy.

I see myself (card seven) as the Son of Wands, desiring self-growth, change and excitement, with enthusiasm for play and the unexpected in my life, rather than the dull and routine. I am also very willful and being quite self-centered.

In my environment (card eight) I find the Eight of Cups reversed. The way of retreat is blocked off. I can't run away, but need to stay. At the same time I can't provide a caring and loving environment all the time—it's too much of a drain. I need to recognize that I need a retreat and time to myself.

For hopes and fears (card nine) I've drawn the Seven of Wands. I'm defending myself and my need to have time for myself and to work. I hope I can hold out against all the forces working against it and I fear I will always be fighting this same battle. I am fearful that I will always be fighting off Casi and her demands on me. Yet I need to learn to stand up for myself.

The final card (card ten) is the Ace of Swords, bringing me opportunites for communication and expanding my concepts, helping me realize I have new choices. I am taking the most important first steps —opening honest communications and peeling away the layers of the problem. It tells me I have to be "just" with both Casi and myself.

The two twos reveal the split I see between Casi and me, or between Casi and my work. The two sevens indicate how I will have to test or try out several options; the two eights, the need to prioritize and reconsider the parameters of the situation.

This reading is not complete. I will continue to expand on it with the "permutations" in Chapter Six. Especially important in any reading is the stage called "Breaking Through Obstacles" (also in Chapter Six), which brings a resolution and completion by discovering the Key to the reading.

Fill in the Celtic Cross Reading form with the cards you received in your reading, then write what you think the cards stand for in your life.

SUGGESTED READING FOR CHAPTER FOUR

On Symbols:

A Dictionary of Symbols. J. E. Cirlot. New York: Philosophical Library, 1962.

On Interpretations of the Cards:

See especially: Butler, Douglas, Fairfield, Gerhardt, Gray, Noble and Pollack in the Bibliography, and the interpretations in Appendix A.

FROM THE NATIVE AMERI-CAN TAROT, created by husband-and-wife team Magda and J. A. Gonzalez and published by U.S. Games Systems in 1982. Contemporary decks are taking more and more liberties with the naming of the Court Cards. The Gonzalezes have this to say about their choice of names: "Native American matriarchs are older women respected for their skills and wisdom. Chiefs are not considered rulers. Rather, they are wise and respected men who have earned their title and its responsibilites. Warriors are young men still proving themselves. Maidens are young women, married or single, who must also prove their worth." The Matriarchs are the essence of spiritual power within, the Chiefs are intellectual power potential, the Warriors are material power activated and the Maidens are emotional power flowing. These ideas are similar to those of the Golden Dawn, in which the Court Cards are associated with the elements so that all Kings have the quality of Fire; the Queens, Water; the Knights, Air; and the Pentacles, Earth. Therefore, the King of Wands is considered to be Fire of Fire (Wands), the Knight of Cups is Air of Water, and so on.

CHAPTER FIVE

THE COURT CARD PERSONALITIES

Most readers find the Court Cards to be the most difficult part of interpreting a reading. You may well be overwhelmed when seven out of ten cards in a reading are Court Cards. The exercises included here are designed to help you create an intimate, personal association with each of these archetypal figures.

When Court Cards appear in a reading, they usually operate in two ways simultaneously. First, a Court Card always represents you, or the person for whom the reading is being done; and second, it may represent someone you know, especially someone on whom you've "projected" part of your personality.

To deal with the second option first, Court Cards often represent someone you know. For instance, a King or a Queen can be your father or your mother, or someone in authority or to whom you look for direction. Kings and Queens are usually mature and able to give advice. They influence the situation in a way described by their position in the spread. Knights are often young men who introduce a spurt of new energy into your life: they invite, entice, encourage and pull you along with their interests. For instance, in a reading for my friend Alice, the King of Pentacles represented her husband Jason, with whom she had a long-established relationship. Then along came Albert, a Knight of Cups type, who became her lover by enticing her with the excitement of the unexpected, with new energy and vitality. Knights tend to be experienced as headstrong and single-focused. Pages can be children, young women or sometimes any person who brings messages and new ideas. They often are serendipitous catalysts for change in your life.

The designs and names of the Court Cards vary among the various decks. For instance, The Crowley/Harris Knight is more mature than the Waite/Smith one, taking the place of the Waite/Smith King, but with more dynamism. The Crowley/Harris Prince is the son of the Knight and Queen and more of a worker, developing his abilities and still learning. The Crowley/Harris Page is called the Princess and is a young woman or girl-child with sensitivity and daring and the ability to take risks and explore new possibilities without fear. The Motherpeace deck features the Shaman, the Priestess, the Son and the Daughter, thus bringing a magical feeling to the deck and suggesting that you have the ability to create your own future.

As I mentioned earlier, Court Cards almost always represent aspects of yourself. In the reading they represent the way you are acting in the situation—those aspects of your identity which you are drawing upon or the mask you put on in any particular circumstance. For instance, do you feel mature and capable, with everything under control? That is, Kingly? Or are you sensitive and receptive to the needs of others, seeking to satisfy those needs to the best of your ability in a Queenly sort of way? Are you an energetic and daring Knight, acting on your desires? Or are you perhaps a Page, new at something, naive and open to learning as much as possible?

Jungian psychology provides a framework for integrating both points of view: the Court Card as yourself *and* as another person. The concept called "projection" refers to projecting (or thrusting) inner qualities of yourself onto other people around you, whether or not they have these qualities. They become shadowy mirror reflections of yourself. It works like this: You notice in other people some of the characteristics that you do not recognize in yourself—both positive and negative. As a result, you tend to let those people act out your own unconscious perceptions of yourself and your own inner situations, or you get angry with them when they don't. For instance, Susan, who was fascinated by books and writing, was living with Thomas, a good carpenter who aspired to write plays. The relationship allowed Susan to continue her fascination without having to attempt to write on her own. She loved to praise Thomas' writing and fire his ego as a way of gratifying her own unrecognized desires, but she also could be quite a nag when he became involved with other things and didn't want to write. If she recognized her own desire to express herself through writing, she would not lay such a heavy burden on Thomas to be always producing. Through the appearance of Court Cards in a spread, you can see what power and abilities you might be "giving away." What roles in your life do you want other people to take on for you? These projections are especially strong across sexes, when a man is discouraged from expressing his feminine side and thus must find a woman to act this out for him, and vice versa. Once you release others from these projections, you release them to be who they really are. You are also free to carry out your own ambitions and desires.

Another form of projection is associated with the shadow self—those negative inner qualities which we try to disown. Note the actions that annoy you in other people. Have you ever acted likewise, or wanted to, but left it to others? Look for these shadow projections, particularly in the Celtic Cross positions of the unconscious (card three), the past (card four) and your hopes and fears (card nine).

A reading containing several Court Cards often refers to your interpersonal relationships and the many different roles you have to play. Sometimes a fragmentation of your energies is indicated by all these different personalities and aspects you are expressing. For instance, there is the executive business woman who is the nurturing mother for her child, the seductive lover to her husband and the respectful daughter to her mother—not to mention the militant feminist to one group of friends and the gracious hostess to another; and then there is her secret life as the student of Tarot and astrology. Each role involves a change of gears, clothes, vocal tone, energy level, focus, etc. We might portray her various roles respectively as: King of Wands, Queen of Pentacles, Queen of Cups, Page of Wands, Knight of Swords, Queen of Wands and Queen of Swords, although you might have picked different cards to express these same characteristics.

Identify five to ten roles which you regularly play and choose a Court Card that best represents you in each role. You may use cards more than once or you may need more than one card to represent a particular role.

CURRENT ROLES IN MY LIFE   CORRESPONDING COURT CARDS

_____   _____
_____   _____
_____   _____
_____   _____
_____   _____
_____   _____
_____   _____
_____   _____
_____   _____
_____   _____

Choose Court Cards to represent the most important people in your life in the aspect you most frequently encounter them.

PERSON   CORRESPONDING COURT CARD

_____   _____
_____   _____
_____   _____
_____   _____
_____   _____
_____   _____
_____   _____
_____   _____

Remember that each of these people has several roles to play and can therefore appear in a spread represented by Court Cards other than the one you selected here. In your daily three-card readings, watch for the various ways in which you and the people close to you usually appear.

THE COURT CARD PARTY

Now it's time to meet all the Court Card personalities. Pull out the sixteen Court Cards in your deck and spread them randomly in front of you. Imagine that they are people at a party.

I feel attracted to:

I would like to avoid:

I feel uncomfortable with:

I feel gay and talkative with:

I feel a secrecy and solitude about:

These seem aloof or rude:

I feel welcomed and warmed by:

To understand the personalities of these Court Cards even better, pick two Court Card figures who might be dynamically attracted to each other. Imagine a dialogue between them about some provocative subject. Write it out on another sheet of paper.

Court Cards: _____ and _____.

Topic:_____.

UNDERSTANDING THE COURT CARDS

The following stimulates the intuitive images you can have of another person. I have adapted this exercise for use with Tarot cards from Frances Vaughan, *Awakening Intuition*. New York: Anchor Press/Doubleday 1979.

First, pick a Court Card that interests you.
Write down spontaneously and without inner criticism the first image that emerges.
Date:

The Court Card I picked for this exercise is:

If the person in this card were an animal, what type of animal would it be?

What type of plant would it be?

If this person were a landscape, what would it be like?

If this person were a body of water, what kind would it be?

> How deep would the water be?

> How clear?

> What temperature?

> Describe its movement:

If this person were a light:

> What color?

> What intensity?

If this person were a geometrical symbol, what would it be?

If this person were a type of music, what would it be like?

If this person were a tool, what would it be?

If this person were a character in history, who would it be?

How would you visualize this person as a little child?

What is this person's energy field like?

What is the energy field like between you and this person?

Take a few minutes to be quiet and receptive to any images that may emerge spontaneously as you continue to focus your attention on the figure in the card.
Write down any additional images which emerge:

Describe how you resemble the card you drew:

How are you unlike it?

If you enjoyed this and it worked for you, repeat this exercise with more, or even all, of the Court Cards. Use the *Court Card Images* chart as a place to record your answers and to give you the opportunity to compare and contrast your images. Some of the Court Cards will be easier to "get a handle on" if you contrast them with others. For instance, how is the Knight of Wands different from the King of Wands, and how would you express this difference in terms of two different kinds of animals?

THE THREE MODES OF TAROT

The story of this next exercise exemplifies the type of synchronicity that occurred while I was working on this book. It confirms the archetypal nature of the Tarot as an expression of the collective unconscious and reveals the inherent qualities that are there for all those who wish to discover them.

I was working on a method to help people understand the Court Cards: What made them different from the other cards? What were the special qualities they possessed? What would be the best way to learn how to use them in readings? I had written most of the other exercises for the Court Card section, when I thought of creating a reading in which the 78 cards were divided into their three natural groupings (or modes): Major Arcana, Number Cards and Court Cards. I realized that one card could be drawn from each stack and integrated in a reading. This evolved into the exercise given here, and I used and tested it in my classes with excellent results. About four months later I was given a then out-of-print copy of *Magic Ritual Methods*, by William B. Gray. Although he gives little space to the Tarot, he does have one section on the Court Cards. In his discussion of how to understand them, he describes the same spread I had just "invented," but with an additional, separate stack for the four Aces. In either case, the reader picks one card from each stack to form the spread. Not only had he "invented" the same spread, but he had discovered it by going through the same process I had—by struggling to understand the Court Cards.

My first reaction was one of dismay: so I had not originated this spread! Suddenly I realized that this incident demonstrates two very important points about the Tarot (and many other metaphysical systems). First, that its archetypal nature manifests not only in the images of the cards but in the very structure of the deck. Anyone who diligently explores the cards is led by them into the "collective unconscious"—Jung's term for the memories and experiences of humankind which are expressed in "archetypal" images. Discoveries like these open the doors to an inner understanding of the way we operate in our quest for self-knowledge.

Second, there is the intuitive asurance that when the time is right, new knowledge will be revealed. Darwin did not originate the theory of evolution. Rudiments of the theory had been published previously. But it was an idea whose time had come. This is also true of the Tarot. While working on this book I have observed it again and again. For example, after I had assigned affirmations to each of the Tarot cards, I attended a lecture by

COURT
CARD
IMAGES

	ANIMAL	PLANT	LANDSCAPE	BODY OF WATER	LIGHT & COLOR	GEOMETRIC SHAPE	MUSIC	TOOL	HISTORICAL CHARACTER	OTHER
KING OF ♀										
KING OF ☿										
KING OF ⚔										
KING OF ⊕										
QUEEN OF ♀										
QUEEN OF ☿										
QUEEN OF ⚔										
QUEEN OF ⊕										
KNIGHT OF ♀										
KNIGHT OF ☿										
KNIGHT OF ⚔										
KNIGHT OF ⊕										
PAGE OF ♀										
PAGE OF ☿										
PAGE OF ⚔										
PAGE OF ⊕										

Angeles Arrien in which she talked about doing the same thing. A list of her affirmations for the Major Arcana appeared in the first *Tarot Network News* only weeks later. It was at this same time that Shakti Gawain published her book, *Creative Visualization*, which popularized "positive thinking" in a new framework of affirmations for personal growth.

The exercise that follows is the one I devised to better understand the differences among the three modes of Tarot cards. The modes are as follows:

COURT CARDS: Mode or method of acting. How are you acting? Your subpersonalities. Masks and personas. What roles are you playing?

MINOR ARCANA: A description of your situation. What are you dealing with?

MAJOR ARCANA: The archetypal energies within yourself that need to be expressed. In what way are you dealing with the situation? What abilities are you using?

(William Gray adds a fourth category, the four Aces, which I have included with the Minor Arcana. You can separate them out at your own discretion. If you use them separately they indicate the aspect of your life that is involved.)

Divide your Tarot deck into three stacks: Court Cards, Pip Cards and Major Arcana. Shuffle each stack and then pick one card, unseen, from each. Write down the card and what it indicates, or a short personalized interpretation, in the sentence format in the adjacent form.

CONTACTING YOUR INNER TEACHER COURT CARD

If you turn back to Chapter One, page 17, you will find instructions for determining your Inner Teacher Court Card. (For this you will need to know in which zodiacal sign your Moon is found.) If you don't have that information, or if you would prefer, you can choose a Court Card that you feel best represents your Inner Teacher. To do this, lay out all the Court Cards and pick the figure you feel most drawn to as a teacher—a personality you could rely on for inner direction regarding your highest potential. Take a moment to quietly sit with this personality; ask your Higher Self if there are any objections to this teacher. If you do not feel a strong "no" or any sense of discomfort, then go ahead with the exercise. Mike Samuels and Hal Bennett in their book, *Spirit Guides: Access to Inner Worlds*, have some good advice for checking the information you receive to see if it is from a "spiritual" source, or what they call "ego static." I sum it up this way:

1) Are your muscles relaxed and do you feel at ease?

2) Is the information nonjudgmental?

3) Is it harmful toward no one?

4) Is it based on love?

THREE
MODES OF
TAROT

COURT CARD	MINOR ARCANA CARD	MAJOR ARCANA CARD

1) What I am experiencing:

I am acting like a _____, a _____
          (Court Card)   *(describe the type of*
_____, in
person you see in that card)

a _____ situation in which _____
   (Minor Arcana Card)   *(describe your*
_____
situation—using action verbs)

because of _____, which describes my need to _____
          (Major Arcana Card)
_____.
(describe what archetypal energies in you need to be expressed)

For advice on how to handle the situation, look at the same cards with the following format:

2) How can I best deal with this situation?

I can use the attributes of _____ to _____
                        (Major Arcana Card)   *(describe*
_____
the best qualities you see in this card)

in order to deal with _____, which expresses my
                        (Minor Arcana Card)

desire for (to) _____
              (describe the situation you have drawn to yourself)

_____

_____,

experienced by my inner _____, the one who _____
                        (Court Card)   *(describe*
_____.
that aspect of yourself which chose to experience the situation)

Design your own sentence formats to express your understanding of the relationships between the modes of the Tarot.

5) Does it please or gratify you? (Or does it bring out your inner doubts and fears? If so, it may be your ego (or shadow-self) speaking.)

Place the Court Card representing your Inner Teacher in front of you. Look at it carefully until you can reproduce it in your mind with your eyes closed. Relax into a deep rhythmic breathing, and ground your energies (as described on page 21).

See yourself as a tree sending roots into the earth, deeper and deeper until they enter a cave in the center of the earth. Then descend down into the cave through one of these roots, as if it were an elevator. Look around. Sense the walls, floor, temperature, colors, furnishings. Don't worry if your impressions are vague and you don't actually "see" anything. You may also make up an imaginary situation.

Your Inner Teacher approaches and kisses you on your forehead to open your sight and to bless and protect you; then touches your heart to make you receptive only to thoughts born of love.

Ask your Inner Teacher to reveal him or herself to you in the most perfect aspect and highest potential. Know that you are entirely safe within your circle of protection. Observe your Inner Teacher; watch how the environment around the Teacher changes and intensifies in color, shape, sound and texture. Don't worry if you have difficulty "seeing." Use all your senses on the inner plane—feel for any subtle change, notice reactions in your own body. Often certain symbols, images and impressions will appear around the figure. Note them.

When you return, write down all impressions. Don't hesitate to use images and metaphors.

My impressions of my Inner Teacher in the most perfect aspect and highest potential can best be described as:

The following is a description of the environment and the objects and images around my Inner Teacher:

Your Inner Teacher Court Card is useful for other forms of guidance. Try some of the following variations:

Breathe deeply, relax and ground yourself. Enter the cave as before and create a comfortable place to sit. Waiting for you in the cave is your guide, your Inner Teacher, who greets you and shows you around the cave. If you don't feel comfortable, ask your Inner Teacher to change the environment until you feel secure and at ease.

Now ask your Inner Teacher to take you to your personal Tarot Helper— someone who can help you read and interpret the Tarot. Allow your Inner Teacher to take you off to the left of the cave to a sunny opening you had not noticed before. The floor rises as you approach the opening, and you see bright daylight outside. You leave the cave and follow a path winding up to the right and around a hill until you come to an elevated meadow. Your Tarot Helper awaits you there. Note what he or she looks like. Give your Helper your Tarot deck. On a cloth or small table your Helper lays out three cards and interprets them for you. If you have difficulty seeing them, ask for only one card. Ask any questions you have about the cards, their meanings in your life, or how to read them.

What does your Tarot Helper look like?

What cards did you receive from your Tarot Helper?

How did your Tarot Helper interpret them?

What other information about reading the Tarot did you receive?

Now that you have made this connection, it will be easier to go back to your Tarot Helper at any time and receive personal readings or have your questions answered.

You can also ask your Inner Teacher to lead you to a Tarot figure who can act as your personal guide and helper for:

1) Healing

2) Problems at work

3) Religious and spiritual guidance

4) Insight into relationships

5) Ideas about creativity

6) Information about past and future lives

7) Political, global understanding.

By allowing your Inner Teacher to lead you to a Tarot archetype, rather than selecting one at random, you may receive unexpected insights and discover new approaches to your problems, just through the type of guide that appears to you in this way. For instance, you may have asked for guidance in a relationship, and to your amazement your Inner Teacher brings you to the Justice archetype. Rather harshly and unemotionally, Justice asks what you want in this relationship. You describe your situation, and Justice then weighs your answer in her scales. Now you realize that you have not been honest with yourself, nor with your partner, in your statement of your desires and needs.

SUGGESTED READING FOR CHAPTER FIVE

On Court Cards:

Magical Ritual Methods. William B. Gray. New York: Samuel Weiser, 1969.

On Projection:

The Tao of Psychology: Synchronicity and the Self. Jean Shinoda Bolen. New York: Harper and Row, 1982.

On Imagery:

Awakening Intuition. Frances E. Vaughan. Garden City, NY: Anchor Press, 1979.

On Spirit Guides:

Spirit Guides: Access to Inner Worlds. Mike Samuels and Hal Bennett. New York and Berkeley: Random House/Bookworks, 1974.

FROM THE THOTH DECK, illustrated by Freida Harris under the direction of Aleister Crowley. The Minor Arcana are laid out in the kabbalistic Tree of Life pattern to demonstrate the relationship between the ten Sephiroth and the Number Cards of each suit. According to Robert Wang in his book, The Qabalistic Tarot, *the Minor Arcana are of the "greatest significance in that they symbolize the real potencies in ourselves and in the universe." They are the "centers of energy" between which we travel on Paths which in Tarot are the Major Arcana. Each Number Card is also assigned a Decan (or one-third) of a zodiac sign (see the Zodiac Lessons and Opportunities Chart given in Chapter One), which is ruled by its own planet. The planets ruling the Decans are assigned consecutively, beginning with the first Decan of Aries as follows: Mars, Sun, Venus, Mercury, Moon, Saturn, Jupiter. They then repeat, in order, through the zodiac. Thus every Minor Arcanum card, beginning with the twos, has an astrological correspondence which colors its interpretation.*

CHAPTER SIX

PERMUTATIONS: READING IN DEPTH

Permutations, according to Webster, are "changes, alterations, rearrangements; the combinations or changes in position possible within a group." By rearranging your Three-Card Spread in Chapter Two, you have already used the concept of permutations. In this chapter the permutations expand on the many possible ways of reading a single Celtic Cross Spread. We have already looked at alternative ways of viewing each position in a reading. Now we will look at rearrangements of the order and position of the cards. Each permutation gives a different perspective on the whole. The principle: maintain paradoxes, seek ambiguity. The resulting creative tension will help you to see everyday events from different points of view, thus increasing your perspective and allowing you more freedom of conscious choice.

Many of the individual permutations have been taught or suggested to me by other people. Through the years I have combined them into my own extended method of reading the Tarot.

Permutations can be used when you seek a deeper understanding of the energies and forces with which you are currently dealing. The more clearly you can see the flow and effect of these patterns in your life, the more you can transform yourself into the individual you want to become.

You can expect to take a significant amount of time when doing a reading using all the permutations—an hour and a half is usual once you are familar with the method. It also takes a commitment to delve deeply into your own (or a friend's or client's) motivations, fears, hopes, plans, concerns, strengths and weaknesses. And you should always take the extra moments needed to thoroughly relax and ground yourself.

You will not be able to master all of these permutations at once. Select one permutation to become familiar with, using it every time you do a Celtic Cross Spread, exploring its nuances and possibilities. Permutation Three (The Whole Person Summary Spread) is the most versatile, as it can be used with almost any other spread. It will help you learn the significance of each suit. Eventually you will develop your own modes of using permutations that work for you. Look upon these as means to express the insights you have gained into the interrelationships of the cards. Each of these permutations can be slightly modified to become its own spread if you find its concepts especially helpful.

REARRANGING THE CARDS FOR FURTHER UNDERSTANDING

First, do a Celtic Cross Spread for yourself following the directions in Chapter Four. Once you have read all the cards using the basic format on page 70 and have a basic understanding of what they mean, you can begin to rearrange these same ten cards into new and different patterns and relationships. The numbers on the cards throughout this section will refer to the original, archetypal Celtic Cross layout positions.

PERMUTATION #1: THE TURNING WHEEL

When trying to understand yourself and your motives, it helps to look at how you have acted in the past and how you might act in the future after internalizing your new lessons.

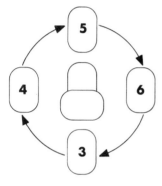

This permutation makes that possible. It was adapted from a Tai-Chi Ch'uan spread designed as a class assignment by Marcia Church.

Imagine the Celtic Cross with a circle around it, connecting the four arms. This corresponds to the Tao and The Wheel of Fortune: everything travels in a circle, eventually returning to itself. Accordingly, in this permutation, we will rotate the four arms of the cross (cards three, four, five and six) one turn clockwise as shown.

Interpret the cards in their new positions, just as if you had originally drawn them that way.

What we are doing here is based on the natural process of any thought and action, which goes through the stages of: 1) idea or ideal, 2) action/assertion, which becomes 3) habit/intuition, and finally 4) letting that go with receptivity to new ideas. The current situation has developed out of past actions (possibly including previous lives) and it influences future behavior. Card five is now in position six, card six in position seven, etc. Now read these cards in relation to each other. In this way you look at what will happen when "what you are currently conscious of" (former card five) becomes your next action (when moved to position six). At the same time, your outer expression of self (former card six) becomes a subconscious habit (when moved to position three), the unconscious basis (former card three) becomes a creative talent from a past life (when moved to position four), and your past-life knowledge (former card four) becomes a consciously directed force (when moved to position five). Rotate the cards a second time and begin again. Continue rotating the cards clockwise and reinterpretating them until they are back in their original positions. Do you see how the "turning wheel" leads to deeper understanding of what these four cards mean?

When looking at the past (as you move the cards clockwise around the wheel), relate the cards to your own experiences, perhaps what you went through last week or a realization of something that happened a year ago. You may even find yourself describing a previous lifetime and how you acted based on your knowledge then.

Similarly, future possibilities for action become apparent when you no longer hide your needs in your subconscious but move them into conscious thought (when card three moves to position five). You can actually watch the wheel of events turn before you and see how the past becomes the present, and how the future is another way of seeing the past. You may wonder how you know whether you are reading what is past or to come. Try reading the cards both ways! Let your intuition tell you.

Example: The Turning Wheel; Permutation #1

Take your Tarot deck and lay out the cards in this example in the basic Celtic Cross Spread. By moving your own cards through the permutation as indicated, this example will be easier to follow.

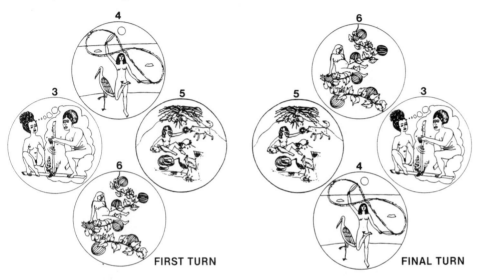

I was dealing with my conflicts about finding time for my work and also time for my daughter. When I began turning the wheel, I found that with the first turn I was ideally trying to keep the peace at all costs (Two of Swords in the fifth position), while asserting that there was a way to work this out lovingly (Strength in the sixth position), yet I was continually evaluating the results (Seven of Pentacles in the third position) and had brought with me the realization that I had the capability to choose what would happen (Two of Wands in the fourth position).

By the time I got to the last turn of the wheel, I recognized that I could consciously evaluate the situation (Seven of Pentacles in the fifth position), assert my power to creatively come up with a solution (Two of Wands in the sixth position), that I have to let go my habit of always seeking compromise (Two of Swords in the third position), and that I need to be receptive to my desire to express my creativity but not let it ride over everything (Strength in the fourth position).

Now go back to a previous Celtic Cross reading of your own that you would like to work with in depth. Lay out the first six cards. Leave the center two cards (one and two) as they are. They won't be used in this permutation but, as always, represent the basic situation around which cards three, four, five and six revolve. In each diagram below, write in the cards as they would appear after rotating them one turn clockwise. Place all the cards in their upright position. Note your interpretations of their new significance in the spaces provided.

In this "past" scenario, I interpret the cards as telling me:

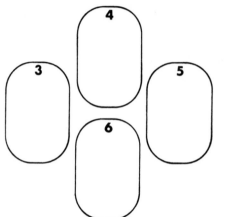

Idea/Ideal (#4)_____

_____

Action/Assertion (#5) _____

_____

Habit/Intuition (#6)_____

_____

Letting Go/Receptivity (#3) _____

_____

Rotate the cards another turn clockwise.

In this next "subconscious" scenario, I interpret the cards as telling me:

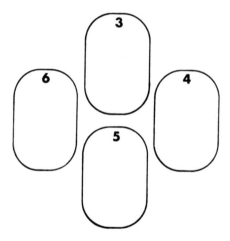

Idea/Ideal (#3)_____

_____

Action/Assertion (#4) _____

_____

Habit/Intuition (#5)_____

_____

Letting Go/Receptivity (#6) _____

_____

Rotate the cards a final turn clockwise.

In this "future" scenario, I interpret the cards as telling me:

Idea/Ideal (#6)_____

_____

Action/Assertion (#3) _____

_____

Habit/Intuition (#4)_____

_____

Letting Go/Receptivity (#5) _____

_____

PERMUTATION #2: PAST, PRESENT, FUTURE

Hilary Anderson, in her class, "The Oracular Dimensions of Creativity," at the California Institute of Asian Studies in San Francisco, taught the following variation on the Celtic Cross.

Rotate the cards back into their original Celtic Cross positions and then sort them into three separate groups as shown by these cards illustrating the sample reading:

GROUP I GROUP II GROUP III

Example: Past, Present, Future; Permutation #2

Continuing with my Celtic Cross example: By moving the cards into their new positions and relationships, I realized that I brought with me from the *past* (Two of Swords, Two of Wands and Seven of Wands) the maturity to be in control and take decisive action. However, along with this came a resurrection of the feeling that I was being opposed and had to fight for my personal needs; yet because of my desire for peace and my attempts at compromise, I had lost sight of the need to act.

In the *present* (consisting of the two heart cards: Eight of Swords and Daughter of Swords, and the cards of myself in the environment: Son of Wands and Eight of Cups) I am enthusiastic about the possibility of new directions for my growth and Casimira's and about the opportunity for each of us to have time and space for retreat. I can now see my way out of my feelings of imprisonment and can open the line for quality communication with Casimira.

My *future* expression (found in the Strength card, Seven of Pentacles and Ace of Swords) suggests that I can be "just" and honest in my communication with Casi, based on my assessment of the situation and my ideals of harmonizing my loving affinity for both Casi and my work.

Now continue with your own reading, using the format for this permutation on the following page.

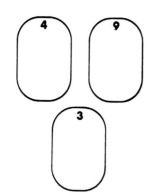

GROUP I—THE PAST: Cards three, four and nine. These cards all relate to the past. Hopes and fears are included in this category because your expectations of future success or failure are based on past experiences. These cards help you to see what lessons you have not yet learned.

The cards which represent my past are:

What issues in the past are still unresolved? What abilities and knowledge that you've previously developed are you drawing on now?

GROUP II—THE PRESENT: Cards one, two, seven and eight. These cards represent yourself (card seven) in your environment (card eight), dealing with the basic situation (cards one and two). They tell you where you are right now.

The cards that represent my present are:

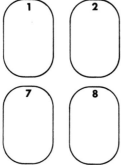

I am _____
                              (description of self based on card #7)
operating in an atmosphere of _____
                                        (describe environment and/or

_____
person portrayed in card #8)
dealing with the basic situation: _____
                                            (describe inner desires as

_____
indicated in card #1)
and _____.
        (describe outer concerns indicated by card #2)

GROUP III—THE FUTURE (in the process of manifesting): Cards five, six and ten. These are forward-looking, visionary, active, conscious. They show you where and how you are manifesting the energy that may shape the future. Eventually, what you think and what you create become your future reality.

The cards that represent the future are:

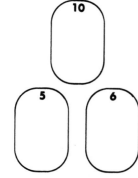

My future expression of _____
                                        (describe your potential expression as

_____
indicated by card #10)
will be the outcome of _____
                                        (describe action indicated by card #6)

_____
and upon _____
                (describe thoughts and ideals indicated by card #5)

_____

Now move the cards around within their own groups. This may tell you more, and suggest further interactions.

PERMUTATION #3: THE WHOLE PERSON SUMMARY SPREAD

This permutation is taught by Angeles Arrien as a further development of her Whole Person Spread. It emphasizes self-understanding in several ways: perceptually, as signified by Wands; mentally, as signified by Swords; emotionally, as signified by Cups; physically, as signified by Pentacles; and archetypally, as signified by the Major Arcana.

Divide the ten cards from your spread into five groups of the four suits and the Major Arcana. (Depending on the cards in your spread, one or more suits may not be represented.) Lay the cards in each grouping in a series of five horizontal rows, one beneath the other (Wands on top, followed by Cups, Swords and then Pentacles). Order the cards left to right, beginning with the Court Cards (King, Queen, Knight, Page) and followed by the Number Cards from Ace to Ten. The Major Arcana form the bottom row and should also be placed in numerical order from left to right. Center each row above the other to create a balanced visual structure, as in the example that follows:

Example: Whole Person Summary Spread; Permutation #3

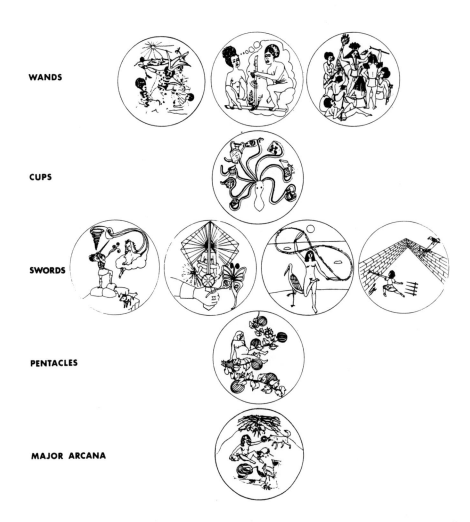

WANDS

CUPS

SWORDS

PENTACLES

MAJOR ARCANA

In this permutation of my example Celtic Cross Spread, I see that I drew three Wands, which indicates that I "perceive" a need to be more creative and expressive in my relationship with Casimira and not give all my power away to her in our relationship. I need my sense of self.

I drew one Cup, which shows my drained emotions and need for retreat and renewal.

There are four Swords, whose preponderance underlines my feelings of being fenced in, always compromising and fighting depression. The emphasis on Swords points to both the struggle I am going through and my efforts at trying to be "reasonable." They also show my need to be honest and fair with both myself and Casimira.

I drew one Pentacle, and seeing this I realize that perhaps I need this time to let my work sit for awhile—to assess where I am going with it, rather than working directly at this time.

I drew one Major Arcana card: Strength. I have the strength and creative ability to come up with a loving solution. The card tells me to be firm in order to control the situation and come to a reconciliation through an understanding of the needs and desires of us both. It does not mean that I love Casi any less.

The preponderance of Wands and Swords confirms I am struggling primarily with issues of communication and fairness about my creativity and self-expression.

Move the spread with which you are working into its new position, following the format on the next two pages. Enter your cards in the blanks provided.

Draw the pattern created by your cards here:

1) WANDS represent the spiritual, creative and perceptive forces at work within you. Yourself as visionary and initiator; your need for growth and activity.

How many Wands do you have? _____
What spiritual and creative forces are at work within you? What are you perceiving, envisioning or initiating?

2) CUPS represent your emotional nature. Your ability to love, relate, dream, imagine.

How many Cups do you have? _____
What is your ability to love, relate, dream, imagine? What are you feeling?

3) SWORDS represent your mental/rational thoughts, your ability to discriminate. Sometimes, your areas of struggle or conflict.

How many Swords do you have? _____
What is dominating your thoughts? Where are you struggling or finding conflict? How are you communicating with others?

4) PENTACLES (DISKS) represent your physical concerns, how you ground yourself, how stable and secure you are. Your ability to devote your energies to work and study are shown here.

How many Pentacles do you have? _____
What are your physical concerns? How are you grounding yourself? How stable and secure are you? How are you using your energies for work and study?

5) MAJOR ARCANA cards represent archetypal forces at work in the situation. Qualities within you that are being called forth and tested. Aspects of yourself involved in the situation.

How many Major Arcana cards do you have? _____
What archetypal forces are at work in the situation? What qualities within you are being called forth and tested? What aspects of yourself do you need to learn about and develop?

Cards that are seemingly negative show the areas in which you need work. Remove these cards and you can see the person you can become after you deal with your fears and insecurities. Any suits not represented usually signify areas of minor concern in the matter. But occasionally it may be obvious that you are avoiding the real issue (the missing suit). For example, in a reading I did about a love affair, no Cups came up. This could sometimes be interpreted as strong emotions not needing attention. But in this case, it was apparent that strong emotions were exactly what the relationship was lacking. It was based on security and convenience, not on feelings. It became clear in discussion that this couple was actually avoiding the realization that there was no longer any love in their relationship.

PERMUTATION #4: YOD HE VAU HE—THE PATH OF HERMES

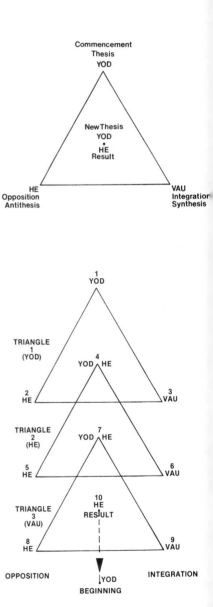

This permutation is based on the work of Papus in his book, *Tarot of the Bohemians*. He describes the structure of the Minor Arcana as a series of three triangles symbolizing a dialectical process of thesis (commencement), antithesis (reaction or opposition) and synthesis (integration), followed by a new thesis. Kabbalistic mysticism states this same idea in the Tetragrammaton, the four letters that spell the name Jehovah or Yahweh: Yod, He, Vau, He, and which represent the process of manifestation.

Each new thesis represents a birth, new order or new action emerging from the center of the previous dialectical triangle, thus forming the image in the margin.

Your Celtic Cross Spread can be rearranged and laid out in this pattern, in order by number, and interpreted according to the following meanings:

CARDS one, four, seven, ten and TRIANGLE one (YOD) all represent thesis, action, creation, commencement, beginning, root, seed. They are initiatory and relate to Spirit and consciousness. They also point out that every new action is simultaneously the result of previous actions and stimuli.

CARDS two, five, eight and TRIANGLE two (HE) all represent opposition, resistance, reaction, reflex, obstacles, contradiction, doubt, preservation. They are emotive and seek to maintain order and preserve the status quo. Inertia.

CARDS three, six, nine and TRIANGLE three (VAU) all represent synthesis, integration, equilibrium, transformation, resolution, transition, passage. They relate to the body. The merging of opposites.

This permutation can be the most intensive and informative of all. A whole new understanding of how each card relates to the others, evolves out of the others and influences the others can be gained through its study. The reading emphasizes the habitual way you have of dealing with life situations. It points to patterns in your actions, which, when you recognize them, can be changed to manifest your own highest qualities.

Example: The Path of Hermes; Permutation #4

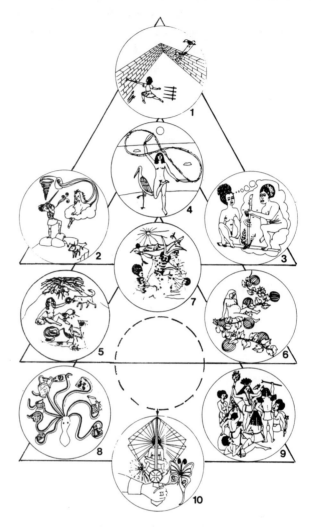

As I continue with my sample spread, I find that this permutation, as always, pulls the reading together and helps me see the patterns of behavior I have established around similar issues.

Card one (Eight of Swords) in the first triangle (Yod) that begins my cycle of actions shows me feeling bound and fenced in, frustrated by what I perceive as limitations.

In Card two (Daughter of Swords), I react against that with the determination to cut through my limitations. Yet the card also represents Casimira, whose need to be with and communicate with me opposes my efforts to break out of my boundaries.

By creatively seeking ways to give quality time to both Casimira and my work as indicated by Card three (Two of Wands), I can regain control over my time and thus integrate the first two opposing energies.

In Card four (Two of Swords), the first card of the second, opposing triangle (HE, known as the beginning of the opposition), I see that I have been trying to compromise. Of course, I have not been satisfied with the result. It is a standoff.

CARD 1: The commencement of the commencement. What are you impelled to begin? What are you trying to manifest?

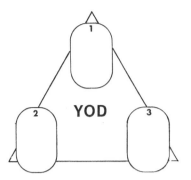

CARD 2: The opposition to the commencement. What opposes this beginning?

CARD 3: The integration of the commencement. How can you integrate the commencement and the opposition (as known by your unconscious self)? What basis for integration is there?

CARD 4: The commencement of the opposition. How do you oppose the new impulse? What in you resists change?

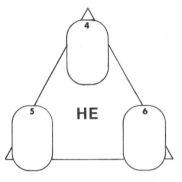

CARD 5: The opposition to the opposition. How do you reassert and envision your desire?

CARD 6: The integration of the opposition. What decision do you make? What action do you take?

CARD 7: The commencement of the integration. How do you begin integrating your desires with your sense of self?

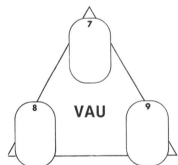

CARD 8: The opposition to the integration. What external considerations do you have to take into account? How might you have to compromise with others?

CARD 9: The integration of the integration. What boundaries and limitations must you learn to work within? What do you need to learn?

CARD 10: The reward or result and the seed of new action. What is the outcome of this cycle? What do you see as the commencement of the new cycle?

In the opposition to the opposition (Card five, Strength), my desire to express my creative self reappears, but this time suggests the ability to lovingly reconcile the needs of both—by being firm and steadfast in my decisions, with total involvement in whatever I am doing at the moment.

To integrate the opposing forces (Card six, Seven of Pentacles), I evaluate the situation and the mistakes I've been making (the lack of quality time and the tendency to react to Casimira rather than act).

The beginning of the integration (Card seven, Son of Wands), the first card of the third triangle (VAU), shows play and adventuring, being flexible, shaking up the old forms with new ideas.

Integration is opposed (Card eight, Eight of Cups) by the emotional drain of trying to placate Casimira and the almost desperate urge to run away. Yet, I remain until I am drained. Do I fear Casi's own independence, her own moving away? Am I failing to teach her to respect and understand the time spent on my work?

To integrate the integration (Card nine, Seven of Wands), I must learn to defend and assert my own needs.

The new cycle (Card ten, Ace of Swords) can commence a new set, a new triangle, a new possibility by opening communications and making a just division of time and energy. The time to begin is now.

Continue with your own permutation. The position meanings are not meant as absolutes, but as examples of how to view the sequence of cards. Write down the cards from your spread in the preceeding diagrams; answer the questions for each card according to your particular situation.

A further permutation is possible, although more complex. Turn the *Path of Hermes* upside down and you have the Kabbalistic Tree of Life with its ten Sephiroth. If you wish to explore the possibilites of this additional pattern, see Chapter Ten for an explanation of the Tree of Life Spread.

BREAKING THROUGH OBSTACLES TO THE HIGHEST EXPRESSION OF YOUR ENERGY

In general, you can now see how the basic Celtic Cross Spread works to describe your situations and provide insights into the connections among different events and/or aspects of your life. Having a clearer perspective certainly helps. You may now see the underlying reasons for asking the question and have a broader concept of what's involved. But what do you do? How do you follow through with the future indications of the cards? Do you have to experience the deception shown by the Seven of Swords? Or the worry indicated by the Five of Pentacles? Not necessarily, because they still represent opportunities for your growth and learning and they need not be experienced in their worst forms. To learn more about how to follow through on what you've learned from a reading, here's a method I call "Breaking Through." Do this with the Celtic Cross Spread or any other spread to discover what is blocking or limiting you, how to break through those blocks and the Key to manifesting your highest qualities in the situation.

Example: Breaking Through Obstacles

In this last stage of my reading, I've picked the Two of Swords, the Eight of Swords and the Eight of Cups as the problem cards that block or limit me. I see in the Two of Swords compromising for the sake of peace and being wishy-washy. The Eight of Swords gives me the feeling I have no choice: I'm stuck in this pattern. And the Eight of Cups shows my sense of exhaustion, wanting to get away.

To break through these blocks, I've chosen the Seven of Wands as representing my ability to defend my beliefs and that I have the power to choose, to perceive creative solutions. With the Seven of Pentacles I can evaluate the situation rather than run from it, and recognize that what I put out I shall receive. Therefore I can change the result by changing my actions.

The Key to manifesting my highest qualities in this reading is the Strength card. The qualities I find in it are love, gentleness, harmony, guidance, perseverance and the strength to do things well and right. The affirmation I draw from this Key is: "I have the strength to persevere in loving gentleness to claim my own needs and to guide Casimira in respecting and claiming hers."

Within 24 hours (and also during the next week) I will spend uninterrupted time focused on Casi, and also in creating worthwhile and enjoyable activities for her to do by herself. Then, should she disturb me at work, I can gently (and guiltlessly) insist that she return to her own projects.

To complete your own reading, first pick out those cards from your spread (usually one to three) which you feel represent problems, blocks or limitations in the situation. Which cards would you like to get rid of, thus leaving the cards you can live with? Place these to one side.

The cards I picked are:
Now describe the specific problem, block or limitation that each of these cards could represent for you in your life:

Next select one card from your spread for each obstacle, a card whose qualities can help you break through that particular block.

PROBLEM BLOCK OR LIMITATION	BREAKTHROUGH CARD	HOW IT CAN HELP YOU DEAL WITH THE OBSTACLE
_____	_____	_____
_____	_____	_____
_____	_____	_____

Now select the one card from your reading that best expresses those qualities which you would most like to develop in this situation. This is your key to manifesting the highest expression of yourself and getting the greatest possible benefit from this opportunity for growth. (Note: Whereas all these cards are to be chosen from the original cards in the reading, you may occasionally feel that no card adequately expresses a Key or Breakthrough concept. By all means, follow your intuition and take your life in your own hands by selecting the cards you need from anywhere in the deck.)

My Key Card is:

What are the qualities in this card that you would most like to develop in yourself?

Using the qualities you have identified, write an affirmation stating that you do possess these qualities. For instance, based on the qualities I have identified as "gentleness, determination, creativity and instinctual needs" in the Strength card, I could write: "I gently but determinedly support and encourage my creative and emotional needs."

My affirmation based on my Key Card is:

Repeat your affirmation three times out loud. Write it on a piece of paper and put it, with your Key Card, in a place where you will see it often, such as on your bathroom mirror or dresser. And repeat your affirmation while visualizing yourself as your Key, several times per day.

Finally, write down something you can do *within 24 hours* that will use the energies of your Key. Make it something simple, so that it will be relatively easy to do and get you effectively started toward your new behavior patterns.

Within 24 hours I will:

This method can give any reading a sense of completion and provide positive indications for action and change. What's more, you choose your own direction for growth by redirecting and effectively using the energies existing in the situation.

EXPANDING THE THREE-CARD SPREAD

The Three-Card Spread described in Chapter Two can be expanded for more information. You can also use the basic three-card format to answer very specific kinds of questions by assigning meanings to each position. Then, after clarifying the question or the issue, you can use those three cards as the introduction to another spread, such as the Celtic Cross.

To start, first relax and ground yourself, purify and shuffle your cards, cut them into three stacks and draw the top card from each stack for a basic three-card reading.

I drew the following three cards: Date_____

_____   _____   _____
       (Body)   (Mind)   (Spirit)
        #1   #2   #3

The issue(s) described by these cards are:

Most people want to know which card is at the bottom of each of the three stacks, so take out those bottom cards too. This second set of three cards is more internal, representing what is hidden or unconscious in the situation. Lay out each of the bottom cards in a row beneath the top cards. Relate the new cards to each other and to the cards above.

The bottom card from each of my stacks is:

_____   _____   _____
       #4   #5   #6

The hidden or unconscious factors in this reading are:

If you find, as I do, that six cards just don't feel complete, then select a third set of three cards. To do this, shuffle each of the original stacks separately, thinking how this card will help with the resolution and completion of the issue. Fan each stack and draw a card from each.

For my third row I selected:

_____   _____   _____
       #7   #8   #9

The resolution and completion of my Body issue (described by cards one and four) as revealed in card seven is:

The resolution and completion of my Mind issue (described by cards two and five) as revealed in card eight is:

The resolution and completion of my Spirit issue (described by cards three and six) as revealed in card nine is:

Finally, shuffle together the three stacks of remaining cards. Cut twice and restack in any order. Turn up the top card. This tenth card integrates the preceding cards and is a key to using the information from all the other cards.

My tenth card is _____ and indicates that the key to integrating the information given by the other cards is:

Asking Questions with the Three-Card Spread

Three cards are to the point when answering many questions. Always try to phrase your question accurately and precisely; write the question down before you begin. The Three-Card Spread can be helpful in the following types of questions:

    Yes-No questions
    Either-Or questions
    Relationship questions

In the following situations you will determine the meaning of each position in the spread, based on what you want to know. Indicate clearly, and in writing, the information you want from each position before shuffling and laying out the cards.

Yes-No Questions

Example: "Should I move to a new apartment in the East Bay in May?" Note the precision of the question. With specific questions like this, put a time limit on the question. You might also want to change your qnestion to, "Is it to my benefit to move to a new apartment in the East Bay in May?" because what do you mean by "should"? Always write this kind of question down, so that you and the "oracle" are precisely sure of what you asked. Bear in mind that Yes-No questions tend to be limiting since there are probably many options you haven't even considered.

As you shuffle the cards, make sure you randomly reverse the direction of some of them. Upright cards are Yes and reversed cards are No, but the middle card counts twice, so you could get a tie for an answer.

In this example there are three counts of Yes and one count of No. Therefore the answer is Yes, at least for the question as phrased, although there is some indication of a change in the future. With new information or a change in circumstances, the answer may change and you may then do a new spread for more up-to-date information.

You might arrive at a tie of two Yes and two No, in which case: a) the out-come is as yet undetermined; b) your best interests are not served by an answer at this time; or c) your question is not appropriately or clearly stated. Also, remember that the Tarot takes the question literally—always be sure you interpret the answer in terms of what you actually asked.

After determining the answer, interpret the cards and their advice in terms of the past, present and future—or any other previously chosen variation of the Three-Card Spread. If you prefer working with more material for inter-pretation, you can use any odd number of cards (five, seven or nine) in the same manner.

Try asking your own question: Date:_____
My Yes-No question is:

The cards I drew for my answer (indicate uprights and reversals) are:

_____ _____ _____
     (Counts once)   (Counts twice)   (Counts once)
       PAST   PRESENT   FUTURE

My answer is:_____, and I interpret the cards to be advising me:

Either-Or Questions

This kind of question implies that you have a choice between two or more options. For example, "Should I go to school full-time or work full-time this fall? I have been working until now."

Before you shuffle the cards, predetermine a meaning for each position in the spread based on your question and *write it down*. Have the left card/position be the option you've already taken, and the right card/position be the new option. You can then read the cards in terms of the past, present and future.

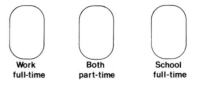

Work   Both   School
full-time   part-time   full-time

As you can see from this example, there is usually a hidden (or not so hidden) third option. The middle card can be designated to indicate your present state of mind. This technique can also be used as a Yes-No spread, so that by its upright or reversed position you get a yea or nay for each option.

Now ask an Either-Or question for which you would like some guidance.

Date:_____

My question is:

Divide the question into its component parts and, if possible, place them on a timeline of the past (or ongoing) option, your present (or an unknown) option, and the future (new) option. Shuffle, reversing the cards if also using the Yes-No option, cut and draw three cards, laying them down from left to right.
The position on the left stands for:

The position in the middle stands for:

The position on the right stands for:

The cards I received indicate to me:

Relationship Questions

This version of the Three-Card Spread gives you a basic understanding of the relationship between any two persons or things.

For example: "What is the nature of Merlin's and my relationship?"

How I relate to Merlin	The relationship itself as an entity	How Merlin relates to me

Or you could ask: "What is the problem between Merlin and me?" If you want clarification of the problem, you could state it as:

My perspective	The problem itself	Merlin's perspective

Or, for resolution of the problem you might state:

My needs and desires in the relationship	A means of resolving the problem or a block to resolving it	Merlin's needs and desires in the relationship

Use this space to design a basic relationship question for yourself and another:

Date:_____

My question is:

I've defined the positions as indicating:
Position on left:

Middle position:

Position on right:

The cards I've drawn in these positions tell me:

PERSONAL MESSAGES IN YOUR READINGS FOR OTHERS

An often overlooked aspect of reading the Tarot for yourself is finding the messages for yourself in the readings you do for other people. For this reason, if for no other, you should always keep copies of the readings you do for others. Later you can go over the reading and its information to see how it applies to you. What can you learn from your own commentary and the insights of the person for whom you did the reading? One example of how this happened for me was when a client felt that the bound woman in the Seven of Swords was waiting for her knight in shining armor to come and save her. Not only did it add to my perception of the card, but it gave me a new perspective on a personal issue I was then dealing with myself.

When doing many readings in a short time, such as at psychic fairs, or when clients pile up, I find that certain cards keep appearing and reappearing. If you keep a record of all the cards drawn, you'll find that several will form, by their frequency, a definite constellation. Pull these cards out and move them around until their relationships form a reading for you.

SUGGESTED READING FOR CHAPTER SIX

On the Tetragrammaton in Tarot:

Tarot of the Bohemians. Papus. N. Hollywood: Wilshire Book Co., 1973. (This is complex and esoteric, therefore not suited to everyone's taste.)

On Designing Your Own Spread:

Choice-Centered Tarot. Gail Fairfield. Seattle: Published by the author, 1982. (Available from Choice-Centered Astrology and Tarot, P.O. Box 31816, Seattle, WA 98103.)

FROM THE MOTHERPEACE TAROT, created by Vicki Noble and Karen Vogel; published in 1982 to represent esoteric traditions in feminist, multi-cultural and contemporary terms. In keeping with their round design, the Major Arcana are laid out in three dancing wheels, each with six cards revolving around a central card, and all of them

revolving around The Fool. To set this up yourself, begin with the cards in order: lay out The Magician, The High Priestess and The Empress separately to start your three arrangements; lay the fourth card, The Emperor, with the first, and so on, creating clockwise circles of cards. The last three cards (except The Fool) go in the center of each wheel.

Note that opposing cards reduce to the same digit, and that the final card of each wheel reduces to the number of the first card. Examine each grouping for related themes. The groups can also be seen to express the dialectic principle of thesis, antithesis and synthesis; or commencement, opposition and integration.

CHAPTER SEVEN

DEALING WITH MOODS, EMOTIONS AND RELATIONSHIPS

This chapter focuses on working with the Tarot in a different way than you are probably used to. In Chapter Two you were introduced to the concept of selecting cards to represent your experiences and looking through the deck to find the most appropriate images. (You can review this technique by rereading page 35.) The exercises in this section are ones that you will want to use in highly charged emotional situations, but work through the exercises now, before the situations actually arise, so that you are familiar with the procedures and what each exercise has to offer.

DEALING WITH DEPRESSION

Some people reach for a Tarot deck when they are feeling moody or depressed. I've found myself shuffling the cards for ten or fifteen minutes and then, upon finally laying out the cards, feeling that they, like everything else, haven't helped a bit. But the following exercise, adapted from a journal technique suggested by Tristine Rainer in *The New Diary* and based on my own experiences when faced with what seemed to be the end of my world, does help.

Try this exercise now, no matter what your mood, so you will remember it and have confidence in its effect when you need it. Take out your deck of Tarot cards and a pen or pencil.

Go through your deck with the cards face up, so that you can see their pictures. Choose several cards that depict how you feel right now.

The cards I chose are:

Now choose *one* card from among these that *most* expresses how you feel.

The card that most expresses how I feel is:

Imagine yourself as a figure in the Tarot card you have chosen and describe, in first person present tense (I am . . .), what is happening in the card and

how you, as the figure in the card, feel. For example, one person chose the Ten of Swords and wrote:

"I (as the person on the card) feel so overwhelmed and listless, and why shouldn't I be with all these swords sticking in my back. They don't hurt but I just can't seem to move. Everytime I do, someone comes along and sticks them a little deeper or adds another sword. Why don't I just give up? I wish I could. But maybe I can hold out until the sun comes up."

Use as many of the objects, colors and images as you can in your description. Experience all the nuances of the card, including things you didn't notice when you chose the card, to describe your depressed state.
I (feel/am):

Once you have completed your description, you many find yourself automatically coming up out of the "depths." The next stage is to choose five cards that picture things you need to be doing or would do—if you could do *anything* you desired. In a few words describe specifically what that action is. For instance, the person with the Ten of Swords chose these three cards: Six of Cups = Return that book to Jamie. Eight of Wands = Go running in the park. Two of Pentacles = Put aside all my responsibilities and take a trip to England.

If I could do anything right now that I wanted or needed to do, I would:

1) Card _____ = _____
   _____

2) Card _____ = _____
   _____

3) Card _____ = _____
   _____

4) Card _____ = _____
   _____

5) Card _____ = _____
   _____

Choose one of the above: _____
Do it immediately.

This procedure can also help you organize your day. For instance: When you are overwhelmed and need to get things into perspective, list five to seven things that you need to do, then select cards that represent these things to you, however personally. Now prioritize by deciding what needs to be done immediately and what can wait. Many Tarot commentators have claimed that the deck is a mnemonic device. Visualizing the cards in a familiar pattern can help you recall, in proper order, any list of things or ideas you desire.

DISCOVERING JOY

There is another exercise suggested by Tristine Rainer, based on the discoveries of Joanna Field chronicled in *A Life of One's Own.* In this book Field relates her attempts to discover what brought her joy, so that she could experience it more regularly and fully in her life.

Choose six cards that describe things that make you feel happy:

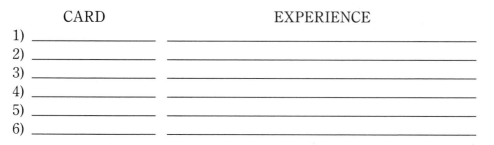

Now think back over the last two days carefully. List every little thing which gave you even a momentary sensation of happiness. Then pick a card to represent each:

EXPERIENCE	CARD

How are your two lists different?

How are they similar?

Joanna Field describes her journey toward discovering joy as a practice of observation. She found that her assumptions about happiness were often radically different from her everyday experiences, and that once she began acknowledging her everyday feelings of joy, they were able to grow and bring her a greater sense of well-being.

Keep a regular (though not necessarily daily) list of joyful happenings—both inner and outer. Observe which cards you keep choosing to represent these experiences.
What are they?

Note when these cards come up in your daily reading charts. Do they come up in similarly happy circumstances or, if different, how are they different?

DATES OF APPEARANCE	CARD	COMMENTARY
_____	_____	_____
_____	_____	_____
_____	_____	_____
_____	_____	_____

CLARIFYING YOUR RELATIONSHIPS

This exercise, based on the work of my student, James Garver, is designed to improve the quality of your personal relationships. By acknowledging the archetypal energies you are projecting and drawing to you in your relationships, you can choose to continue or change your behavior to harmonize with your inner needs.

Use the entire 78-card deck. When selecting cards, go quickly though the entire deck, pulling every card that seems appropriate (if you hesitate over a card take it); then narrow your selection down to from three to seven cards before finally selecting the one with which you will work. Decide before you begin whether you are working on emotional/sexual relationships, familial or friend relationships, or work relationships.
Answer these questions before selecting any cards:
1) What needs to be clarified in your relationships?

What needs do you want to satisfy in your relationships?

Go through the entire deck of Tarot cards and select the ones that seem to illustrate how you see yourself in a relationship. Narrow these cards down to from three to five. List the cards you have picked:

Pick the one card from among these that best represents you in your relationships:

What qualities in this card portray how you act in relationships?

What qualities and images appear in all the cards you picked above?

2) What is your fantasy of the ideal partner for you in a relationship?

How would he or she act in the relationship?

Go through the deck again and pick out the cards that represent this kind of person and narrow them down to from three to five of the most expressive cards:

Looking at the cards, what stands out among them? What images and qualities are similar in each card and what are they?

Which single card from those above best represents your most ideal partner?

Why?

3) Put the card you picked for yourself and the card of your ideal partner together on the table before you in some way. How would they relate to each other?

Flip through the deck and pick out several cards to represent the way they might interact:

Which of these best describes their ideal interaction?

Describe this interaction:

4) You've probably been describing a totally positive interaction. Pick out a card that might represent how the two of you would negatively interact, such as in a fight:
What does this card say to you?

5) Look at the four cards you've chosen. When viewed together, what do they say to you about your potential relationship?

6) Of the cards you chose to represent your ideal man or woman, do any remind you of current people in your life? (If not, pick a card most like an important person with whom you are or were in a relationship.)
What card?_____ With whom?_____
Associate this card and the card you picked for yourself at the beginning. Discuss their interaction:

Pick out some cards that express this actual relationship:

Describe what is going on in each of these cards:

How do you *feel* in these situations?

7) What action do you need to take in order to transform your current relationship into your fantasy one?

Select a card that best expresses your ability to create the kind of relationship you want and deserve:

What can you do *immediately* to begin this process of transformation?

Now, create a mandala for affirming the qualities you value in a relationship. Take the following cards from the exercise you have just completed. Place them as indicated by number in the six-pointed Star Relationship Mandala illustrated below.

Your ideal self in a relationship: _____(1)
Your ideal partner in a relationship: _____(2)
The way you would interact: _____(3)
The way you would interact in a negative situation: _____(4)
Your ability to create the relationship you want and deserve:

_____(5)

Lovers Card or Two of Cups _____(6)
Put your mandala (or a photocopy of it) somewhere in view for several days; look at it frequently.

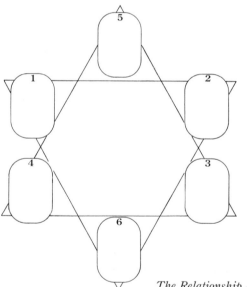

The Relationship Mandala

YOUR INNER MASCULINE AND FEMININE

What is masculine and what is feminine in an individual is, regardless of what is said in books, a very personal and relative experience. The following exercises, when done together with several other people, illustrate the diversity of concepts of masculine and feminine. When done alone, they can help you sort out your own experience of those "masculine" and "feminine" sides of yourself and how they interrelate.

Exercise A:

Give yourself plenty of space to lay out cards. The rug or floor works well and allows you room to stand back and get the entire picture. Take the Major Arcana cards and sort them into the following groupings, according to how they express gender to you: feminine, masculine, androgynous (a balance of masculine and feminine) or non-sexual. Or instead of groupings, you may place the cards in a continuum with no hard and fast divisions. Play with the visual effects you can create.

Draw a picture here showing how you arranged your cards:

What qualities do your feminine cards seem to have in common?

What qualities do your masculine cards seem to have in common?

What qualities do your androgynous cards seem to have in common?

What are the qualities of the cards you selected as nonsexual?

Which feminine card most clearly depicts your own inner feminine self?

Why?

Which masculine card most clearly depicts your own inner masculine self?

Why?

VARIATIONS FOR FURTHER WORK

1) Write down a dialogue between your chosen feminine and masculine cards on any relevant issue.

2) Bring in an androgynous card as a mediator or for a new point of view.

3) Introduce a nonsexual card to your discussion, perhaps to sum up what the real issue seems to be.

4) Take a large sheet of brown paper (or tape several together). Lie down face up on the paper and have a friend draw an outline of you. Lay the Major Arcana cards within the outline of your body, placing them where you feel they most appropriately belong.

Exercise B:

Many of the cards have been linked as pairs by Tarot commentators, such as The Emperor/Empress, Moon/Sun, etc. See if you can sort all the Major Arcana into pairs of complementary (not necessarily masculine or feminine) energy. Again, work on a rug or other large space and try as many variations as possible.

POSSIBLE CARD PAIRS

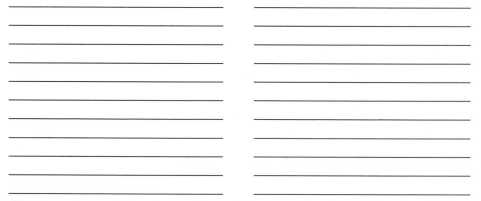

Which cards would work equally well in several pair combinations? What are the alternate pairs they form?

Which don't seem to pair well at all?

What have you learned about the cards that you didn't realize before? (Such as similar or opposite images in the cards, or new relationships among them.)

A COMPOSITE RELATIONSHIP SPREAD

This spread is a variation of the Celtic Cross Spread in which you and your partner both draw cards; the reading is for that third entity, the relationship between you. Use this spread to gain understanding about the dynamics of your relationship.

Both persons shuffle the deck in turn. Designate one of you as Person "A" and the other as Person "B". First, Person A cuts the deck into two stacks. Person B chooses one of the stacks, Person A the other. Both shuffle their individual stacks, then fan them and intuitively select the following cards, placing them in the traditional Celtic Cross layout:

CARD 1: A's heart in the relationship.

CARD 2: B's heart in the relationship.

CARD 3: The basis of the relationship. What the couple is not yet consciously aware of. B selects this card.

CARD 4: The relationship in the past. Also the talents, skills and abilities to relate which have been developed. B selects this card.

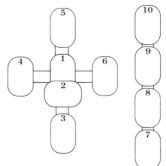

CARD 5: The conscious goals and ambitions of the couple in the relationship. A selects this card.

CARD 6: Decisions before the couple and their ability to act on them together. A selects this card.

Taking turns, shuffle together the remainder of the cards. Make one large fan.

CARDS 7 and 8: Each person draws a card to represent "myself as I see myself," each person's self-image in the relationship. Therefore, for each person there is designated a card of the self and a card of the "other."

CARD 9: That issue or problem which must be overcome or resolved in order to develop the relationship. This card is drawn by either person.

CARD 10: That quality or tool which will help both achieve a new depth in the relationship. This card is drawn by the person who did not draw Card Nine.

Both persons together interpret each of the cards, bearing in mind that their personal and interpersonal responses are more important than the objective meanings of those cards. Ideally, you synthesize a picture of your interaction, coming to some realization of how each of you helps to create the entity of the relationship.

ANGIE'S RELATIONSHIP SPREAD

This second relationship spread, originally taught by Angeles Arrien, shows the actual interaction between two people. Do this spread only when both persons are present; as in the previous spread, the subjective reactions and joint interpretations are an important dynamic. This spread works with friends, family members and business partners as well as lovers. Two decks are needed, preferably of the same design. If only one deck is available, lay out one person's cards, write them down, gather up all the cards, reshuffle and lay out the second person's cards. Then pull the first set of cards from the deck so you can see the entire pattern.

1) Each person, working with a complete deck, shuffles while consciously thinking of the relationship; each of you divides your deck into three stacks. One of you is designated "A," the other, "B."

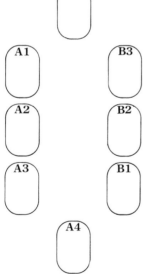

2) Each person: Shuffle your first stack while thinking about "what you give" in the relationship. Fan the stack and select a card, placing it in your position one.

3) Each person: Shuffle the second stack while thinking about "your own self-esteem." Fan the stack and select a card, placing it in your position two.

4) Each person: Shuffle the third stack while thinking about "what you receive" in the relationship. Fan the stack and *have your partner select a card from your stack*, placing it in your position three. You then select a card from your partner's stack, placing it on his or her position three.

5) Each person: Gather the remaining cards in your three stacks and shuffle them together while thinking about "what you want" for the relationship. Fan the cards and select one, placing it in your position four.

When reading the cards, turn up A1 and B3 first—what you give and what your partner receives. Then turn up B1 and A3—what your partner gives and you receive. Follow with A2 and B2, then A4 and B4.

Note especially any cards that appear in both readings. Be prepared to discuss your relationship honestly—both the good and bad aspects, as in this spread it often happens that situations appear which have long gone un-spoken.

SUGGESTED READING FOR CHAPTER SEVEN

The New Diary: How to Use a Journal for Self-Guidance and Expanded Creativity. Tristine Rainer. Los Angeles: J.P. Tarcher, 1978.

A Life of One's Own. Joanna Field. Los Angeles: J.P. Tarcher, 1981.

FROM THE VOYAGER TAROT, collaged by Ken Knutsen under the direction of Jim Wanless (1984). *Major Arcana cards are laid out in the Whole Self Mandala which Wanless describes as "a symbolic portrait of yourself and your world." The cards in the ten positions were selected for this photograph by Wanless to represent one possible ar-* chetypal pattern that can express the essences of these positions. They are: *1) Fool-Child for spirit—your archetypal personality; 2) Balance for head—your mental state; 3) Priestess for heart—your emotional state; 4) Hermit for legs—your physical state; 5) Moon for the left side—your feminine nature; 6) Sun for the right side—your masculine nature. These* six form your Inner Self. Surrounding them are the cards representing your world: *7) Fortune for your finances; 8) Emperor for your work; 9) Empress for your home; 10) Lovers for your relationships. The results of your past actions and the seeds of the future are depicted here as the changes you choose to make in the present.*

CHAPTER EIGHT

PROSPERITY AND PLANNING

*The ability to make decisions according to the purpose
and potentiality of one's own being is the most essential
factor in constructive and meaningful growth.*
Haridas Chaudhuri

TURNING POINTS AND MAJOR MILESTONES

In order to take control of your life you need to see it in broad perspective.
You can get such an overview by listing twelve or more turning points in
your life, representing choices and decisions you have made in the past,
and/or ones made for you. Turning points, milestones, or stepping stones
are points where you could have continued on as you were, but you chose
another option or direction. In making your list, consider times when it seems
that destiny chose for you, times you experienced long anxiety over a crucial
decision and also times when someone else seemed to make an important
choice for you. The important thing is to identify twelve major steps that
brought you to where you are today.

For example, I listed the following:

1)	Went away to college.	Three of Pentacles
2)	Broke my engagement.	Eight of Wands
3)	Involved with theatre.	Seven of Cups
4)	Moved to Atlanta.	Two of Wands
5)	Quit job to go to Europe.	Eight of Cups
6)	Returned to Florida by myself.	Four of Swords
7)	Married.	Two of Cups
8)	Divorced.	Eight of Swords
9)	Taught first Tarot class.	Six of Pentacles
10)	Moved to San Francisco and got job at college.	Seven of Wands
11)	Discovered womanspirit.	Three of Cups
12)	Formed partnership and gave birth to child.	Ace of Cups

Use the worksheet on the following page to list these twelve turning points
in your life. Next, correlate each point with a different Minor Arcana card
(any of the 40 cards from Ace through Ten of each suit), choosing the one
that most nearly describes or illustrates each event.

TURNING
POINTS
WORKSHEET

WHY? Major Arcana	EVENT AND PERSONAL SIGNIFICANCE	WHAT? Minor Arcana	WHO? Court Card
1.			
2.			
3.			
4.			
5.			
6.			
7.			
8.			
9.			
10.			
11.			

Finally, write a short description of the significance of each event as you've interpreted it in the card you chose, using the Turning Points Worksheet on the previous page.

Which suit appears most often?

Why do you think it predominated? Does it suggest anything about the reasons for your choices?

If you wish to go further, select a Court Card to represent the aspect of yourself that desired or instigated each turning point. For example, did your inner masculine or inner feminine aspect predominate in making these decisions? Were you actively or passively involved? Were you concerned with money or security? Love and passion? Creative self-expression? Pain and anger? Did you want to establish and build, or nurture, or learn? Don't hesitate to use a King even if you are a woman, or a Page if you are a man—examine those *inner* qualities and energies from which you acted and choose accordingly. You can use the same card more than once.

What cards appeared most: Kings, Queens, Knights, Pages?

Do you see any outstanding significances in the cards you've chosen?

Have you clarified any of your actions?

Think about how each turning point came about. Was it through a choice or decision you made? Did someone else decide for you? Or did it "just happen"—by fate, by chance or through some inner guidance?

Choose a Major Arcana card from the list below for each of your twelve turning points to indicate *why* you made the choice you did. One Major Arcana card can describe several events. Or you may find you need two or more cards to accurately indicate why you did what you did.

FOOL: From foolishness, innocence or naivete.

MAGICIAN: From the exercise of your own will.

HIGH PRIESTESS: Because of inner self-guidance, a woman's influence or to keep something secret.

EMPRESS: Your mother made the decision for you.

EMPEROR: Your father made the decision for you.

HIEROPHANT: Because of teachings, tradition or society and family expectations.

LOVERS: For the sake of love or because of a lover.

CHARIOT: To "prove" yourself and your abilities or to protect someone else.

STRENGTH (LUST): Because of a strong desire for creative self-expression or self-growth.

HERMIT: Because of a search for spiritual development or upon the orders of a guru or spiritual teacher to whom you've pledged obedience.

WHEEL OF FORTUNE: Because of chance or fate. Or because of "right timing," such as the completion of a cycle.

JUSTICE (ADJUSTMENT): To redress a wrong or because it was "just." Or for a legal reason.

HANGED MAN: As a sacrifice or while drugged or mentally unstable.

DEATH: Because of the death of something or someone. As a means of severing the past or letting go of something.

TEMPERANCE (ART): To bring you into balance or for health and healing.

DEVIL: For power, control or mischievousness. "The devil made me do it."

TOWER: To break down or break out of a situation or while acting in anger.

STAR: By "divine guidance." Because of the belief in an ideal.

MOON: Instinctually. In confusion. "Compelled" by something. Because of a dream or an intuitive feeling.

SUN: For pure joy and love of life. A feeling that this is the best choice you've ever made.

JUDGMENT (AEON): Because you recognized a new (and unexpected) possibility and direction in your life—a new vision and purpose.

WORLD: As an integration of all parts of yourself. To express a totality of being. To express freedom in a restricted setting.

Which Major Arcana cards came up most frequently?

What do these cards tell you about your method of action?

Which cards did you not use at all?

FOR FURTHER WORK

Go over this again several months from now. Use a different colored pen and write in major milestones that you now can't believe you overlooked. Review your responses and see if you feel the same way, noting your new thoughts in the margins.

CLARIFYING YOUR OPTIONS

Having looked at your past experience and past choices using the Tarot, now you are ready to use it for making conscious and personally meaningful choices in the future. The first step is to see and clarify all your options.

This spread is a further development of the Three-Card (or Either-Or) Spread described in Chapter Six. It answers the questions of what to do when you have more than two or three options.

Use this reading for situations in which you feel you have to choose from among two or more options that you can clearly identify. It is important to state your options clearly and specifically before you begin, although you can also designate a position to describe a previously unseen option.

Turn to the Clarifying Your Options Spread Sheet on page 133. Write each option or choice under one of the card blanks in the top line. Since you will use only as many cards as you have options, cross off the unnecessary ones. Not all the choices need be feasible at this time. You are seeking guidance about directing your energy, and the least likely option may generate more possibilities once you have clarified and defined it.

For example, at a time when my work situation was very shaky and unclear, I drew the cards to help me see what I really wanted to do. My options were:

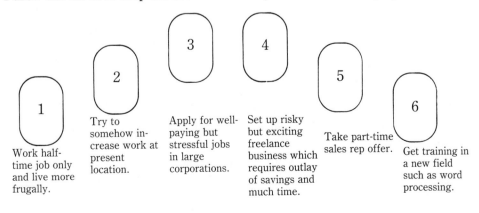

1 — Work half-time job only and live more frugally.

2 — Try to somehow increase work at present location.

3 — Apply for well-paying but stressful jobs in large corporations.

4 — Set up risky but exciting freelance business which requires outlay of savings and much time.

5 — Take part-time sales rep offer.

6 — Get training in a new field such as word processing.

I was trying to do all this simultaneously, yet realized the necessity of putting more concentrated effort into one or two of these options. In fact, in the act of writing down my first five options, the sixth one emerged from what had previously been only a vague possibility, for I now recognized it as feasible. And I did learn word processing and was able to type and edit this book using a computer.

Several other cards can be added to your spread to help clarify issues and bring greater insights in making your decision, such as:

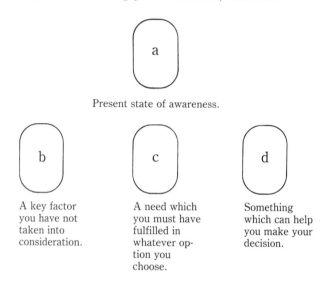

Present state of awareness.

A key factor you have not taken into consideration.

A need which you must have fulfilled in whatever option you choose.

Something which can help you make your decision.

If a "negative" card appears in any of these last positions, it may indicate an obstacle in making that decision, but does not necessarily mean it would not be ultimately rewarding.

Clarifying Options: Shuffle and Method

Shuffle your deck and divide it into as many stacks as you have options. Take the top card from each stack and lay it face down in position. Gather the remaining cards, reshuffle, cut twice and restack. Drawing from the top, take a card for each remaining position. Before looking at your cards, read the rest of this section.

When using the cards to make choices, interpret the cards themselves, but also pay attention to what you experience as you turn over each option card. Do you want it to be a "good" card, indicating success in that option? Do you hope it will show failure so that you can let go of that option? Are you apprehensive? Are you tense or relaxed? Are you afraid to look? Why? Do you remember flipping coins two out of three times to get an answer? And when it wasn't the answer you wanted, you decided to go for three out of five, and then four out of seven—until you finally got the answer you really wanted all along. Here too, you may at least find out what you actually want.

As you interpret each card, how do you respond: Relief? Frustration? Do you try to justify certain interpretations more than others? Do you brighten up or feel let down? Notice your body reactions: tension, nerves. These responses are keys to what your inner self is trying to tell you. Learning to notice and "listen" to these inner reactions will more finely attune your intuitive abilities and your knowledge of yourself. In time, as you make your decisions and observe the results, they will help you discover when you are using intuition and when it is self-deception.

Which option(s) are you the most anxious to interpret positively?

Which option(s) do you feel relieved to put aside for the time being?

Are there any surprises? What are they?

Now read the additional "insight" cards you have chosen. What additional considerations must you take into account?

Sum up the information you received. Prioritize your options based on this information, if appropriate.

You can do this spread again whenever you have significantly more information about your options, or when you realize you are seeing the situation in a new light. The reading is based on current conditions; as they change a new reading will offer more clarification.

THE FIVE-YEAR FANTASY

The purpose of the Five-Year Fantasy is to acknowledge your hopes and dreams for the future. This recognition gives you the opportunity to take advantage of options that will bring you closer to your goals. For instance, in 1980 I wrote in my 1985 fantasy that I was living in Mexico. Several months later I accepted a sudden opportunity to live in Mexico, even though it meant canceling a planned vacation in Peru and risking not being able to return to my job. Another part of this same fantasy was the publication of a (at that time unplanned) book on Tarot—this one! And even though I returned to the States in a year, rather than remaining for five, I've never regretted my decision to live out my dream.

Visualize the most exciting, fascinating and ideal future you can imagine for yourself five years from now. See the circumstances in as much detail as possible. Be specific as to your environment, work and achievements. Do not censor any ideas as too outlandish or silly. *Anything* is possible in your fantasy, and the wilder and least likely the better—demolish your habitually safe thinking! Can you make yourself gasp a little with the daring of your ideas? Is your mouth watering at the anticipation of such delight? Are you feeling yourself swelling with pride at what you might achieve?

Take your Tarot deck and fan it. Select a card, sight unseen, to signify yourself creating your fantasy. This goes in position one: the center of the following layout. There are seventeen cards (positions) in this Fantasy Mandala, which represents The Star, symbolic of hopes and visions for the future. As you go through the rest of the instructions, write the cards you received in the mandala layout.

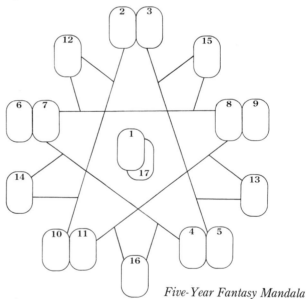

Five-Year Fantasy Mandala

For positions two through eleven, look through the deck (face up) and take your time to choose cards that represent your fantasy according to the meanings given below. Combine and blend together the meaning of each pair of cards. As a personal example, The Magician and the Six of Pentacles paired as cards two and three might represent my vision of success for this book (five years hence). The Magician symbolizes the communication of my ideas, while the Six of Pentacles (Success) disburses royalties from sales. The figure in the Six of Pentacles holds a scale, strengthening the idea that success is based on public judgment. From another viewpoint, this pair of cards also represents the magical exchange of knowledge and energy I hope to get from my readers.

The date (five years hence) is _____.

POSITION 1 (select unseen):

You, creating your fantasy. This "blind" card will give you some idea of how you go about creating your fantasies. If a negative card appears, you may choose not to continue this exercise at this time, as a positive framework is essential for the magic to work.

POSITIONS 2 to 11:

Next select five pairs of cards that describe your ideal future five years from now. Go through the deck (face up), considering various trial pairs until they feel right.

2 & 3 A major accomplishment recently achieved.

4 & 5 Your work/professional situation.

6 & 7 Something exciting in your life—a relationship, travels, hobby or creative project.

8 & 9 Talents and abilities you have mastered.

10 & 11 Your home environment.

POSITIONS 12 to 17:

Gather the remaining cards, shuffle and fan them *face down*. Now draw six cards representing the following areas:

12 Intellect   15 Breakthroughs in Consciousness
13 Creativity   16 Money and Power
14 Love and Sexuality 17 Your Ideal Self

These cards will provide insights when considering your personal development over the next five years.

If you perceive any of the cards you drew unseen as blocks or obstacles to achieving your goals, then choose a card whose qualities will help you break through these blocks. Place it over the obstacle card.

To consolidate your vision, write a letter to a friend, as if you haven't seen him or her in a long while. Use the current day and month, but five years from now. Tell your friend what you are doing, based on images you selected for your Star Mandala. Feel yourself, your joy, your pride and your sense of accomplishment.

In using the Five-Year Fantasy with my advisees in college, I find *most* achieve much of their fantasy within *two* years and sometimes are already beyond their wildest dreams. To me, this shows that this spread, with its combination of deliberated "fantasy vision" cards and drawn "insight" cards, is a highly effective means of achieving personal goals.

CLARIFYING MONEY ISSUES AND YOUR PROSPERITY MANDALA

Many people feel that more money would solve all their problems, yet it is a common cliché that wealthy people often find themselves unhappy or dissatisfied. In bringing money into your life, you need to manifest the kind of prosperity that is right for you. To do this, you need to know what you like and don't like about money and why you deserve it. The following exercise helps you clarify your feelings and create opportunities to bring appropriate prosperity into your life.

In this exercise, you look though your deck and pick those cards that seem "appropriate." Use your own personal associations when looking at the cards. For instance, the Six of Pentacles, which in the Waite deck shows a wealthy man distributing money to beggars, might be your boss doling out a minimal salary while he rakes in the profits from his workers' labors. However, you might see the card entirely differently—as receiving a grant, or giving money to charity, etc. In other words, interpret the cards broadly yet specifically in your own terms.

Date_____

1) Pick several (three to five) cards that represent what prosperity means to you.

Describe what prosperity means in terms of images you have chosen. (Are there any common images among the cards?)

Which of these prosperity cards necessitate(s) money?

Which ones require some other factor to a greater extent than money?

Name the other factor(s):

2) Pick several cards to represent what scarcity means to you:

Describe the situation(s) in the cards you chose:

Which ones could be remedied with money?

3) Money means security for many people. Pick cards that describe what security means to you:

Are there any common factors in these cards?

What do they tell you about your own sense of security?

How important is money to this security?

4) Money is one method of rewarding people in our society. Pick cards to represent things for which you deserve to be commended and acknowledged:

What specific achievements of yours do these cards represent?

Pick a card that shows how you would ideally like to be rewarded for these accomplishments:

What does the picture on the card describe?

5) Pick several cards to represent what you hate most about money:

What do they have in common?

What does this mean to you?

What needs to be resolved for you to feel good about money?

What card might represent such a remedy?

6) Imagine yourself prosperous and happy. Pick a card to indicate this image of yourself:

Do you remember any time when you actually felt this good? Describe the situation:

7) Pick one or more cards to represent your feelings of anxiety and tension about money:

What kind of situation do these cards describe?

Feel the tension in your body created by thinking about this anxiety. Now slowly relax your body, allowing the tension to drain out of your feet and into the earth. Breathe deeply in and out three times. Relax your forehead, jaw, shoulders, chest, hands, stomach, guts, legs, toes. Select a card which shows you totally relaxed and at ease:

Pick another card which represents the universe providing abundantly for all your needs:

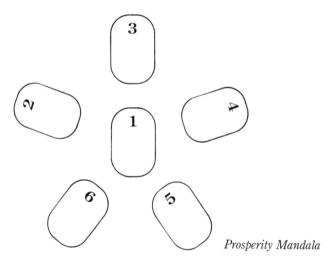

Prosperity Mandala

Take the last card you selected (showing the universe providing abundantly for all your needs) and place it in position one.

Arrange around it the following cards, which you have already selected from the deck:

Position 2) The card that most shows you relaxed and at ease.

Position 3) The card that most shows you prosperous and happy.

Position 4) The card that remedies your negative feelings about money.

Position 5) The card that most shows how you will ideally be rewarded for your accomplishments.

Position 6) One (or more) cards that represent what prosperity means to you.

This is your Prosperity Mandala. Keep it where you can look at it often. Every night, before going to sleep, see yourself as prosperous and happy. Recreate what that feels like in your body.

List the main qualities that you see in the images of your Prosperity Mandala:

Use these qualities to write a statement affirming prosperity in your life (such as, "The universe abundantly provides for all my needs."):

Visualize your mandala and say your affirmation aloud three times before the bathroom mirror each morning and last thing before you go to bed. This is one way to use the Tarot to magically bring what you want into your life.

PLANNING WITH THE TAROT

When planning or problem-solving, remember that decisions are only one stage of a vast cycle of ever-changing events. Moreover, all plans can go astray. Therefore, any plan should have contingency options. The following spread allows you to view the problem itself, define your final goal and the steps necessary to get there, and suggest additional options.

This process can be summarized with the following questions:
1) What?—The Goal
2) Why?—The Purpose
3) What with?—The Resources
4) How?—The Steps
5) When?—The Time Frame
6) Who knows?—Fate

Get your Tarot cards; relax, ground and center yourself.

1) GOAL

The first thing is to define your problem; or, in other terms, to assert your goal. What do you intend to do? This could be something direct and practical, such as getting a job or solving some problem in your work; it could also be something creative or spiritual.

Look through the deck face up and select one or more cards that represent your intentions.
The card(s) I selected:

My goal/intention/problem is:

2) PURPOSE

The second stage is to examine *why* you want this. The answer will give you the basis on which to evaluate the effectiveness of your final effort. Let's say you want to get a job: Is it just for the money? Or to get experience in your field? To meet people? To get away from home or family? To keep you from doing something else? It's worthwhile to think about and define your motives. There is usually more to this than meets the eye, because the reasons why people do things are seldom simple. Therefore, for this stage of the spread, you look at three aspects of your intention.

Shuffle the deck, fan it face down and choose unseen three cards. These represent the physical, mental and spiritual reasons *why* you intend to achieve your goal.

The cards I chose are:

_____   _____   _____
      Physical   Mental   Spiritual
They tell me:

3) OBJECTIVES

The third stage is to acknowledge and facilitate your objective(s). What must you learn or use in order to carry out your project?

Look through the deck face up and select one or more cards that represent the following three kinds of learning: 1) Skills and abilities necessary to carry out your plan; 2) Knowledge and information required; and 3) Attitudes or feelings you must change to open yourself to new possibilities.

The cards I selected are:

_____   _____   _____
  Skills & Abilities   Knowledge & Info   Attitudes & Feelings
These cards tell me that I need to develop myself in the following ways:

4) HOW

The next stage of planning is to determine the actual steps you need to take to complete your project.

Shuffle the deck, fan it face down and choose unseen three cards that represent the steps toward your goal.

The steps I must take to achieve my goal are:

CARDS	STEPS TO TAKE
_____	_____
_____	_____
_____	_____

5) WHEN

The fifth step is to ascertain the time frame involved. It need not be absolute, but must be specific. The time frame lets you know if you are operating according to plan or if you need to reconsider what you are doing.

Select a card or cards, face up, from the deck to represent when you expect to complete your project, according to the following information. (You can also select a time card for each of the "steps" in the last section.) Time equivalents are determined from the Minor Arcana by multiplying the number on the card by:

> Wands = Days (For example, the Ten of Wands = ten days.)
> Cups = Weeks (For example, the Five of Cups = five weeks.)
> Swords = Months (For example, the Two of Swords = two months.)
> Pentacles = Years (For example, the Seven of Pentacles = 7 years.)

The Major Arcana refer to the month indicated by their astrological referent. For instance, Justice (which corresponds to Libra) refers to from September 23 to October 22. (See pages 16–17 for the dates referred to by each card coresponding to a zodiac sign.) The cards that correspond to planets refer to the number of years equivalent to the number on the card. They time future events and/or past events that led up to the situation. The Court Cards refer to stages of development: Pages are beginnings, Knights are the process itself, Queens indicate maturity and fruition, and Kings indicate completion.

I plan to complete this project by:

_____	=	_____
Time Card(s)		Date

6) FATE

This last stage uses what I call the "wild cards." These two cards indicate unseen factors with which you have to deal. They can come up anytime and anywhere and may mean restructuring your plan and time frame.

Shuffle the deck, fan it face down and choose two unseen cards. These cards represent:

_____	_____
Something you need to take into consideration	An unseen opportunity or possibility

I need to take into consideration:

I should watch for the following opportunity or possibility:

The Planning Mandala

In creating your mandala out of the preceding exercise, use what you learned in "Breaking though Obstacles" in Chapter Six to find cards that will help you break through any blocks or limitations which appear. Mark your Key Card with a star.

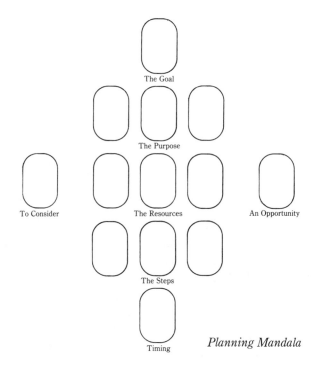

Planning Mandala

SUGGESTED READING FOR CHAPTER EIGHT

The Universal Traveler: A Soft-Systems Guide to Creativity, Problem-Solving and the Process of Reaching Goals. Don Koberg and Jim Bagnall. Los Altos, CA: William Kaufmann, 1976.

Design Yourself. Kurt Hanks, et al. Los Altos, CA: William Kaufmann, 1973.

Prospering Woman: A Complete Guide to Achieving the Full, Abundant Life. Ruth Ross. Mill Valley, CA: Whatever Publishing, 1982.

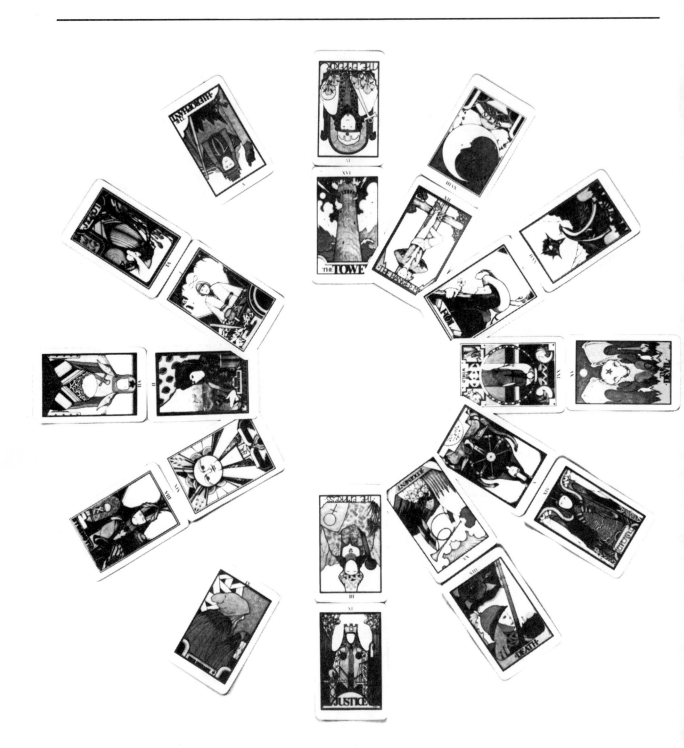

FROM THE AQUARIAN TAROT, illustrated by graphic artist David Palladini and published in 1970. The Major Arcana are here laid out in the basic horoscope wheel. On the outer wheel are the signs of the zodiac, and on the inner wheel are the planets that rule them. Aries (The Emperor) begins the horoscope on the left horizon, known as the Ascendant. It is ruled by Mars (The Tower). Moving counterclockwise are Taurus (The Hierophant), ruled by Venus (The Empress, who serves double duty elsewhere); Gemini (The Lovers), ruled by Mercury (The Magician); Cancer (The Chariot) at the nadir, ruled by the Moon (The High Priestess); Leo (Strength), ruled by the Sun (The Sun); Virgo (The Hermit), ruled by Mercury (The Magician, who is elsewhere); Libra (Justice) on the Descendant, ruled by Venus (The Empress); Scorpio (Death), ruled by Pluto (Judgment); Sagittarius (Temperance), ruled by Jupiter (The Wheel of Fortune); Capricorn (The Devil) on the midheaven or M.C., ruled by Saturn (The World); Aquarius (The Star), ruled by Uranus (The Fool); and Pisces (The Moon), ruled by Neptune (The Hanged Man).

CHAPTER NINE

BECOMING CONSCIOUS OF
WHAT YOU CREATE

This chapter contains a potpourri of Tarot methods using other tools for consciousness with the Tarot.

YOUR BIRTHCHART MANDALA

You can interpret your own Natal (or birth) Chart even if you know very little about astrology, by setting it up using the Tarot cards. You will need an accurate natal horoscope constructed for your time and place of birth. If you don't have a birth chart, you can inexpensively order one from Neil Michelsen's Astro Computing Service, P.O. Box 16297, San Diego, CA 92116 (cost $3.00 at the time of this writing). Send your birth date, exact time of birth (preferably from birth certificate or family Bible) and birthplace (include exact longitude and latitude if you know them). If you do not know your birth time, you will receive what is known as a "Solar Chart," adequate for general purposes.

You will also need twelve sticks or pieces of yarn about three feet long. Lay the yarn or sticks out in a horoscope wheel as illustrated so that there are twelve segments. These are called "houses."

Find the zodiacal sign on the ascendant, or First House, of your chart: your ascendant is at the left side of the horizon line of your chart. Then use the table provided to find the zodiacal sign which begins each of the houses of your chart.

Beginning at the ascendant, place the following Major Arcana cards of any Tarot deck in a counterclockwise direction around your mandala, to correspond to the sign of each house. They will be in the same sequence as given below, but will begin with *your* ascending sign. (Occasionally a sign [and its opposite sign] is "intercepted" and will therefore be found *within* a house rather than on a cusp [between two houses]. In this case some other sign [and its opposite sign] will appear on two consecutive house cusps. This is found more often in far northern or far southern latitudes.)

Indicate the house position of each sign of the zodiac and its corresponding Tarot card on the chart below: (The "cusp" is the line which begins the house.)

     Aries: The Emperor is on the cusp of House #_____
     Taurus: The Hierophant is on the cusp of House #_____

145

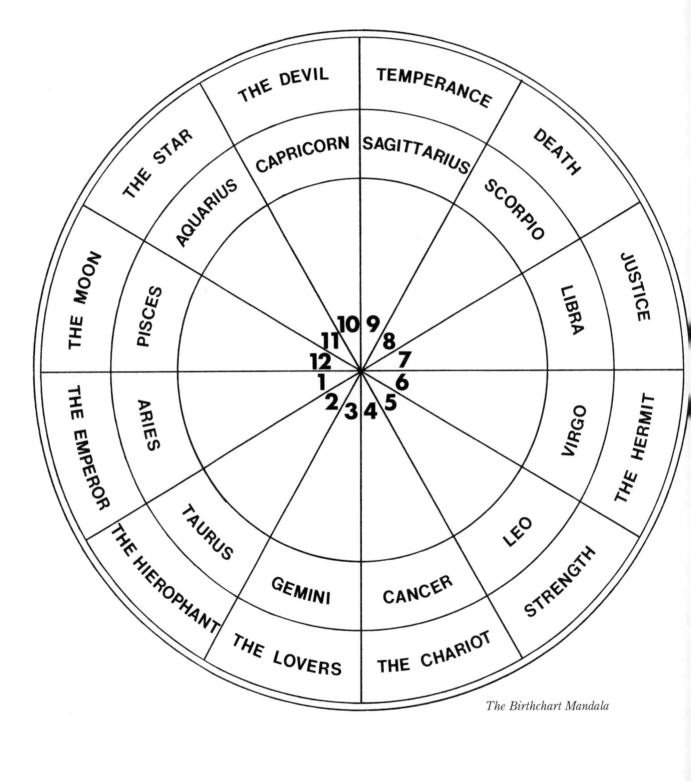

The Birthchart Mandala

Gemini: The Lovers is on the cusp of House #_____

Cancer: The Chariot is on the cusp of House #_____

Leo: Strength/Lust is on the cusp of House #_____

Virgo: The Hermit is on the cusp of House #_____

Libra: Justice/Adjustment is on the cusp of House #_____

Scorpio: Death is on the cusp of House #_____

Sagittarius: Temperance/Art is on the cusp of House #_____

Capricorn: The Devil is on the cusp of House #_____

Aquarius: The Star is on the cusp of House #_____

Pisces: The Moon is on the cusp of House #_____

Next, find each of your planets on your natal chart and place the corresponding Major Arcana card in the appropriate house near the sign it is in.

Sun: The Sun is in the sign _____ & House #_____

Moon: The High Priestess is in the sign _____ & House #_____

Mercury: The Magician is in the sign _____ & House #_____

Venus: The Empress is in the sign _____ & House #_____

Mars: The Tower is in the sign _____ & House #_____

Jupiter: The Wheel of Fortune is in the sign _____ & House #_____

Saturn: The Universe/World is in the sign _____ & House #_____

Uranus: The Fool is in the sign _____ & House #_____

Neptune: The Hanged Man is in the sign _____ & House #_____

Pluto: Judgment/Aeon is in the sign _____ & House #_____

By placing your cards in a circle, you have your basic Birth Chart Mandala, incorporating all 22 of the Major Arcana; use it to meditate on as a whole, or you can "read" it as follows:

The planets are your "vital energies." Signs show how those energies manifest—the way they behave—while houses show where in your life (in what area—home, work, relationships, etc.) they appear—that is, how they externalize themselves in your life. For example, my Moon in Libra in the Twelfth House could be stated as: "My High Priestess (Moon) energy expresses itself in a Justice (Libra) way in The Moon (Twelfth House) area of my life." This could also be said several different ways, using keywords that refer to the cards, such as: "I trust my inner feminine (H.P.) to equalize (Justice) my individual expression with societal and collective needs (The Moon)"; or "I make decisions (Justice) intuitively (H.P.) when obstructed or confused (The Moon)"; or "I am receptive (H.P.) to the truth (Justice) about the unknown and the mysterious (The Moon)."

High Priestess in Justice in Moon

Interpreting Your Birth Chart

1) Interpret the cards according to their house position, using the following meanings for each house:

FIRST HOUSE—(Emperor) Your physical body and appearance. Early environment. Your personality and self-expression. Your interests.
In the First House I have the following planets which describe:

SECOND HOUSE—(Hierophant) Your possessions and financial standing. What you value. Personal creative abilites, especially in music and voice.
In the Second House I have the following planets which describe:

THIRD HOUSE—(Lovers) What you think. Studies. Communication. Short journeys. Ability to relate to your environment. Brothers and sisters and neighbors.
In the Third House I have the following planets which describe:

FOURTH HOUSE—(Chariot) Your heredity. The beginning and ending of life. Your home and parents. Physical and emotional security.
In the Fourth House I have the following planets which describe:

FIFTH HOUSE—(Strength) Your creative expression. Self-expression. Procreation and your children. Love affairs. Adventures and speculation. Entertainment.
In the Fifth House I have the following planets which describe:

SIXTH HOUSE—(Hermit) Self-improvement. Your health, hygiene and nutrition. Service and work.
In the Sixth House I have the following planets which describe:

SEVENTH HOUSE—(Justice) Your relationships and partnerships. Legal matters. Contracts and agreements. Either cooperation or enmity. In the Seventh House I have the following planets which describe:

EIGHTH HOUSE—(Death) Sex. Death. Transformation. Other people's money and inheritances. Occult and psychic experiences. Deep exchanges of energy.
In the Eighth House I have the following planets which describe:

NINTH HOUSE—(Temperance) Your personal search for meaning. Philosophy. Higher Education. Religion. Dreams. Long journeys. Publications. Teaching.
In the Ninth House I have the following planets which describe:

TENTH HOUSE—(Devil) Your honor. Prestige. Status. Fame. Professional career. Ambitions. Employers. Mother or father.
In the Tenth House I have the following planets which describe:

ELEVENTH HOUSE—(Star) Your goals and objectives. Friends and social life. Groups and clubs. Reform and revolutions. Humanitarianism. Hopes, ideals, aspirations.
In the Eleventh House I have the following planets which describe:

TWELFTH HOUSE—(Moon) What is hidden, unseen or unexpected. The personal and collective unconscious. Your relationship to the roles and structure of society. Self-undoing, obstructions and limitations. Karma. Seclusion. Institutions.
In the Twelfth House I have the following planets which describe:

2) For more depth, examine your "aspects." Aspects are determined by the mathematical relationships among planets. Each sign has 30 degrees, for a total of 360 degrees in the horoscope circle. Your planets' positions are given by sign, degree and minutes. For instance, venus might be at 17 degrees 13 minutes (17° 13") of Capricorn, or just past the middle of that sign. For our purposes use the following concepts to relate any two, three or four planets which are "in aspect" to each other:

CONJUNCTION—Planets within 8 degrees of each other blend their meanings. They work together and augment each other.
My planets which are conjunct each other:

OPPOSITION—Planets opposite each other (180 degrees), within 8 degrees. These represent two contradictory parts of you that yearn for opposing things in a seesaw or push/pull manner. It's hard for you to feel you can have both.

My planets which are in opposition to each other:

SQUARE—Planets at a 90-degree angle (or three signs apart). Indicates conflicts and tensions between the two planets' energies, which you struggle to reconcile. Often indicates areas of great strength and determination.

My planets which are square each other:

TRINE—Planets at a 120-degree angle (or four signs apart). Indicates things that come easily to you. Talents and natural abilities you have not had to work for. These planets work harmoniously together.

My planets which are trine each other:

These are the main aspects, although there are many others, such as the sextile (60 degrees apart) and semi-sextile (30 degrees apart), which are mildly harmonious and offer opportunities; also the semi-square (45 degrees apart) and inconjunct (150 degrees apart), which are troublesome.''

As an example, if you had Saturn (The World) conjunct Pluto (Judgment) conjunct Mars (The Tower) in the sign Leo (Strength) in the Ninth House (Temperance), you would first look at these conjunct planets (represented by The World, Judgment and The Tower) as a Three-Card Spread. Judgment in the middle links the two others. They speak about a breakdown of old order and the buildup of a new one in a process of transformative realization. You would be likely to accept radical changes in your philosophical constructs and would even welcome them. You would probably be impatient with others' conventionality and might even lash out in anger at those who seem too rigid or limited. In the sign Leo (Strength) you would dramatically and creatively express your beliefs and philosophy (Ninth House).

The World
Judgment
The Tower

THE HOROSCOPE SPREAD

The Horoscope Spread can be used with your Natal Chart or by itself. It gives you a general overview of your life at this time. I find it to be especially useful when I'm feeling depressed or frustrated but not exactly sure what the problem is—the source of my confusion. By seeing in which house any obstacle or problem cards appear, I can locate the source of my distress.

Relax, ground and center yourself. Purify and shuffle the Tarot deck, cut and lay out thirteen cards counterclockwise, beginning with the ascendent (First House). Place the last (thirteenth) card in the center; this indicates your current ability to integrate all twelve areas of your life.

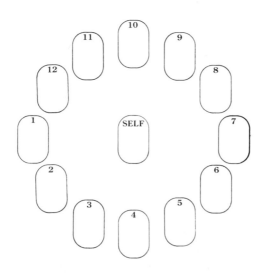

Interpret each card according to the meaning of its house position as given on page 148. Decide which cards represent blocks, obstacles or problems. The houses in which these cards appear represent areas in which you are uncomfortable and have something to resolve.

Find a card in the spread that can help you break through each block (usually one breakthrough card per problem card). These cards are from other areas of your life that are especially strong right now and in which you can focus energy productively. They also represent keys to dealing with your problems.

Finally, select the Key Card from your reading: the image representing those qualities you would most like to be manifesting in your life right now. Name those qualities and create an affirmation of them in yourself. Determine what immediate action you can take using those qualities.

If you know your Natal Chart well enough to work with it more extensively, place the cards you've drawn for this spread around your own horoscope chart, including the current transits and progressions, if you have them. Note the problem and breakthrough cards as they relate to what's going on in your chart.

HOROSCOPE SPREAD SUMMARY SHEET

House	Card	Qualities/Problem/Breakthrough
1	_____	_____
2	_____	_____
3	_____	_____
4	_____	_____
5	_____	_____
6	_____	_____
7	_____	_____
8	_____	_____
9	_____	_____
10	_____	_____
11	_____	_____
12	_____	_____

THE MAJOR ARCANA SPREAD

I find this spread similar to working with a horoscope because all the Major Arcana cards are present, just as all the planets and signs are present in your horoscope. As someone once said, "Everyone has Saturn somewhere in their chart"; so too does everyone have The Devil, Death and The Tower somewhere in themselves. In this spread you can see exactly where they are currently functioning.

This is basically a Celtic Cross Spread that unravels as a spiral, then snakes back around, encircling itself. Many decks with no pictures in the Minor Arcana (for instance, the Tarot de Marseilles) have very powerful Major Arcana that work well in this spread.

Relax, ground and center yourself. Purify and shuffle the cards and cut into three stacks. Then restack and lay out the cards face down in numerical order as given in the diagram.

Turn up the first ten cards only; note your first impression of each card and its relationships. Then turn over the rest of the cards and read them all in depth. The three, four, five and six cards have two modifying cards each, which blend to give additional information about the top card. Pay special attention to where your Personality, Soul, Year and Sun-sign Cards appear. Use the following position meanings, or combine them with your own Celtic Cross meanings.

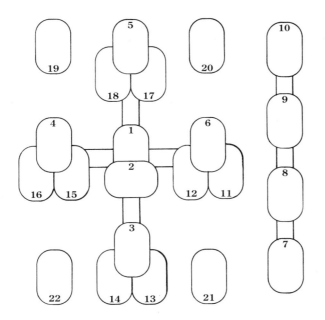

Cards one and two: What is the inner (one) and outer (two) focus of your energies? What conflict or tension is in your heart?

Cards three, thirteen & fourteen: What are your subconscious needs and desires which form the basis of the situation?

Cards four, fifteen & sixteen: What talents or abilities do you bring with you that will assist or hinder you? What opportunities are you most receptive to?

Cards five, seventeen & eighteen: What are you thinking about? What are your ideals and ambitions in the situation?

Cards six, eleven & twelve: How will you act and use your abilities in the near future? What decisions will you make?

Card seven: How do you see yourself in the situation?

Card eight: How do others see you in this situation? What is the environment in which this takes place?

Card nine: What lesson do you need to learn?

Card ten: What is your individual expression in the future, based on your thoughts and energy expression in the present?

Card nineteen: How are you expressing your yin or feminine energy?

Card twenty: How are you expressing your yang or masculine energy?

Card twenty-one: What are the limitations and structure you must deal with?

Card twenty-two: What are the possibilities and magic that you can take advantage of?

USING A CRYSTAL PENDULUM WITH THE TAROT

You can use a pendulum with your Tarot cards to gain clarity in your readings and gain more information than you can get with either alone.

Scientists affirm that you only use about ten percent of your brain's potential—the rest lies beyond your conscious reach. Any mechanism that can help you to tap even a little of the unknown ninety percent can be a boon. For example, hypnotism and brain stimulation can reveal memories and knowledge you didn't know you had. The pendulum is another means of tapping the vast possibilities of your inner wisdom. Used in conjunction with the powerful images of the Tarot, the pendulum can help to open and stimulate the expression of your intuition.

Dr. Freda Morris, in her book, *Self-Hypnosis in Two Days*, describes the movement of the pendulum as being controlled by your unconscious, which "is always answering questions, but normally you are unable to receive this information." The pendulum magnifies imperceptible body impulses into visible movement. You yourself can train your unconscious impulses to act in a predictable manner through positive reinforcement. The goal is to identify movement of the pendulum in one direction as meaning "yes" and in the other direction to mean "no."

Using a quartz crystal as the weighted end of a pendulum makes it into an extremely sensitive psychic current detector and amplifies your intention in using it.

To make a crystal pendulum, hang a small piece of crystal from a cloth cord, piece of leather, or gold or silver chain. (Quartz crystals can be inexpensively purchased from gem or rock shops. Ask for a mineral sample—the quartz in its natural state. But if quartz is unavailable to you, make do with what you have—a button hung from a piece of string will work.)

If you wish to wear your crystal as a pendant, the chain should be about 27 inches long, so that the crystal hangs just at the point where your breast bones separate. By wearing your pendulum, you help to attune it to your vibration and to your heart. (More information on crystals and how to purify them is given in the next chapter.)

First you must find out which directions of the pendulum swing indicate yes and no *for you*. To learn how your pendulum works, hold the string about eight to twelve inches above the crystal weight, so that its point is suspended an inch or so above your palm. Ask an objective question which you definitely know is *false*, such as, "Is my name Mary, Queen of Scots?" Ask the question out loud and repeat it one or two times. This is not asking a "trick" question, for your intention is to open communications and establish a relationship with your pendulum by finding out the movements that are particular to your relationship. The pendulum may move in any direction or it may not move at all. Now ask a concrete, specific question for which the answer is definitely yes, such as, "Was I born in _____ (your birthplace)?" or "Is my car a _____?" You should get a different movement in this case. For some people it will be easy to get a consistent yes-no response immediately, but others will have to be persistent in working with the pendulum, trusting that meaningful responses will eventually develop as they learn to listen carefully to their subtle body impulses.

Once your pendulum is ready to use, try some of the following:

PICKING OUT A TAROT DECK: Ask your pendulum which deck is most in harmony with your spirit as you hold the pendulum over each deck in turn. Observe which way it moves and how strongly. However, don't let this be the sole criterion as to the deck you choose. (For an excellent discussion of how to choose a Tarot deck, refer to *Choice-Centered Tarot* by Gail Fairfield.)

The pendulum can be helpful for choosing an appropriate container for your Tarot deck. I went through all my decks and their wraps in this way to determine the most harmonious containers and ended up rearranging several. I felt much relief and satisfaction at the results.

TO DECIDE WHICH DECK to use in a particular reading: You may get several yes responses, but which one is wildly enthusiastic?

TO DETERMINE YOUR MIND/BODY/SPIRIT STACKS in a three-card reading: When first developing your intuition, you may have difficulty specifying the stacks. First note carefully what you feel from each stack and then use the pendulum to verify your sensations by asking if one stack is your body stack, for instance. After doing this once or twice, you will no longer need the pendulum because of the clearly associated sensation you will have developed with each stack.

TO CLARIFY THE MEANINGS of cards in a spread: Hold your pendulum above the card and ask questions about its particular significance in your life. Remember that since we are dealing with a symbolic system, more than one answer can be true. For instance, you might have asked if the Knight of Wands represents your boyfriend. But the Knight of Wands might *also* be your own burning desire to creatively express your ideas. And of course it is important to understand how these two referents relate to each other in terms of the other information in this spread. You can always ask via your pendulum if there are additional significances to the card that you haven't yet acknowledged.

TO SELECT CARDS FOR A READING: You can use your pendulum as a kind of dowsing rod by holding the cord only two or three inches above the crystal weight. Fan the cards from which you wish to choose and fill your mind with the question or position meaning while moving the crystal over the cards. Look and feel for a subtle magnetic pull toward a particular card.

TO DETERMINE WHICH QUESTION TO ASK: Simply ask if your question is the most appropriate one while holding your pendulum over your open palm or over the question written on a piece of paper.

SUGGESTED READING FOR CHAPTER NINE

On Astrology:

Astrology: A Cosmic Science. Isabel M. Hickey. Watertown, MA: Published by the author, 1970. (35 Maple St., Watertown, MA 02172.)

Saturn: A New Look at an Old Devil. Liz Greene. New York: Samuel Weiser, 1976.

On Pendulums:

Self-Hypnosis in Two Days. Freda Morris. New York: Dutton, 1974.

Huna: A Beginner's Guide. Enid Hoffman. Rockport, MA: Para Research, 1981.

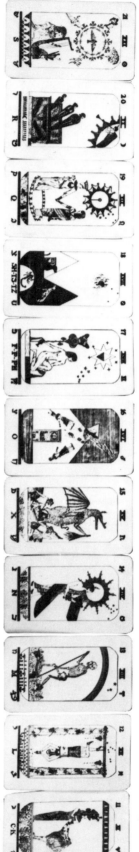

FROM THE EGYPTIAN TAROT, designed by C.C. Zain and originally published by the Church of Light in 1936. The Major Arcana are laid out in two rows of eleven cards each. According to the neoplatonist, Iamblicus, as translated by Paul Christian in The History and Practice of Magic, *they were presented in the sacred vaults under the Great Pyramid to the initiate before the final test of the Sacred Mysteries of Thoth-Hermes. The Sphinx, says Manly P. Hall, was the place of "second birth," the "womb of the Mysteries," and a secret passageway connected it to the Great Pyramid. It was along this passage that the originals of the Tarot were lined. The Pastophore, or "Guardian of the Sacred Symbols," gave the aspirant encouragement in the difficult tests by explaining these symbols, "the understanding of which creates in the heart an invulnerable armour . . . The Science of Will, the principle of all wisdom and source of all power, is contained in these twenty-two Arcana or symbolic hieroglyphs."*

CHAPTER TEN

HEALING

*Illness is a message from your body telling you that you
need to change something in your life..*
Dr. Mike Samuels

Illnesses are sometimes the means used to solve personal problems. In the book, *Spirit Guides: Access to Inner Worlds*, Dr. Samuels says to ask yourself, "Are you willing to give up what you get from having that illness—or get it in another way?" Only you can know the answer to that question; that is, whether you are willing to go within and ask what you would have to give up to be healed.

"Moreover," he says, "as one learns to locate areas that cause discomfort and disease and to seek positive changes which bring comfort and health, one is assuming control of their life and control over the direction that life will take."

You probably know when you are out-of-ease (dis-eased), although you may not know exactly what is wrong. The doctors themselves usually can only find the direct cause of your "symptoms," and not the real cause of the dis-ease. They treat the symptom—to make it go away and hope that it won't reappear somewhere else or in another form. Often the prescribed rest and relaxation and perhaps enforced change of diet help you more than anything else. But you still have not dealt with the real cause of your dis-ease.

The Tarot can help you by first pointing out to you that something is amiss—that there is something you need to let go of or uproot or some problem that needs to be solved. It can also help show you those habitual patterns of getting what you need in life that may not be beneficial to your health. It can be an early warning device, a reminder that there are things you need to face up to in order to manifest the most healthy and harmonious being you can be. Cards to watch for that can indicate situations conducive to ill health are: The Hanged Man, Death, The Tower, The Devil and The Moon. Also the Hierophant, The Hermit, Justice, Temperance and Judgment/Aeon, when appearing with the former cards, can indicate physical problems. Among the Minor Arcana note the appearance of the Five, Seven and Nine of Wands; the Four, Five, Seven and Eight of Cups; the Three, Four, Five, Seven, Eight, Nine and Ten of Swords; and the Five and Eight of Pentacles. Although none of these cards in themselves signify definite illness, they do indicate situations of stress, confusion and anxiety that can lead to physical problems.

If you have a sense of dis-comfort or dis-ease, you can try the following Chakra Spread as a personal diagnostic tool to determine areas of your body that might be blocked from normally healthful functioning.* Use it whenever you feel "out-of-ease" or "dis-comforted" with anything—in your self, your relationships, your work, your creativity.

CHAKRA SPREAD

The Chakra Spread can help you discover the psychological source of your illness and pinpoint areas of your body that need to be brought back into balance. This spread focuses on seven physical, psychological and spiritual energy centers within the body which have been noted and used primarily in Eastern cultures. Chakra means "wheel" in Sanskrit, and the chakras are envisioned as spinning discs located along the spinal column; also as lotus blossoms with varying numbers of petals. Each chakra has its own color, forming a rainbow blend, beginning with red at the bottom or Base Chakra and culminating in violet at the Crown Chakra. When your chakras are "clean" they become smooth conduits for the flow of psychic energy. When "dirtied" by stress and bad habits, or cluttered with old emotions and unfinished business, they block the smooth flow of energy and cause dis-ease. For instance, a block in your communications (Throat Chakra) might result in a sore throat. Yet, if you seek further you might find your inability to communicate generating from a deeper block—perhaps a feeling of powerlessness housed in your solar plexus and potentially giving rise to problems with digestion of your food.

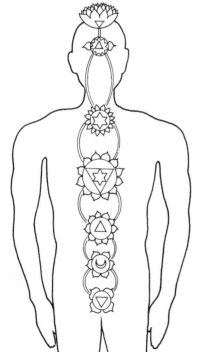

The Chakra Spread is an eclectic blend of the Eastern concept of the seven centers with the Western vision of the Tree of Life, which can also be overlaid on the human body. It too has seven levels, but three of those levels have two positions. The levels with dual positions have to do with balancing your feminine/masculine, inner/outer, unconscious/conscious, receptive/assertive selves. I use ten cards for the Chakra Spread because it integrates so well with the Tree of Life Spread presented next. The two spreads may each be used as a further development of the other, or separately.

To use the Chakra Spread, first thoroughly formulate your questions concerning your illness or dis-comfort and decide which area of your body is displaying the most obvious symptoms.

Relax, ground and center yourself. Purify your deck and shuffle it thoroughly, concentrating on your desire to see what might be causing dis-ease in your body and where it can be found. Cut the deck into three stacks

*See Gail Fairfield's book, *Choice-Centered Tarot*, for an excellent example of creating a spread to get at the personal roots of any illness and to develop the means of transforming the experience into an opportunity for learning and self-development.

and restack it in any way. Then lay the cards out in the positions and order given in the adjacent diagram.

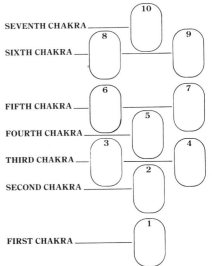

1) The Base, Sacral, or Root Chakra (in Sanskrit, *Muladhara*; color red). This governs your feet and legs and shows how grounded and down-to-earth you are. It is your basic survival instinct and will show your vigor, vitality and general life energy level. Your genes and hereditary factors are based here and also your roots in the past. Habits are usually fixed at this level.

2) The Second, or Spleen Chakra (in Sanskrit, *Svadhisthana*; color orange). This chakra is concerned with survival of the species and therefore your sexuality and emotions. Anger and fear will especially show up here if felt deeply. It shows how you process stuff in your body (especially your intestines)—how it is or is not assimilated. Your instinct to nurture and take care of others is found here.

3A&B) The Third, Navel, or Solar Plexus Chakra (in Sanskrit, *Manipura*; color yellow). Two cards are to be drawn here. This chakra shows how you use or express your vital energies. It indicates your sense of power or powerlessness and your will to achieve. Your ego projections come from this place, as do your attitudes and prejudices. Cordings or emotional connections to others emanate from this point and when you leave your body for astral travel, you leave and return through this chakra. The digestive functions are here. Your ego is most vulnerable here; this is where you receive those psychological solar plexus punches. Great diversity between the energies of these cards (the left one represents your will and ego, and the right one contains your emotional connections) can indicate stress and tension.

4) The Fourth, or Heart Chakra (in Sanskrit, *Anahata*; color green). This is the center of universal love. Your ability to experience compassion, strength and understanding is found here. It is also the center of your sense of time as established by your heartbeat. Your ability to heal both yourself and others is here. This chakra is associated with your lungs and breath (*prana*).

5A&B) The Fifth, or Throat Chakra (in Sanskrit, *Vishudda*; color blue). The throat is your center for speech, self-expression and communication. If you are clairaudient or mediumistic, this is where it will show up. Blockage indicates you are holding back something that needs to be said, usually stemming from your lower chakras. Two cards are drawn for this position representing your inner and outer communications.

6A&B) The Sixth, Brow, or Third Eye Chakra (in Sanskrit, *Ajna*; color indigo). This chakra is the seat of your inner as well as outer sight, visions, fantasies and dreams. It indicates your ability to visualize and is the source of your thoughts; thus of the first impulse to manifestation—making real what you think. Your psychic abilities are developed here as well. The card on your left is right-brain (left-hand) oriented, while the card on the right refers to your left-brain (right-hand) functions.

CHAKRA
SPREAD
FORM

Page One

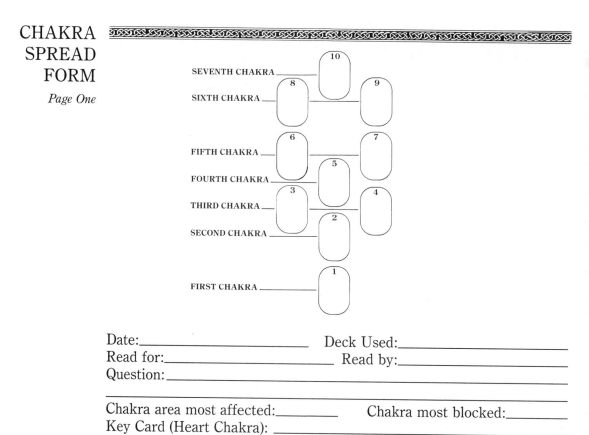

SEVENTH CHAKRA ___

SIXTH CHAKRA ___

FIFTH CHAKRA ___

FOURTH CHAKRA ___

THIRD CHAKRA ___

SECOND CHAKRA ___

FIRST CHAKRA ___

Date:_____   Deck Used:_____

Read for:_____   Read by:_____

Question:_____

_____

Chakra area most affected:_____   Chakra most blocked:_____

Key Card (Heart Chakra): _____

1) ROOT CHAKRA. What is at the root of, or the basis for, your problem? How vital and energetic are you? What habits are you tied into?

2) SPLEEN CHAKRA. How are you using your sexual energy? What emotions are you feeling deeply? What are you trying to assimilate or take in? Whose energy and problems are you taking on?

3A&B) SOLAR PLEXUS CHAKRA. Who or what are you strongly connected to (card B)? Who's in control (card A)? What ego blows have you sustained (A), or dealt out to others (B)? What convictions do you hold (A&B)? (Note conflicts between the energies of the two cards.)

4) HEART CHAKRA. What is your ability to heal yourself? Is your heart in it? What is the Key to your healing process? What must you accept with unconditional love?

5A&B) THROAT CHAKRA. What does your unconscious or Inner Self have to say (card A)? What are you actually communicating (card B)? To whom? How are you expressing yourself? Are your inner and outer selves in harmony?

6A&B) BROW CHAKRA. What are your dreams or intuition telling you (card A)? What possibilities are you seeing and what would you like to manifest (card B)?

7) CROWN CHAKRA. What do you hope will be the result of your healing? What can assist you in your healing process?

7) The Seventh, or Crown Chakra (in Sankskrit, *Sahasrara*; color violet) is your connection with Source. It is the entrance place for cosmic energy. Your highest aspirations and knowledge of Truth are found here. Many systems do not even place this chakra in the body but above it, connecting you directly with the will of the Spirit.

The card representing your Heart Chakra is the key card in any health reading. Even if some cards indicate problems, a positive card here means you can heal yourself if you choose. If, however, a very negative-seeming card comes up here, say the Nine of Swords, then you are denying yourself your ability to get well—perhaps by refusing to see yourself as worthy of love. Without self-love, healing is not possible.

THE TREE OF LIFE SPREAD

The Tree of Life is a complex meditational and philosophical system stemming from the Jewish mystical inner teachings called Kabbala. It is composed of ten circular "Sephiroth" which symbolize the attributes of the Creator; also, the containers of "Hir" essence reflected in "WoMan." the ten Sephiroth are connected by 22 Paths corresponding to the Major and Minor Arcana cards. Like the Tarot, the Tree of Life also sets forth the eternal principles operating in all human beings. It demonstrates the connections among body, mind and spirit, and therefore mirrors to us the state of our being, including our health and physical well-being. As there are many books elaborating on the connections between, and meaning of, the Tarot and Kabbala (see the reading list at the end of the chapter), I will not expand on them here.

Although there are ten Sephiroth, they are placed on seven levels which, as mentioned before, roughly correspond to the seven chakras. The Tree of Life Spread, therefore, uses the same layout as the Chakra Spread and can be integrated with it for more depth. Of course, it may also be read alone.

As with the Chakra Spread, begin reading from the bottom (Malkuth) up to the top (Kether)—even though the numbers begin with ten to accord with the traditional numbering of the Sephiroth. Each position expresses psychological and physical aspects of your being. Once you have interpreted the meanings of your cards, read them again from the top (Kether) down to the bottom (Malkuth). A form for recording your spread follows the descriptions of the Sephiroth and their interrelationships. The psychological attributes of the Sephiroth are as follows:

10   MALKUTH ("Kingdom"; the four elements; the colors citrine, olive, russet, black)—Manifestation. Outcome. Physical result and vehicle. Environment. Home. The Body. The Senses. Basis for the situation. Daily life.

9   YESOD ("Foundation"; the Moon; the color violet)—The subconscious foundation of the matter. Mood and atmosphere. Imagination. Fantasy. Visioning. Psychic and clairvoyant activity. Past lives or karmic foundations. Habits. Dreamwork. Collective unconscious.

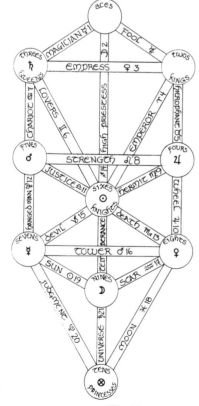

The Tree of Life

8 HOD ("Splendor"; Mercury; the color orange)—What you think. Logos-intellectual reasoning. Knowledge of truth/falsehood. Verbal expression and communication. Craft. Skills. Science. Technology. Plans. Ambitions. Magic. Symbols and metaphors. Wit. Mischievousness.

7 NETZACH ("Victory"; Venus; the color green)—What you love. Eros. The desire behind your motivations and intentions. Inspiration. Emotional likes and dislikes. Relationships to others, especially sexual. Pleasure, both aesthetic and sensual. Where you find beauty. Appreciation. Feelings.

6 TIPARETH ("Beauty"; Sun; the color yellow)—Self. Identity. Individuality. The heart of the problem. Health. Visualization. Balance. Central goal or purpose. Ability to sacrifice for your ideals. Intention. How you are recognized.

5 GEBURAH ("Severity"; Mars; the color red)—Challenges. Conflict. Readjustment. What you experience as obstacles, frustrations, disharmonies. Expression of anger, aggression. Breakdown of habits and complacency. Expressions of power. Leadership.

4 CHESED ("Mercy"; Jupiter; the color blue)—Opportunities. Gifts. What life is giving you to help you on your way. Resources. Aids. Helpers and assistance. Virtues. Ways in which you have recognition and power.

3 BINAH ("Understanding"; Saturn; the color black)—Internal image of Mother. Yin qualities. Anima. Inner knowing, and understanding to be gained. Material values. Limits and boundaries of life; the pain of coming to terms with your limitations. The basic structure or form of a thing. The vehicle that contains the essence.

2 CHOKMAH ("Wisdom"; the zodiac; the color grey)—Internal image of Father. Yang qualities. Animus. Creative and energy outflow. Initiative. Assertiveness. The wisdom and knowledge potentially acquirable. Outer, abstract values and ideas. The essence.

1 KETHER ("Crown"; the color white)—Sense of purpose and meaning. Highest ideal. Source or reason for your question, especially spiritual. Means of reconciliation.

DA'ATH—When you have completed reading all the cards, fan the unused cards remaining in the deck and select one to be the Da'ath Card. This card goes midway between Kether and Tipareth. It represents the will to bring your highest aspirations down into manifestation. It is your inner, hidden knowledge of the potential of your highest self. It represents a critical point in your development. But do you have the desire to use it? Warning: this knowledge cannot be used for material success or ego gratification or it will lead you astray.

The Lightning-Flash Sequence

Now read the cards from the top—Kether—down to Malkuth in what is called the "lightning-flash" sequence—as numbered from one to ten. As sug-

THE TREE OF LIFE SPREAD FORM

Page One

Date:_____ Deck Used:_____

Read for:_____ Read by:_____

Question:_____

_____

Highlighted Paths:_____

Highlighted Sephiroth: _____

10   What is grounding and centering you? How does it physically manifest? What is the environment?

9   What is the mood or atmosphere of the situation? What is happening on the astral, unconscious dream level? What is the subconscious foundation? What psychic or clairvoyant (or past-life) activities are involved?

8   How are you thinking and communicating? How are you using magical skills? What is the truth of the matter and is it being expressed clearly?

7   What desire is behind your motivations? How are you relating to others? What do you love? How are you experiencing pleasure or beauty?

6   What is the heart of the problem? How is your health and sense of vitality? What is your goal or intention? How are you seen?

5   What are you experiencing as challenges, obstacles, frustrations and disharmonies? What habits and barriers must be broken through? Where are you expressing aggression or anger?

4   What opportunities and gifts do you have? Who or what is assisting you? Where is your power and how is it recognized?

3   How are you bringing your ideas into form? What can you learn from limitation and boundaries? How is your inner feminine (mother-image) manifesting?

2   What is your energy outflow? How are you taking the initiative and being assertive? What wisdom can you gain from this situation? What values are you upholding of the inner masculine (father-image)?

1   What is your highest ideal in the matter? What is the spiritual reason for this reading?

DA'ATH—What is the hidden knowledge that can help you manifest your highest aspirations? Are you ready to use it?

What are your sexual dynamics and polarity, as indicated by Geburah/ Tipareth/Netzach?

How are you communicating, traveling and philosophizing as expressed by Hod/Tipareth/Chesed?

How can you achieve a transformation of self through the energies of the Middle Pillar—Kether/Tipareth/Yesod/Malkuth?

gested by the name, this will often result in a burst of recognition of the meaning of this spread for you.

Relating the Sephiroth

Finally examine your spread from the following structural points of view:

The Geburah/Tipareth/Netzach cards form a diagonal indicating your sexual dynamics and polarity.

The Hod/Tipareth/Chesed diagonal will indicate your communications, thoughts and philosophy. Also travel, writing, publishing and teaching.

The Middle Pillar of Kether/Tipareth/Yesod/Malkuth shows you how to achieve transformation of self.

Highlighting the Paths

Refer to the Tree of Life diagram to find the paths corresponding to the Major Arcana. The Major Arcana cards appearing in the spread can also be placed on their own paths, indicating that those paths are especially active. They point out vital links and connections in the situation. A path is described by the Sephiroth it connects; for example, the High Priestess connects Kether to Tipareth.

Highlighting the Sephiroth

The Minor Arcana cards are seen as emanating from the Sephiroth corresponding in number; that is, the Aces correspond to Kether, etc. The Court Cards have their correspondences as follows: Kings—Chokmah, Queens—Binah, Knights/Princes—Tipareth, Pages/Princesses—Malkuth. You can place these cards from your spread on their appropriate Sephiroth to find which you are focusing on at this time.

TEMPERANCE: THE HEALING ANGEL

Once you have some idea of what is the matter, and you are ready to work on it, then the Tarot can again be helpful. The Tarot contains powerful images for helping you create the reality you want. They work within your inner consciousness. You can choose to place before you the images of what you want to manifest for yourself.

Temperance

The Temperance image is especially powerful in healing. By invoking the "angel" of this card, you call on the wisdom and knowledge of all the healing arts, ancient and modern. This card depicts the archetypal Healer mixing an elixir that brings the energies and flow of your body and mind back into balance. This figure is known by many Taroists as The Alchemist. She/he is your own personal physican, who can prescribe the medicine necessary to help you heal yourself.

To get in touch with the Healing Angel of the Temperance card, first relax completely and put yourself in a light trance (see page 21).

Enter into the card and approach your Healing Angel, who smiles at you in greeting. Tell your healer why you have come. Ask her to check out your body, and stand while the Healing Angel puts down her vases and runs her hands all over your body about an inch or two from its surface. She is checking you head to foot for tension, imbalances and blocked energy flow. She then realigns imbalances, gently opens blocked passages and sweeps away fatigue and tension. You will feel refreshed and eased by this loving and caring touch, this sensitivity to your energy field. Notice as her hands move along your body how each part relaxes and releases its tension and anxiety. Notice where she hesitates or spends more time. These are areas in which you need additional work. Thank your angel. Now ask her what seems to be blocking you from healing. Your angel answers:

Ask her what you can do to release the block. Your angel answers:

Ask her what you need to do to bring yourself back into balance. Your angel answers:

Now see yourself become the Healing Angel. Feel your long robes hanging to the ground. One of your feet stands in cool flowing water and one foot is placed on firm warm earth. You draw your sustenance and nourishment up through your feet. Pick up the two urns and place in each the things needed to be brought into balance. Now begin to combine them, pouring from one into the other, back and forth, mixing and combining until a new substance is formed in the air between them. This is an object that symbolizes your own personal healing elixir—your means of being healed. Ask your Inner Self what it is for, how you are to use it and where. Accept whatever thoughts come.
What is your object:

What is it for?

What kind of actions does it suggest that you take in order to be healed?

Where in your body should you apply this healing elixir?

Place it wherever is most appropriate to let it do its healing work.

Affirm to yourself that you are willing to heal yourself and bring your energies back into balance by using the symbol and the suggestions you received from your Healing Angel. You now feel relaxed and whole and you can feel the healing process taking place within.

Step back from your Angel. Thank her again and take your leave by stepping out beyond the boundaries of the card, which is now just cardboard in front of you. Feel the ground beneath your feet supporting and "grounding" you. If you feel "heady," bend over and place your hands flat on the ground and breathe into it for a moment, then stretch.

In a meditation I did with the Temperance Angel, I was told by her:

"I am the healer who is a clear channel. The solar disc on my forehead represents the Crown Chakra. Energy freely enters here and leaves through my Heart Chakra, mediating the energy flowing through my heart and giving shape and form (the square) to spirit (the triangle within the square). I simultaneously draw the energy up from the earth and the sea while I breathe in *prana*. I allow these elements to mix within me in temperate, balanced proportions. . . . Belief heals. I am your belief in a part of yourself which is a perfect part of the universe."

In doing psychic healings, it is important to be a channel for the healing energy of Source. To help me do this, I visualize myself becoming the Temperance Healing Angel, thus allowing the healing force to flow freely through me without my own ego getting in the way. "I" am no longer doing the healing, but an impersonal archetypal force is working through me unimpeded by me and my ego. By doing this my own energies are not drained. I feel reenergized yet relaxed—as if I too had received a healing (which in truth I have).

The next chapter continues on the subject of healing, but with the special emphasis on using quartz crystals with the Tarot.

SUGGESTED READING FOR CHAPTER TEN

On Healing:

Spirit Guides: Access to Inner Worlds. Mike Samuels, M.D. and Hal Bennett. New York & Berkeley: Random House/Bookworks, 1974.

The Well Body Book. Mike Samuels, M.D. and Hal Bannett. New York & Berkeley: Random House/Bookworks, 1973.

On the Tree of Life:

The Qabalistic Tarot: A Textbook of Mystical Philosophy. Robert Wang. York Beach, ME: Samuel Weiser, 1983.

A Practical Guide to Qabalistic Symbolism. Vol. 1: *On the Science of the Tree of Life*. Vol. 2: *On the Paths and the Tarot*. Gareth Knight. New York: Samuel Weiser, 1978.

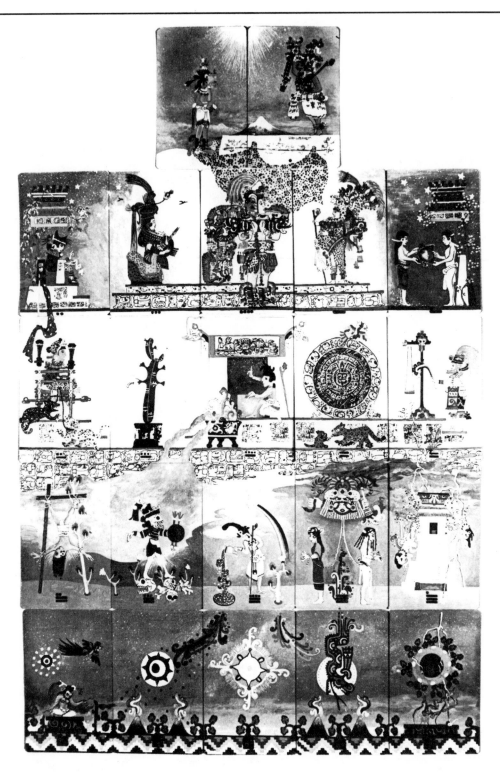

FROM THE XULTUN TAROT, created by Peter Balin and based on an image that came to him on December 21, 1975 of the completed *Major Arcana in Mayan dress joined in one picture. When he later wrote about the Tarot in his book,* The Flight of the Feathered Serpent, *he said, "The use of the Tarot calls for* a 'detached watching,' the mind first must allow total freedom to discover." He relates it to the roots of the word intelligence, which means "to see between the lines." The five levels of Balin's Tarot picture could refer to the five worlds that Mayan mythology says have been created: the world of spirit, the world of mind, the world of the emotions, the world of pure physical manifestation and this fifth world of movement. The sixth sun, which the Mayans predicted as beginning around 2012 A.D. with the destruction of our present world, is called the world of "consciousness."

CHAPTER ELEVEN

CRYSTALS AND TAROT

This chapter continues with methods of using Tarot primarily for healing, in conjunction with another powerful tool: quartz crystals. Crystals have recently been rediscovered for their use in meditation and protection, but above all, for their ability to psychically intensify and focus thought forms.

I had been working with crystals for some time and felt a growing need to somehow integrate them with Tarot, but wasn't quite sure how to do so. My breakthrough occurred while I was visiting a Tarot class in Bolinas taught by my friend Jim Wanless. As the evening drew to a close, I was standing next to a woman with flowers in her hair, who asked me if I had ever used a pendulum with Tarot. Shivers suddenly ran up and down my spine—this was it! "No, I haven't yet, but I'd like to," I responded eagerly, feeling that something important was about to happen. "How do you do it?" She smiled widely and said, "Oh, you know!" And then she turned away as if she knew that was all she needed to say.

I went home that night and wrote nonstop, producing the major part of this chapter on crystals and the material on pendulums in Chapter Nine. Since then, I've thoroughly checked what came that night and have needed to make very few modifications.

According to Merlyn, my friend and crystal caretaker of Hawaii, crystals are the flowers of the mineral kingdom. They are the highest stage of mineral life and literally grow into existence as intricate and beautiful natural formations. In ancient times, rock crystal was believed to be permanently frozen water from heaven. There are over 2,000 different kinds of crystals, with quartz being the most abundant kind.

Quartz, or "rock crystal," is silicon dioxide (SiO_2), with a hardness rating of 7 and a specific density of 2.65, and is found in the shape of a hexagonal prism terminated at one or both ends by a six-sided pyramid. Besides the clear variety, quartz comes in a range of colors: purple, called amethyst; yellow to orange, known as citrine; pink, called rose quartz; and brown to gray, called smoky quartz. Crystals have "lay lines," which are like fingerprints—no two are the same, and they grow in spirals with either left- or right-handed twists. Quartz passes a greater range of the light spectrum than glass, with less frequency distortion. Optically superior to glass, quartz is used in fine lenses for precision equipment.

Quartz crystals demonstrate what is called the piezoelectric effect, which means they undergo mechanical distortion when subjected to an electrical input. As a result, dependent on their physical parameters, they resonate within narrowly defined frequency ranges and are universally used to control oscillator circuits of broadcasting and other electronics apparatus, and in precision timepieces. Conversely, the piezoelectric effect also enables crystals to produce an electric output when mechanically distorted. This property makes them useful as transducers in phonograph cartridges, microphones and strain gauges. Finally, our revolutionary computer technology is entirely based on the incredible memory capability of silicon crystal "chips."

Crystals are also personal healing tools that can assist us in many ways. First and foremost, they are amplifiers and magnifiers of intention. Therefore, be mindful of your intentions. "Set your intentions clearly so the universe will know what to provide," says Merlyn.

Crystals are used for healing, divination, magic and dreamwork, protection, rain-making, intensification of visualizations, contacting of guides and teachers and as teachers themselves (because a crystal will let you know what it is for). Quartz also absorbs positive ions and emits negative ions.

CRYSTAL LORE

Some say that your first crystal should be given to you, but if you are drawn to own one, to hold it in your hand and gaze at its gleaming surfaces and rainbow lights, then go ahead and purchase it for yourself, but don't haggle over the price. You will then be a crystal caretaker.

Crystals are thought to have been the powerful energy source of Atlantis. The American Indian teacher, Oh Shinnah, speaks of electrical generators from ancient South America that exist in museums, powered by crystals and still working. Crystals have the greatest efficiency of any known energy transfer process.

Native Americans, Egyptians and the ancient Irish buried their dead with a piece of rock crystal connecting them to the light of the spirit even while interred in a dark grave. Crystals are worn today by some Native Americans as pendants, hanging between the solar plexus and Heart Chakra. Since the solar plexus is where you receive external stimuli into your body, a crystal in that vicinity can purify the energy you receive—if that is your intention. (And it doesn't hurt to carry your own negative ion generator wherever you go.) Be sure that any crystal you wear or use is open at both ends, so that the energy can pass unobstructed through the crystal. Pendants should be fastened with a wire or band around the crystal, not a closed cap.

There are many famous historical crystals housed in museums and private collections; the majority of them were used for sacred or occult purposes. Crystal balls are among the most outstanding examples, including Dr. John Dee's crystal ball of smoky quartz with which he made prophecies for Elizabeth I. Currently in private hands is the famed Mitchell-Hedges skull found at the Mayan site of Lubaantum in British Honduras (now Belize). This skull, with lower jaw separated, was carved from one piece of extremely clear quartz crystal. It was found beneath an altar and was believed by its finder to have been used for ritual divination and worship in Atlantis. The fact that this skull and others found in Central America are those of women leads me to believe that they come from a time and place in which women were spiritually powerful.

Native peoples of various lands have venerated rock crystal, believing it to contain living spirits who can work good or ill upon the possessor and those he knows. They are wrapped well—usually in leather, kept well-washed, and sometimes bathed in blood to feed them. In some tribes, each member received one at birth; it was said to contain the light of his/her spirit. These personal crystals were then kept safe in caves except when used for ritual purposes. Crystals were used by the Cherokees to find lost objects, especially horses, and by the native Australians to make rain.

In Europe, water in which a crystal had soaked was used for numerous medicinal benefits, including relief from anxiety and diarrhea, production of milk in nursing mothers, to staunch bleeding and cure giddiness. Today many people keep a small crystal in their drinking water to "sweeten" it. A crystal placed on cuts and burns seems to draw out the pain and aid in healing. Placed against the temples for a headache, it works much like an ice pack. Crystals were even used by the Romans to cool themselves on hot summer days and held in the mouth by the Chinese to quench their thirst.

Probably their main use throughout the ages has been for meditation and in religious practices. Their clarity, inner rainbows and prism effects are all reminders of the light of Creator, the spirit of the Great God/dess. By meditating on the inner light and clarity one can penetrate the darkness of ignorance and gain insight into the design and intention of Creator, or at least the Higher Self. By staring deeply into the depths of a crystal one can concentrate and focus attention (as hypnotists well know) on whatever tasks are at hand.

PURIFICATION OF CRYSTALS

Because a crystal takes on so many external energy vibrations, positive ions and prevailing intentions, it is essential to purify your crystal regularly. Always treat a crystal with respect and love and you will receive it back in greater measure.

There are many ways to purify and cleanse a crystal. The most common method is to soak it in sea water overnight. Sea salt and spring water will also do. The salt absorbs energy from the crystal. This water should then be poured someplace where nothing can grow. If you have just received a crystal or feel that it needs an especially deep purification, then soak it for seven days and seven nights.

The sun recharges a crystal and gives it light energy. Place it in the sun as often as possible and soak it in a clear glass in a window where it will pick up the sun's rays.

Other methods of purification include:

1) "Smudging" the crystal in the smoke of cedar, sage, sweetgrass, rosemary or other local herbs, especially those used by the native peoples of your area. This cleans the energy fields around you for clear thought and communication and revitalizes you.

2) Burying it in the earth, especially when a longer, deeper purification is necessary.

3) Visualizing it filled with pure white, gold or "Christ" light.

4) Blowing out the impurities with your breath.

5) Wiping it with a cloth; cotton or silk are best.

6) Holding opposing sides and exhaling sharply while simultaneously pulling the energy out of the tip with your fingers. Do this three times so all the faces are cleansed.

Remember that your intention is as important as any method you use.

CRYSTALS AND TAROT

Immediately following is a summary of the ways in which crystals can be used with Tarot cards. Each of these ways is discussed in detail in the remainder of this chapter.

As a pendulum, for clarifying information and selecting what is appropriate to work with. (See Chapter Nine for a discussion of this.)

To purify your deck and protect it, and to harmonize the reading atmosphere.

To focus on your question and amplify your intention for the reading.

To record a reading.

To infuse a crystal with a Tarot archetype for healing and magical work.

To protect a sacred place or work space.

For meeting your Tarot archetypes and guides, and for amplifying your Tarot visualizations.

Using Crystals to Purify and Protect Your Tarot Deck

After using your Tarot deck, place a freshly purified crystal on top of it. This will both cleanse and protect the deck while you are not using it. Some people always keep a small crystal in their Tarot wrap with their deck. You could also reserve a special crystal pendulum only for Tarot use, wrapping the string to hold the bag or container closed. Be sure to cleanse your pendulum regularly in salt water and smudge everything often.

Using Crystals to Focus on Your Question, to Amplify Your Intention and to Harmonize the Atmosphere for a Reading

For this, you may use the same crystal that you always keep with your deck, being sure to cleanse it often with light if nothing else. Hold the purified crystal in your right hand and breathe your question into it. Speak aloud when you do this. Thus you have set your intention and made it clear both to yourself and the universe. Keep the crystal before you while shuffling and reading the cards and look at it often to keep your attention focused. Since a crystal generates negative ions, it will also keep the atmosphere harmonized and healthier.

Using a Crystal to Record a Reading

Crystals have memories, perhaps the longest natural memories on the planet. Not only will your crystal remember everything in a reading that occurs in its presence, but you can retrieve that information. A crystal will not speak to you in words, of course, but by holding the crystal in your left hand, you can recall the essence and occasionally the very words. Sit quietly, breathe deeply and evenly, relax and open yourself to the information recorded in the crystal. This can be especially helpful if you later want to write about the reading in a letter to a friend or record its significance in your journal.

Infusing a Crystal with a Tarot Archetype

You may want the essence of a particular Major Arcana card to energize a crystal for a special use—for instance, healing. This can be for a temporary or permanent purpose.

Crystals held in your hand act to magnify both the healing intention and the energy flow through your hands. For instance, in the case of a sore throat, the healer imagines a blue ray of light directed through the crystal and flowing out from its point sweeping over the person's sore throat, cooling and soothing the inflamed tissues. By visualizing the crystal imprinted with a Tarot archetype (expressed in its highest ideal) you can expect to draw on great transformative powers. You are calling upon and expecting extra-normal things to happen, things that cannot be explained logically. And they can and do happen. You are also tuning into and exercising astral and psychic forces and energies: angels, gods, goddesses, the planets, the universe.

TEMPORARY INFUSION

First, decide which card (or cards) are appropriate to your purpose. Second, purify the card and your crystal (which has already been cleansed in salt water) in cedar or other herbal smoke.

For a temporary purpose simply place the crystal on the card. State your intention three times aloud and ask for the essence of the card to enter the crystal for your purpose. You may leave them in place overnight, or the crystal may be used immediately. If you know the images on your cards very well and can visualize them clearly and accurately, then simply visualize the card and breathe your intention into your crystal. The energy will remain until you purify the crystal of your intention.

PERMANENT INFUSION

To permanently imprint the essence, place both the card and the crystal upon it under the light of a full moon for three nights (the night before, of, and following the full moon). The full moon attracts, pulling energy toward it, and therefore the essence of the archetype draws upward into the crystal upon the card. Be sure the moon sign harmonizes with your purpose. Finally, pass the crystal three times through a sacred wood fire that you've made yourself only for this purpose.

Both the temporary and permanent methods of infusing a crystal can be done ritually within a ward-set circle (see page 180).

Here are some guidelines for the use of Tarot archetypes in infused crystals:

FOR HEALING:

TEMPERANCE—For rebalancing auras, healing guidance, general psychic healings, combining essences.

THE TOWER—For breaking down or burning away obstructions, cancers.

DEATH—For cutting off, releasing, easing transitions (combine with The Star and Strength).

STRENGTH—For strengthening organs, especially the heart.

THE DEVIL—(Use sparingly) For increasing sexual energy and low drive (combine with Strength).

THE MAGICIAN—For assistance in diagnosis (combine with Judgment).

THE SUN—For vitality, relaxation, general good health, masculine/feminine balance (combine with The Moon).

THE MOON—To pull or draw out, to relax or bring on sleep.

THE STAR—For cleansing and purification and to free one from fears; good for stress.

THE WORLD—For limiting or constricting and to help someone make the most of a limited or constricted situation.

FOR MAGIC AND PSYCHIC DEVELOPMENT:

THE MAGICIAN—For focus and attention and the use of magical implements.

THE HIGH PRIESTESS—Especially for clairvoyance, for psychic and Tarot readings, for inner guidance and protection.

THE HANGED MAN—For altered states, mystical visions.

THE DEVIL—For sexual magic.

THE STAR—For ritual work.

THE MOON—For past lives, dream work, astral travel, magic in general.

THE EMPRESS AND THE HIEROPHANT—For grounding and centering.

THE LOVERS AND TEMPERANCE—For alchemical works.

Actually, all the Major Arcana have a magical purpose, or more specifically, an alchemical or kabbalistic one. The above listings are only to give you some ideas.

FOR RELATIONSHIPS:

THE LOVERS, STRENGTH and such pairs as SUN/MOON, EMPRESS/ EMPEROR, etc.

IN GENERAL:

THE MAGICIAN and the planet MERCURY—For magic, communication and intellectual pursuits.

THE HIGH PRIESTESS and the planet MOON—For inner wisdom, Tarot consultation, past lives, receptivity.

THE EMPRESS and the planet VENUS—For conception, nurturing, the arts.

THE EMPEROR and the sign ARIES—For starting new projects, building, authority, self-assertion.

THE HIEROPHANT and the sign TAURUS—For teaching, public speaking, singing, grounding.

THE LOVERS and the sign GEMINI—For choices, nervous tension, love relationships and the balance of masculine and feminine energies.

THE CHARIOT and the sign CANCER—For victory and as a guardian protecting the home.

STRENGTH and the sign LEO—For desire, creativity, courage and the heart.

THE HERMIT and the sign VIRGO—For journeys, spiritual seeking and patience.

WHEEL OF FORTUNE and the planet JUPITER—For change, expanding your resources and luck in gambling.

JUSTICE and the sign LIBRA—For legal and money matters, contractual agreements, clear thinking and truthfulness.

THE HANGED MAN and the planet NEPTUNE—For surrender, mystical visions and inducing altered states.

TEMPERANCE and the sign SAGITTARIUS—For general healing, angelic guidance, combining remedies, returning balance.

THE DEVIL and the sign CAPRICORN—For stirring things up, for mirth and play, to increase sexual energy, for low vitality.

THE TOWER and the planet MARS—For burning away, breaking down (especially habits).

THE STAR and the sign AQUARIUS—For meditation, cleansing and purification, rituals, spirit guidance, freedom and liberation.

THE MOON and the sign PISCES—For dreamwork, to hide something, for receptivity, for magic.

THE SUN and the SUN—For success, finding things, creativity, recognition, childbirth, good health, relaxation.

JUDGMENT and the planet PLUTO—For visualizing, critical perception, transformations and transitions.

THE WORLD and the planet SATURN—For psychic protection, dance, integration.

Protecting with Crystals and Tarot: Setting Wards

When working with a magical spread, or for healing at a distance, you may want to place your work within a circle of energy and protection. This is called "setting wards." You want to focus the energies from each of the four directions upon a single point at the center and then imagine there is a glowing ball of white light. This gives power to the focus of your attention, allowing it to expand into manifestation, as you visualize the white light expanding.

You need a white cloth about two to three feet square spread on the ground or upon a small table. In the center of your cloth place any Tarot magic spread you are working on, Tarot mandala or single Tarot card representing qualities you want to develop or someone you want to heal. You may also include a picture of the person you want to heal.

Place one small white candle somewhere in or near the center. At each of the four directions, place a candle whose color represents that direction. Beginning in the east and moving clockwise:

East: Yellow, white or pale blue—Air—Swords
South: Red, orange or gold—Fire—Wands
West: Blue, light green or indigo—Water—Cups
North: Black, brown or deep green—Earth—Pentacles
(White candles may be used if the other colors are not available.)

Next to each of the four outer candles, place a crystal pointing in toward the center. Under each crystal place the Ace from the suit that corresponds with that direction. Place a fifth crystal, pointed up, on the card or picture you have placed in the center.

Sit in the east. Take sea salt, preferably in the rock crystal state, and draw a circle around the whole, touching and connecting each of the four crystals and the four lights.

Turn to the east and say something like: "Guardian of the Powers of the East, from where the sun rises and all new things begin, guide and protect me. May my work (state what it is) partake of your light and my thoughts and intentions be crystal clear and in harmony with the universe." Light the candle and visualize a beam of golden light, like the rising sun, flowing through the point of the crystal and into the center.

Turn to the south and say: "Guardian of the Powers of the South, land of burning deserts, guide and protect me. May my work (state what it is) partake of your light and my perceptions and creative inspiration be crystal clear and in harmony with the universe." Light the candle and visualize a beam of red light, like fire, pouring through the point of the crystal and into the center.

Turn to the west and say: "Guardian of the Powers of the West, home of lakes and streams and rivers, guide and protect me. May my work (state what it is) partake of your light and my love and emotions be crystal clear and in harmony with the universe." Light the candle and visualize a beam of blue light, like a stream, flowing through the point of the crystal and into the center.

Turn to the north and say: "Guardian of the Powers of the North, of caves, earth, and dark places, guide and protect me. May my work (state what it is) partake of your light and may I be safe and secure and all my senses crystal clear and in harmony with the universe." Light the candle and visualize a beam of black, green or ultra-violet light coming through the point of the crystal and into the center.

Light the white candle in the center and visualize all the colors of light meeting to form a sparkling clear rainbow that slowly grows, engulfing all the light to the edge of the circle, so that the crystals seem to merge in a circle of light. This light gives energy and vitality to your work symbolized in the center. Visualize what you want to accomplish. For instance, you "see" your friend become filled with a healing light that burns out her illness and restores balance to her cells. Or you "see" yourself in the studio of your dreams, light streaming from the skylight, your easy chair in one corner and work space in another.

Spend what time you need to concentrate on your work. Then complete and close the process by ritually opening the circle. Begin in the east saying, "I thank you, O Guardians, for your guidance and protection," (blow out candle) "and I accept this light to cleanse myself." Take the crystal and place the "matrix" (the broken-off end) against your forehead, inhale and feel the last of the light being absorbed through your forehead and passing through your body, cleansing, renewing and purifying it; then out your feet on the exhale, into the earth. Moving clockwise, repeat with the red, blue and green candles, and finally the central white light.

When working with more than one person, you can have a different person address each direction, but all members in the group should inhale each color in order to remain in balance.

If you wish to work on a project for several days, you may leave your work space set up, but candles should be lit each day. On the last day allow the center candle to burn itself out.

Using a Crystal for Tarot Visualizations

As previously mentioned, crystals are amplifiers and magnifiers of intention. by holding a crystal in your right hand you can magnify and amplify your intentions to visualize clearly and realistically, to have your senses experience vividly and to remember everything that happens in your visualization. It is helpful for clarifying and intensifying your affirmations and for remembering them after the visualization is over. Remember: "Set your intentions clearly, so the universe will know what to provide!"

The following is a powerful visualization developed by Dale Walker of Sunol, California, for use with your crystal:

Hold your crystal in your right hand, breathe, relax and ground yourself (see page 21).

Imagine you are outside in a grassy meadow. The sun is shining high overhead on a warm spring day. You place your crystal on the ground before you and watch as it slowly grows bigger and bigger until it is the size of a small house. A door opens in one side and a ramp extends down to the ground. You enter into your crystal. As you look around inside, bring all of your senses into play: what are the walls like, and the floor? What do you smell? What do you hear? Is there anything to taste? What is the temperature and does it change as you move around? As you get to know the inside of your crystal, it will probably change to suit the circumstances. Stand in the very middle, under the apex of the point. Look up. What do you see? Go down below, deep within the matrix. What do you find there?

Once you are thoroughly familiar with the inside of your crystal, you can begin creating a suitable environment for the purpose of your visualization. For instance, imagine two chairs, a rug, a bookcase, a visualization screen (like a TV or movie screen perhaps) and anything else that makes you feel comfortable and right at home. Sit down in one chair and invite your Tarot Guide to join you in the other chair. Take this opportunity to ask for Tarot guidance or to have your questions answered.

The inside of your crystal is an excellent and very safe place to work when doing any healing, or for your Healing Angel to do a healing for you. You can also meet other guides within your crystal.

When meditating on a particular card, infuse your crystal with that card, enter the crystal and meditate on the card from within.

You will find that the bookcase or video library you created inside your crystal can be a never-ending source of information about crystals, Tarot, healing and the universe. Pull out one of the records and take a look at what it contains.

I find that walking down the street late at night is much safer if I walk inside my crystal, and it never hurts to add a little Chariot or some dancing Universe energy.

When you've completed your work inside the crystal, be sure to thank your guides who always travel with you. Leave your crystal via whatever means you like. See the crystal grow smaller and smaller until it is the size of the crystal in your hand. When your consciousness returns to the hand holding the crystal, open your eyes. Take several deep breaths, exhaling deeply into Mother Earth to ground your excess energy, and stretch.

A variation on this is when you want to "crystallize" a dream. Put your crystal under your pillow or next to the bed (double-terminated or "Herkermer Diamonds" are excellent for this). In a way similar to the visualization process above, enter your crystal, find your dreaming room, make your dream intention clear and fall asleep inside your crystal. Use your crystal to help you remember your dream in the morning.

In summary, I have found crystals to be a good tool to use in conjunction with Tarot readings and meditations, especially for harmonizing and balancing the atmosphere, and for helping me focus my attention and clarify my intentions.

SUGGESTED READING FOR CHAPTER ELEVEN

On Crystals and Healing:

Healing Stoned: The Therapeutic Use of Gems and Minerals. Julia Lorusso and Joel Glick. Albuquerque, NM: Brotherhood of Life, 1981. (110 Dartmouth, SE, Albuquerque, NM 87106.)

Precious Stones: Their Occult Power and Hidden Significance. W. B. Crow. London: Aquarian Press, 1968.

The Way of the Shaman: A Guide to Power and Healing. Michael Harner. New York: Harper & Row, 1980.

On Ritual:

The Spiral Dance: A Rebirth of the Ancient Religion of the Great Goddess. Starhawk. New York: Harper & Row, 1979.

Mother Wit: A Feminist Guide to Psychic Development: Exercises for Healing, Growth and Spritual Awareness. Diane Mariechild. Trumansburg, NY: Crossing Press, 1981.

FROM A MAJOR ARCANA
DECK created as a Tarot-class project. These collaged images exemplify
how a unique, personally significant
deck may be created, in this case using contemporary figures such as
Harry Houdini as the Magician and
Gertrude Stein as the High Priestess.

The cards are laid out in a pattern
that represents one possible evolution
of the Three-Card Spread and the archetypal concepts at the root of it.
Here the Magician and the Virgin
Priestess (esoterically the ever-present
Now and Memory) are viewed as a
pair. Their intercourse or interaction

(Will and the magnetically attractive
opposition to it) create something
new. The High Priestess is
transformed into the pregnant Empress. Ideas take on form. As a
future is conceived, time begins. Love
is born.

CHAPTER TWELVE

DESIGN
AND CREATIVITY
WITH THE TAROT

Throughout this book you have not only been observing your own life through the Tarot, but actually designing it as well. In this final chapter you have the opportunity to design and creatively express yourself using the Tarot for inspiration. The areas I will cover are: designing your own spread, designing your own deck, Tarot art and creative writing with Tarot.

DESIGNING YOUR OWN SPREAD

You have already been given numerous spreads with which to work. They can probably give you information about most of your questions. The spreads will work better for you as you become thoroughly familar with them— understanding their nuances, the kinds of information they can give you and what they can't. Thus you develop confidence in the completeness of the reading.

To take the next step into Tarot, you will want to design, modify and create your own spreads in order to express your personal philosophy, world view, style and concerns.

Following are some ideas for different ways to design a spread. Keep a notebook of spreads that you and your friends design. (Please send me a copy if you'd like to share them.)

1) Base the design on your understanding of a metaphysical or physical structure, such as the Chakras, Tree of Life and Tai-Chi Ch'uan (or Turning Wheel) spreads given in this book. For example, you might design spreads based on such diverse structures as a DNA helix, a house plan with different "rooms" or the key ideas of psychosynthesis.

2) Consider the numerological purpose of your spread, based on the number of cards in it: For example: 3 = creativity, new combinations and harmony; 4 = structure, what's established, four directions; 9 = mastery and completion. Use whatever ideas these numbers mean to you, or refer to Appendix A, the Minor Arcana Number Cards, for inspiration.

3) Assign each card in your spread a Tarot archetype that represents the meaning of that position. For instance, Angeles Arrien designed a spread

called the Path of Rebirth, which uses nine cards beginning with Death and continuing in sequence through The World. The first card, in this case Death, sets the theme of the reading—what you must let go of and how you will experience rebirth and transformation. It is a spread examining struggle and self-discovery, culminating in ascent through the birth canal and back into The World.

4) "Your layout is a map of your questions," says Gail Fairfield in her book *Choice-Centered Tarot*. She suggests you begin with your question and all your concerns and issues. You can then design a spread on the spot by assigning a card position to each core concern. Since your first step is to clarify your question and all its component aspects, Gail says that sometimes you will not even need to spread the cards—just clarifying the question may give you the answer. See Chapter Five on "Expanding the Three-Card Reading," which gives a simple example of this.

5) Begin with any basic spread (the simpler the better). After reading the cards in the spread, you can ask for clarification or more information about any card or issue in the spread. Fan the remaining cards and draw a card to give you that information. You can also do an entire reading in this way, asking questions spontaneously and drawing cards to answer them. It is especially important to tape this kind of reading because it tends to move fast, developing and passing through many ideas quickly.

6) Begin with a theme such as relationship, money, healing, dreams. Determine the major elements (or patterns, needs, concerns) and give each of them a position. For instance, a Relationship Spread will involve at least two people (or two or more aspects of self) and perhaps questions of communication, sex, support and so on. Rather than dealing with a particular situation, you are trying to discover a spread that could apply to anyone working with your chosen theme.

7) Translate psychological/social/economic/spiritual theories of behavior into positions for a spread. Use gestalt, role-playing, design and planning formulas.

8) Begin with a traditional spread, and then through meditation, contemplation, use and just playing around ("What if I move in a spiral instead of up and down?" etc.), change and further develop the spread based on your own insights. Modify it to suit you by asking yourself:

Do the visual and geometric patterns suggest internal relationships among cards?

Is the spread divisible into more basic component structures such as past/present/future, conscious/unconscious or right brain/left brain?

Can I gain anything by moving the cards around?

Is anything unresolved? Am I left hanging or could additional cards resolve it?

Would phrasing the position meanings differently (turning them into questions, seeing them as metaphors) work better for me?

Make a list of themes, theories, ideas that could be turned into spreads:

What kinds of questions have you not found an adequate spread for? (Break them down into their component parts and see what you can do with them.)

DESIGNING YOUR OWN DECK

"But I don't know how to draw!" Yes, if you are like me, that may be your stumbling block, yet there are many other ways to produce your own personalized deck of cards. It is worth the time and effort, as it will teach you volumes about the Tarot and about yourself. You don't even have to do an entire deck—begin with one card, such as your Personality, Soul or Year Card. Make one for a friend for his or her birthday. It is not even necessary to stick to traditional Tarot concepts. Here are some suggestions on how to do it:

1) Make a collage deck. If it is a little too large to shuffle, you can make photographs or photocopy reductions of the completed set for use in your own readings. Old magazines can be found in second-hand bookstores, Goodwills and at garage sales.

2) Make a photographic deck. You can take pictures especially for your deck, creating costumes, finding sets, props and friends who look the part. Another way is to go through your own collection of snapshots and choose those that represent the qualities of each card as they have appeared in your life: your father and mother as The Emperor and Empress, your child's first steps as The Fool, a rainbow over a waterfall for Temperance, etc.

3) Hand-color a black-and-white deck such as the B.O.T.A., Church of Light/Egyptian, Rolla Nordic or Amazon Tarots—to name only a few. You can either follow traditional color arrangements or go totally wild with your own impressions.

4) Add to the colors of an existing deck or otherwise embellish it. The soft colors of U.S. Games' version of the Rider-Waite-Smith deck work well for this. The new metallic pens can add a richness impossible in conventional printing processes.

5) Even if you are not an accomplished or natural artist, nevertheless it is entirely possible that you could paint a personally meaningful deck. Remember that much so-called "primitive art" is dominated by nonprofessionals and often carries a "presence" of deeply felt power. But if that's not for you, commission (or work with) an artist to draw or paint your vision. This follows the tradition of many established decks, for which one person was the conceptualizer and another the artist.

6) Put together your own deck from endless different sources. Ffiona Morgan did this while waiting for her own deck (the Matriarchal Tarot) to be completed by the artist (which took years). She cut out 78 circular pieces of cardboard and glued on them her favorite cards from many different decks, pictures from magazines, drawings by herself and friends and photographs of people. Hers is a constantly evolving and changing deck and often has images on both sides of a card. The deck is somewhat bulky in size, but she handles it with dexterity and ease in a reading.

TAROT ART

In my college Tarot classes, students have always had to prepare either a final paper or a creative project. Over the years I have seen Tarot expressed through the media of: batik, silk screen, enamelwork, music, song, clothing, containers, jewelry, perfume, paintings, drawings and photographs. Very few of my students who created these Tarot projects could be called artists or craftspersons, yet their projects repreatedly demonstrated to me that artistic facility of some kind is latent in almost everyone and only needs the stimulus of something they want to express.

There have also been Tarot plays, Tarot novels, Tarot record albums and Tarot art shows.

Pick one Tarot card which appeals to you strongly and reproduce its essence in some tangible way. Use your hands. What symbols do you want to include? Are pictures even necessary? What medium appeals to you?

Explore the colors in the card you have chosen. For frustrated nontalented artists like myself, take a watercolor set, dampen an entire piece of watercolor paper and drop on swirls of color that match those in your card; don't worry about representational pictures.

CREATIVE WRITING AND TAROT

Many people have used Tarot either as a theme for their writing or as the inspiration behind it. Sometimes its influence is readily apparent and sometimes not. A Tarot image can be a starting point or the entire piece. When reading a book, especially on mythology or psychology, I frequently find that the Tarot cards could have been used as illustrations. Yet the author may have had no awareness of the cards themselves.

If you have carefully worked through the exercises in this book, you might find, in going back over the material, that the seeds of several poems or stories exist in your intuitive writing pieces. Those in which you described what you saw in the card are often especially good. The following is a description I wrote of the Empress card from the Crowley-Harris Thoth deck while taking a writing class in Mexico with author Pierre Delattre.

Crowley-Harris

THE EMPRESS

She gathers in the energy around her—
Ripples and currents of vibration
Wave, parting before her hands,
Hurrying to follow her sweeping movements.
In the heart of her being is poised
A blue flower, a half-opened lotus
Which now widens, shimmering,
To reveal a pure white center.
The waves of energy collect in it.
Her left hand gathers the energy,
Her right hand remains still,
Ready to send it out again.

She uses her right hand to direct the cards,
To move them here and there,
To interpret for herself
Their meanings.

At her feet,
An aperture forms deep in the earth.
She sinks her roots heavily from her strong trunk,
Searching for nourishment she needs
From Mother Earth.
She breathes out,
And the roots sink deeper,
Spreading, reaching.
She breathes in,
And coursing up through her feet and legs
Comes a feeling of solidity,
Self-assurance,
Composure,
At-one-ness with Nature.
She breathes out and in again,
This time the rising currents fill
The blue flower in her heart,
Engorging it with sensation.
Transforming into a pure white light,
The current sweeps up her spine.

She breathes out.
It pours from the top of her head
And meeting with a
Golden crown above her,
Creates a rainbow shower of light
Completely engulfing her.

She sits encapsulated in a perfect
Oval of moving, flowing colors,
Her left hand receptive to the outer currents
And her right hand prepared
To express whatever she should find
In the cards before her.

She sits,
Senses alert,
Body straight but relaxed,
Eyes gazing ahead,
Ears finely tuned
To the gentle, hovering
Song of intuition.

Many writers have been inspired by Tarot images in their writing. Others, such as W.B. Yeats, while never using the images directly, found in the Tarot, according to Kathleen Raine, "a means of apprehending the unchanging, universal aspects of reality."

A friend recently told me how he received his first deck of Tarot cards from a writer/artist friend: "He gave me a deck of Tarot cards and a book about them and said, 'Here, every good poet should know the Tarot inside and out.'" (Aethelaid Eldridge to Patrick Flynn.)

The following are some of the poems and stories that have been inspired by the Tarot and its images. The first piece by Robert Creeley is a word-picture of one card:

from ZERO: THE FOOL
by Robert Creeley

"With light step, as if earth and its trammels had little power to restrain him, a young man in gorgeous vestments pauses at the brink of a precipice among the great heights of the world; he surveys the blue distance before him— its expanse of sky rather than the prospect below. His act of eager walking is still indicated, though he is stationary at the given moment; his dog is still bounding. The edge which opens on the depth has no terror; it is as if angels were waiting to uphold him, if it came about that he leaped from the height. His countenance is full of intelligence and expectant dream. He has a rose in one hand and in the other a costly wand, from which depends over his right shoulder a wallet curiously embroidered. He is a prince of the other world

on his travels through this one—all amidst the morning glory, in the keen air. The sun, which shines behind him, knows whence he came, whither he is going, and how he will return by another path after many days . . ."
—from PIECES, 1969.

The following poems, while still focusing on one card, are more wide-ranging.

LE CHARIOT
by John Weiners

A flame burns in the morning.
It is the empty bag of horse

That carries the sun across the sky
And lights the love that blinds your eye.

It turns the night to infinite noon.
Changes the course of the unearthly moon

To ride in your heart instead of heaven.
This is the card that reads as seven.

—from THE VOICE THAT IS GREAT WITHIN US, ed. by Hayden Carruth, 1970.

from SIX OF CUPS
by Diane Wakoski

Poem on a Card

Pretend means something different every time.
The two children gathering flowers
in the high walled garden,
filling their cups with blossoms,
must see that there is a star,
white-hot, as it fell from the sky, burning its way down
on top of each receptacle,
but they do not seem to be aware that it changes the contents
in any way.
They hand each other the cups;
perhaps they touch the stars floating on top
as if they were hot cookies
or pieces of gingerbread fresh from the oven.
The cups are toys that they hand one another for examination
and sampling—proud of ownership,
proud of each pretty star.

If I put my hand on one of their stars,
my hand would disintegrate into a lump of carbon in a minute,
without even a chance for me to reflect and draw back.
I have to keep my hand away from that ten-thousand-degree star.
But still they hand each other the cups,
smiling and bowing,
presenting for love
something I do not need them to tell me the value of.
They could as well hand me the cup
with a coral snake inside
curled up like a carved face.

—from INSIDE THE BLOOD FACTORY, 1968.

THE EMPRESS #8
(FROM THE TAROT DECK)
by Diane Wakoski
To D. di P.

That snake that peeps out from under your foot
        —are you stepping on it
            or sheltering it (under your high arch)?

Do you have both powers
or
only the
appearance of
both?

—from SMUDGING, 1974.

PRINCESS OF DISKS
by Diane di Prima

There is a whole
spectrum of her, it ranges
from the green lady veiled
w/leaves who rules
the jungle, who seldom
raises her eyes, to the
desert woman, whose red hair
is the sunset, whose naked body
is clay whose eyes
seem empty because they are the precise blue green
of the empty desert sky
                        behind her head
blue green of turquoise of evening
                    & her feet

fade into the sand.
               She is mountain woman who walks
at dusk her skin
                    & robes of silver grey & too
the wylfen she-bear
                         dryad the small
spirits of mushrooms
                    she is a rainbow of women, yet
she is not all of them
                    Ice queen & mermaid
belong to her sister, the one
who carries the cup & there are others
invisible, or they move too fast, she belongs
to the spectrum you see.

—(previously unpublished)

from THE QUEEN OF WANDS
by Judy Grahn

 . . . .
And I am the Queen of Wands.
The people honor me.
I am the torch they hold over their own heads
as they march march like insects
by the billions
into the bloody modern world,
over discarded corpses of their ages past,
always holding me, aloft or in their arms,
a flame in the hand of the statue,
a bundle of coals
in their inflammatory doctrines, calling me
a chalice of fire,
essential light,
the Flama
and the stuff of which their new world will be made.
Sophia (Helen) they call me, enlightenment,
"God's light," wisdom, romance, beauty, being saved,
"Freedom" and the age of reason.
Progress, they call me, industrial revolution,
"People's rule," the future, the age of
electronics, of Aquarius, of the common man and woman,
evolution
solar energy and self-reliance. Sexual self-expression.
Atomic fission, they call me, physics, relativity,
the laser computations in an endless sky of mind,
"science," they call me and also emotion, the aura of
telepathy and social responsibility, they call me

consciousness, "health," and love
they call me, bloom of Helen.
Blush upon her face, and grace.
. . . .

—from THE QUEEN OF WANDS, 1982.

Some poems have been written to describe Tarot readings, such as in
this poem by Duncan McNaughton:

The back fence
the ancient Celtic cross

It reappears in the autumn . . . the terminal Flower:
The picturing card for number Five
Reads *Death* aloft, or placed to cover
The head of one who would survive . . .

With July gone by yet my rosetree alive—
In the phase of Six, opposing the player,
The Tower of God, abolished . . . I dive
Wounded, on wings of an injured prayer

Toward earth for entry, to the house of Seven
Held by *the Devil:*   that intercession
Be done & waiting in between day's heaven
and night, denied appointed destination . . .

My Star that draws in me alone
Abides in the sign of its empty Throne.

—from A PASSAGE OF SAINT DEVIL, 1976.

WHAT MADE TAROT CARDS AND FLEURS DE LIS
by Philip Lamantia

What made tarot cards and fleurs de lis
        chariots my heart to shackled towers
The priestess maps apocalypses
        Swords catch on medused hair
            Mandolins woman in a garden

They scaled the wall, they fell from a wall
Fleurs de lis illuminated on an eyeball

        came out of the wall

        they fought in a flower.

Symbologies systematized from sweat suctionings
made theatrical cruelty extend souls on a pensive
cloud turn turning incendiary incentives ON!

      They came to PEACE
and wailed in gavottes
      monsters cooled their mothers
in bubbling craters
          angels
  dropt leprous booty
On a high flung season they blackened blood,
          climbing the walls

A fleur de lis on a charging horse swam up
    into the moonclad Knight
his lady on a wall
      raped
         moon struck by wands
clapt in a bell, his lady shook fleurs de lis on the wind

      Mandolins
   in a bile styled peace
       explode!
  Knights go scattering swords
The Tripled Queen on a resinous wall
       apparitioned
as fleurs de lis
    luminescent
  under burnt out flesh
suddenly galed
     TAROTED
on medieval   stained   glass

—from SELECTED POEMS 1943–1966, 1967.

There have been numerous novels written about the Tarot or using the Tarot
in a scene. The following is an excerpt from a novel about the Tarot in which,
as the cards take on a life of their own, the characters in the novel assume
mythic proportions.

from Charles Williams' THE GREATER TRUMPS

The cards shook in her hands; she looked back at them, and suddenly one
of them floated right out into the air and slowly sank towards the floor;
another issued, and then another, and so they followed in a gentle persistent rain. She did not try to retain them; could she have tried she knew she
could not succeed. The figures before her appeared and disappeared, and
as each one showed, so in spiral convolution some card of those she still held

slipped out and wheeled round and round and fell from her sight into the ever-swirling mist.

They were huge things now, as if the great leaves of some aboriginal tree, the sacred bodhi-tree under which our Lord Gautama achieved Nirvana or that Northern dream of Igdrasil or the olives of Gethsemane, were drifting downward from the cluster round which her hands were clasped. The likenesses were not in her mind, but the sense of destiny was, and the vision of leaves falling slowly, slowly, carried gently upon a circling wind that touched her also in its passage, and blew the golden cloud before it. She grew faint in gazing; the grotesque hands that stretched out were surely not those of Nancy Coningsby, but of a giant form she did not know. With an effort she wrested her eyes from the sight, and looked before her, only more certainly to see the dancers. And these now were magnified to twenty times their first height; they were manikins, dwarfs, grotesques, yet living. More definitely visible than any before, a sudden mingled group grew out of the mist before her. Three forms were there—with their left arms high-arched, and finger-tips touching, wheeling round a common center; she knew them as she gazed—the Queen of Chalices, holding her cup against her heart; and the naked figure of the peasant Death, his sickle in his right hand; and a more ominous form still, Set of the Egyptians, with the donkey head, and the captives chained to him, the power of infinite malice. Round and round, ever more swiftly, they whirled, and each as it passed seemed to stretch out towards her the symbol of itself that it carried; and the music that had been all this while in her ears rose to the shrieking of a great wind, and the wind about her grew cold and strong. Higher still went the shrieking; more bitterly against her the fierce wind beat. The cold struck and nipped her; she was alone and her hands were empty, and the bleak wind died; only she saw the last fragments of the golden mist blown and driven upon it. But as it passed, and as she gaspingly realized that her lover and friends were near her, she seemed yet for a moment to be the center of that last measure; the three dancers whirled round her, their left hands touching over her head, separating and enclosing her. Some knowledge struck to her heart, and her heart ached in answer, a dull pain unlike her glorious agony when it almost broke with the burden of love. It existed and it ceased.

Henry's voice said from behind her, "Happy fortune, darling. Let's look at the cards." . . .

—from THE GREATER TRUMPS, 1950.

In this final selection, a Tarot reading was actually used to create the plot and the characters for a romantic novel. The reading was then incorporated into the story itself. Throughout the writing of the novel, the two authors would periodically draw cards or do additional readings to clarify the motives of characters and to further develop the plot. The story is of a woman, who after the sudden death of her husband moves across country to a house he was building for her on the beach in Carmel. There she discovers her own creative abilities and loses her fear of being on her own. This is from their original Tarot reading as it appears in the book, demonstrating how the plot unraveled for the authors.

from QUEST OF THE HEART
by Cybil Damien (Kathleen Goss and Dori Gombold)

"Now, let us look at the energy flow in your life right now." Mara continued. "Something is in the process of flowing out—and what is it?" With a dramatic flourish she turned over the card on the right to reveal a mournful figure in a black cloak looking down at three overturned cups, while behind him two full cups stood unheeded.

"The Five of Cups, Ellen. You see—you are getting ready to remove that black robe of mourning that holds you to the past. When you do, you will be able to turn around and face the future and the full cups that are waiting for you."

"But what is in the two cups?" Ellen asked eagerly, yet a bit apprehensively.

"I am a counselor, not a fortune teller. Remember, the future is very fluid, very malleable. You hold it in your mind the way a potter holds a vase on his wheel—molding it, shaping it until it is placed in the kiln where it hardens. That is when the future becomes the present. Until then, it is yours to create. But look closely at this card." She held it out to her. "Look at the symbols in the background. There is a house near water, and a bridge. Bridges symbolize transition. You are leaving a place of mourning and going to a place that offers you a new life. And there is a house—the house will be a catalyst."

Ellen drew in her breath. "Yes, there is a house, on the beach in Carmel. I came out here to see it."

"The house will bring changes into your life. It may frighten you at first, because it represents the unknown, but you need not be afraid; the change will be for the better. . . ."

"And now," Mara said, turning over the card on the left, the last remaining card, "let us see what is getting ready to flow into your life. . . .And there he is, the Knight of Wands!"

The authors chose to take the appearance of the Knight of Wands quite literally. He arrives on the scene, a dashing figure, riding a horse through the sands of Carmel beach.

—from an unpublished manuscript.

TELLING YOUR OWN STORY

Here are some ideas for getting to know the Tarot better and for writing stories at the same time.

The Fool's Tale

Fairy tales are often about the youngest or only child, or a simpleton, or a fool who is set some great task. She/he ultimately succeeds because of naivete and innocence and by being friendly and kind, especially to animals (who are wise and helpful). She/he is usually assisted by magical gifts given by the creatures and people she/he has helped. The prize is most often marriage (if male) to the daughter of a king, and thus he becomes the king and wise ruler over the land; or (if female) to Prince Charming, and they live "happily ever after" in a faraway kingdom. The marriage re-establishes order in the society and represents the reattainment of balance.

Write a fairy tale about a Fool using the images in The Fool card in some way: Who is she/he? Why the odd costume? What is the task and why must it be accomplished? What is in the shoulder bag? Why the rose and the red feather? How is the dog involved? Why is the Fool on the edge of a cliff? Where has he come from and where is he going?

A Story Through the Suits

This exercise leads to a better understanding of the sequencing of the cards in the Minor Arcana suits:

Pick any suit and make up a story illustrated (and based on) the cards in that suit *in order from Ace through Ten*. The Court Cards can be used as the characters in the story if you wish.

Creating a Plot

Let the cards themselves create a plot for a short story or novel. The Celtic Cross Spread works well for this:

Either select a court card to represent the main character or pick one from among the sixteen Court Cards at random. The Court Card you have chosen for your main character is:

What kind of story is this to be? (Mystery, romance, comedy, adventure, fantasy or what?)

Shuffle all the cards while thinking about creating a story for this person. Cut and lay them out in a Celtic Cross Spread. You can have a good time and end up with an interesting storyline if you interpret the cards as literally as possible. For example, if the Knight of Wands comes up, you could actually have a red-headed fellow appear on the scene riding a horse, or at least riding in a red Porsche. Once you've laid out your cards, write down the storyline in the spaces that follow.

Cards One and Two are _____ and _____, describing the basic conflict:

Card Three _____ represents something the main character doesn't know, which is at the base of the matter:

Card Four _____ represents something from his or her past that must be let go:

Card Five _____ represents what is on his or her mind:

Card Six _____ represents what comes next:

Card Seven _____ represents the self-image of the main character:

Card Eight _____ represents the environment:

Card Nine _____ represents the lesson to be learned—what change the character must go through:

Card Ten _____ suggests the ending:

Make up your mind about the style and form, add other characters and events, flesh out your basic storyline and there's your original story.

EPILOGUE

You write your own epilogue. At the beginning you were asked to define Tarot as you saw it at that time and to project what you would like to learn by working with it. Now it is time to review what you have learned and evaluate its worth in your life. There is no need to have read or done every exercise given here. The fact that you are reading this now qualifies you to answer the questions now and whenever you want to do so again in the future. Is Tarot a tool that you will continue to use, and if so, in what ways? Only you can decide what is to come after this book.

Date:_____

Has your personal definition of Tarot changed? What is it now?

What methods and techniques have you found most useful? (And why do you think they worked better for you than others?)

What methods, techniques or ideas did you disagree with or decide not to use? Why?

What were some of the more noteworthy things you learned as you used this book?

What would you like to do with Tarot in the future?

INTERPRETING
THE CARDS

These interpretations of the cards are designed to help you identify specific areas in your life and your psyche that are involved in the situations pictured in your readings.

It is best to learn the meanings of the cards in context, not by memorizing each one.

Keywords

When you look up a card, read through the keywords and concepts, watching for those interpretations that seem to relate especially to your situation. Write your own favorite keywords in the margins.

Questions

Read through the questions, noting any images that fly through your head in response to each. Focus upon the one or two questions that apply most to the situation you are asking about. Answer them as concretely and specifically as possible, modifying the information for the position in which it appears in the spread (past, present, future, self, others, etc.).

Affirmations

Sample affirmations are given to help you use the highest energy of each card. Create your own affirmations based on the qualities you admire in each card and what you want to manifest in a particular situation.

Dating the Cards

Note the date of your reading in this workbook next to each card you received. In this way you can see what cards you get and how often, over any period of time. You can also tell when cards drop from significance, what cards you've not yet received and when they first appear. Those cards that appear often in any given period are ones you may wish to work with further in order to discover what you need to learn from them. You can also indicate position in a spread through simple codes such as: "CC4" for Celtic Cross position #4, or "B" for the body position of the Three-Card Spread.

Getting the Most from Each Card

By doing the exercises given in Chapters One and Two you've found that the images on the cards contain keys to their meanings. The specific deck you use should influence your interpretations if you are reading the images. The following list summarizes some of the suggestions given previously in this book. Before or after looking up interpretations, you can:

1) Simply describe in your own words what you see pictured in the card.

2) Become a figure in the card and talk about who you are and what's going on. Use the first person singular, present tense.

3) Dialogue with figures in the cards using intuitive writing.

4) Free-associate and use intuitive writing when relating to images in the card.

5) Express first impressions and sensory reactions to seeing the cards.

6) Give meaning to colors, shapes and symbols in the cards. Then interrelate the individual meanings of the symbols into a composite whole.

These same suggestions apply in understanding the relationship between two or more cards.

Make the Interpretations Your Own

Use the margins for writing down additional interpretations of the cards that you want to remember, personal affirmations and to change meanings which don't work for you.

Correspondences

Each Major Arcana card has an astrological correspondence of planet or sign and a corresponding Hebrew letter indicated below the card name. Each Minor Arcana card is associated with a planet in a sign, and each Court Card is related to a combination of two of the elements: earth, air, fire and water. In these correspondences, I have mostly followed the Order of the Golden Dawn designations. See Appendix C for more information about Major Arcana correspondences.

THE MAJOR ARCANA

0
THE FOOL

Uranus   Aleph

Leaping off into some new phase of life. Free-spirited. Carefree. Being open
to experience. Acting on impulse without thought or plan. Spontaneity.
Something unexpected or unplanned. Childlike enthusiasm. Innocence. Lack
of inhibitions. Footloose and fancy free. Being silly. Frivolity. Folly. The
choice you are making may appear foolish or not well thought out to others.
Trusting in the universe. No sense of worry or fear. Feeling protected. Experiencing life in the here and now—from moment to moment. Optimism.
Travel and vagabonding. Expect the unexpected with this card.

QUESTIONS TO ANSWER:

In what area of your life are you operating entirely on faith and trust? Where
are you going? What are you feeling foolish about? What would be fun to
do if you could do anything you wanted?

SAMPLE AFFIRMATION:

"All possibilities are open to me as I boundlessly experience the here and
now."

1
THE MAGICIAN

Mercury   Beth

Consciousness. A sense of self. Focusing your attention on a project or goal.
Singleness of purpose. Commitment. Being in control. Dexterity. Skill.
Manual ability. Craftiness. Cunning. Cleverness. Mischievousness. Organiza-
tional skills. Manipulating nature and others to harness their energies.
Magical and occult powers. Communication. Using skills of writing, speak-
ing, persuasion. The animus, or one's sense of self.

QUESTIONS TO ANSWER:

Where are you focusing your energy? Are your objectives clear? What skills
and abilities are needed in this situation? How are you communicating with
others? What do you want others to believe or see?

SAMPLE AFFIRMATION:

"I am a willing channel for the manifestation of spirit in the world."

2
HIGH PRIESTESS

Moon   Gimel

Deep inner wisdom. Inner knowing. Good judgment. Psychic or mediumistic ability. Esoteric knowledge. Access to the *Akasha*. Independence. Self-reliance. In quiet retreat. Seclusion. Objectivity. Receptivity. A mystery or secret. Something hidden. Something in your memory that you need to look at. Recollection. Dreams. Astral travel. The anima, or female sense of self. Seeking guidance and counsel, especially from a woman. Paying close attention to the natural rhythms and cycles of your body and emotions. Habits. The menstrual cycle. Moods and changeableness. Thinking by comparison and contrast, pros and cons.

QUESTIONS TO ANSWER:

What rhythms or cycles do you need to be aware of? What knowledge are you seeking? What do you need to remember or "discover"? What are you concealing? Is it appropriate to do so? How can you best use your intuitive, psychic or dream abilities at this time? Who is seeking your counsel, or whose are you seeking?

SAMPLE AFFIRMATION:

"The knowledge that I seek is within myself awaiting my question."

3
THE EMPRESS

Venus   Daleth

Maternal urges. Your mother or another woman in your life who is nurturing and motherly. Mother Earth. Grounding your energy. The anima. Artistic and aesthetic inspiration through a woman. A flow of creative thought and action, but often undisciplined and in need of pruning and organization. Fertility. Making new combinations. A desire to give birth to something remarkable. Awareness of your own sense of beauty and grace. Attraction and charm. Self-indulgence. Seeing the abundance and harmony in everything around you. Prosperity. Attention to the body, the senses. Promotion of good health for growth and well-being.

QUESTIONS TO ANSWER:

How are your nurturing and mothering qualities being used right now? What creative projects are growing and developing? What are you attracting to you? Who is inspiring and nurturing you? How are you indulging your senses?

SAMPLE AFFIRMATION:

"I am a fertile garden in which creativity can be nurtured to fruition."

4
THE EMPEROR

Aries   He

Father-figures. The Animus. The Boss. The King. A male influence, or your inner male. Lording it over things. A benevolent dictator and the security that comes under his rule. An executive familiar with power. Established leadership. Ambition to reach the pinnacle of success. Power to achieve ambitions. Authority. Confidence. Assertion. Beginning and initiating new things. Action as the road to fulfillment. Life, passion, vision. Ordering, planning, building. Ordering your thoughts and energies. Seeking stability. Experiencing wholeness and unity within the self; integration of the elements, the four functions, etc. Repression of natural urges for the good of society. Creating a stable situation in which to function. Protecting and supporting something/someone. Possession. Ownership. Seeing natural and human resources as raw materials for building and construction. Relying on reason, power and stabilization.

QUESTIONS TO ANSWER:

Where do your ambitions lie? What are you organizing, building, doing? What kind of Emperor are you—energetic and imaginative, or rigid and unreceptive? Who is establishing guidelines, parameters and structures in your life? Who has the power and authority, and how is it being used?

SAMPLE AFFIRMATIONS:

"I have the power and discipline to achieve my highest ambitions.

5
THE HIEROPHANT

Taurus   Vau

A teacher, animus figure or mentor. Intuitive guidance. Teaching and education, especially education in the traditions of one's society. Communicating and teaching others what you have learned. Giving or receiving advice. Following a guru, system, philosophy, tradition or ethical system. Spiritual discipline. The rules of obedience and loyalty—to a guru, organization, work, country, etc. Blessings. Identification with a culture or any kind of group in which you abide by their beliefs and rules. Conformity. Understanding the rules and manners of the existing hierarchy. Learning how to play the game. It furthers you to seek out an authority in the field, to make new allies. Assertion of moral laws of good and evil. Conventional morality. Following the internalized rules of a culture. Listening to the dictates of your conscience. Feeling oppressed by the "shoulds" and "oughts" of life. Repression of free thinking, causing you to react with unorthodoxy, new and revolutionary ideas or gullibility. Feeling betrayed by the system. Problems involving public versus private conscience.

QUESTIONS TO ANSWER:

Who are you looking to for assistance, direction or learning? What law or rule do you feel you have transgressed? And who would hold you accountable? What traditions are you upholding? What traditions are you rebelling against? What are you learning?

SAMPLE AFFIRMATION:

"I commit my obedience only where and when my higher self directs."

6
THE LOVERS

Gemini   Zain

Synthesis. Combining elements of head and heart, feeling and intellect. The union of what is divine in us and in the universe. The coming together of opposites. Thinking about relationship. Working with a partner or in preparation for partnership. Your relationships are mirroring your own inner sense of worth; how you feel about yourself can be seen in how your partner relates to you. Choice between security and a risk of some kind, or between the old and the new. Choice between something respectable but dull and something greatly desired but morally improper. Responsibility. Taking responsibility for your choice and actions. Using free will. Freedom from inhibitions, guilt, conditioning, bondages. Love that can exist only in the absence of restrictions. Recognition of duality. Balanced decisions that require your conscious and subconscious minds to be in agreement. Involvement in a process of cooperation. Recognition of masculine and feminine characteristics of self and others. Need to integrate them within yourself.

QUESTIONS TO ANSWER:

What significant relationship are you involved in? How does this relationship mirror your own sense of self-worth? What choice or decision do you need to make? What responsibility will you have to take based on your decision? What needs to be combined, synthesized or brought together?

SAMPLE AFFIRMATION:

"I choose to be free from inhibitions, guilt and bondages in all my relationships."

7
THE CHARIOT

Cancer   Cheth

Self-control. Self-discipline. Victory over the instincts. Successfully controlling some situation through the force of your personality. Confidence, optimism and faith in your own abilities. Bravado. Control of your physical environment and your body. Control over nature by force of will or technology. Having a sense of direction, a plan. Harnessing all your forces toward your purpose. A strong division between your work and your feelings. You "mirror" the actions and emotional feelings of those around you. Being extremely receptive and sensitive to emotions around you, you need your armor for self-protection, thus putting on a mask of detachment. Development of the personality—the outer mask presented to the world. Your identity in the world. Your ego-mask. Testing what you have learned. Proving yourself and your abilities. Dependence on your skills and abilities to move you instinctively through challenges. Setting forth on a journey, especially one of personal development. Making progress. Unresolved contradictions and tensions that are brought under control. Imagining yourself to be beyond human limitations. Pride. *Hubris*. Ego-inflation coming from success and popularity. Victory. Mastery. Conquest. Triumph.

QUESTIONS TO ANSWER:

What mask (persona) are you presenting to the world? What emotional reactions are you hiding? What contradictions and tensions are you struggling to maintain control over? Where have you experienced recent victory or success in your life? What progress are you making in testing your abilities in the world?

SAMPLE AFFIRMATION:

"By harnessing all my forces toward my purpose and controlling my fears, I victoriously meet my challenges."

8
STRENGTH/LUST

Leo   Teth

Love as a source of strength. Finding the strength to begin or continue with some difficult project despite fear and emotional strain. Strength to endure despite all obstacles. The drive or will to survive. Lust for life. Trying to keep your emotions in hand; learning to handle intense emotional situations calmly. Acting passionately and having strong desires. Intense emotions. Sexuality. Love for what you do. Enthusiasm. "Lust" for your own creativity. Courage to take risks. An abundance of vital energy. Reconciling opposites or with an enemy, and integrating disparate energies into a formidable force. Wrestling with a problem that requires perseverance to solve. Harnessing natural energy so that you can work in harmony with it. Love without judgment. Learning to love the beast. Being freed from the forces of repression. Understanding others by being able to imagine yourself in their place. Courage and perseverance.

QUESTIONS TO ANSWER:

How strong is your love? How are you being called upon to show courage and perseverance? What do you desire to create? What inner passions need to be expressed and reconciled? What is the "natural" or instinctive thing to do?

SAMPLE AFFIRMATION:

"I courageously persevere in the loving reconciliation of my lower and higher selves."

9
THE HERMIT

Virgo   Yod

Withdrawal. Solitude. Turning away from or abandonment of conventions through inner conviction. A search for something. Research. Preoccupation with details. Examining something concealed or hidden. Patience. A vision quest. A journey. Timing. Time management. Prudence. A need to plan and take things slowly, feeling your way carefully. Mastery of what you have been working on. A teacher or guide to help you in your inner search. Help and advice from a teacher, guru, counselor, friend. Instruction from an expert in your field, or acting as such a guide for others. Prudence, caution, discretion. A time to observe but keep silence. Refraining from comment. Making plans secretly. Introspection. Completion of a cycle. Maturity. Interest in illness and health: hypochondriac or healer.

QUESTIONS TO ANSWER:

What are you doing with the time you have to yourself? What are you looking for? Or what do you need to know? Who can help you find out? What concerns about time do you have? What do you need to keep silent about? What would be the prudent thing to do? What do you need to complete?

SAMPLE AFFIRMATION:

"I patiently follow the guidance of my higher self on the path to enlightenment."

10
THE WHEEL OF FORTUNE

Jupiter   Kaph

The laws of karma and reincarnation. The natural consequences of our actions. Cycles and turning points (such as a Saturn-return). Initiation. Finding cycles and recurring motifs in your life. Changes in the circumstances of your life (in which you may have had no choice). Optimism. Generosity. Chance. Adapting to change. A shift of fortune. Moving, or changing jobs. Expansion of situations in your life, bringing in new resources, people, money. Luck. Unexpected windfall. Recognition for something you have done. Coming into the limelight. Having a central focus or purpose around which everything revolves. Or being stuck in a rut. Asking the Oracle, or seeking to have your fortune told. Beginnings and endings, the change of seasons. Circular thinking. *Hubris*. Excessive pride. Extravagance; overindulgence.

QUESTIONS TO ANSWER:

What life-changes are you experiencing? How are you adapting to these changes? What effects are you feeling from circumstances you put in motion previously? Is there something you need to resolve? How are your horizons expanding?

SAMPLE AFFIRMATION:

"I rely on the universe to bring me the experiences I need to manifest my full potential."

11

JUSTICE/ADJUSTMENT

Libra   Lamed

A decision needs to be made. Deliberating on which action to take. Action suspended until a decision is reached. Needing to establish equilibrium, poise, balance and harmony. Finding the equilibrium between understanding and action, truth and justice, self and other. Balancing your accounts. Decisions concerning money or compensation for your work and time. Contracts. Fair exchange of energy through money, goods or work. The ability to see both sides of an issue. The ability to discriminate and peel off outer layers to perceive real motivations. Weighing all the factors: the benefits and the liabilities, the good that you want to keep and the bad that you want to sever. Negotiating. Arbitrating. Playing the middle person. Facilitating. Recognizing the truth about yourself. Concern over the justness of a situation. Wanting to "justify" your actions, needing to feel they are morally right or acceptable. Making plans and being aware of possible reactions and consequences. Taking responsibility for your actions. The law of cause and effect. Receiving the consequences of your past actions. Reacting to previous actions. Finding an appropriate response. Involvement in a legal situation: lawsuit, contract, traffic ticket, etc. Equal partnership.

QUESTIONS TO ANSWER:

What decisions are you weighing? What are the pros and cons? What consequences are you experiencing as the result of some previous action? What is the appropriate compensation (or "energy exchange") needed to balance the situation? What do you need to do to be true to yourself?

SAMPLE AFFIRMATION:

"I am willing to be true to my self in all my decisions."

12

THE HANGED MAN

Neptune   Mem

Listening to your inner self even if it seems opposite to what you would have thought. A need to reverse your established order of doing something. Looking at things from another point of view. Unconventional behavior. Feeling hung-up about something. Blocked. Limited. Waiting. Anxious. Suspended action. A time of stagnation and frustration. Illness. Mental breakdown. Losing touch with reality. Straightening out your affairs, cleaning up loose ends. Seeking counseling or therapy. Psychic abilities or a psychic experience. Seeing things others can't. Sacrificing something. Martyrdom. Masochism. A need to examine your motives for giving up your personal time, space and psychic needs to others. Victim consciousness. Feeling sorry for yourself. Loneliness and isolation; "nobody cares". Use of drugs or alcohol to escape your problems. Trying to evade responsibility. Total trust in and surrender to a higher force or being. Suspending judgment and even expectations in the hopes of receiving higher knowledge. Making the mind into a clear, reflective vessel. Meditation. Suspending disbelief. Rite of Passage. Initiation or transition from one state into another. Devotion to a cause. Patriotism. Subsuming your sense of self to a cause or another person. *Maya*. Illusion. Not seeing things as they are.

QUESTIONS TO ANSWER:

What do you expect from the sacrifices you are making? What are you devoted to? How are you hung-up? What do you need to get straight? What do you need to give up? What are you trying to escape? How are you seeking higher knowledge?

SAMPLE AFFIRMATION:

"I am willing to suspend my personal comforts for the richness of the spirit."

13
DEATH

Scorpio   Nun

Being stuck in old patterns. Constipated. Need to eliminate the restrictive habits and blocks, outworn ways. Ill-at-ease with an old situation or belief. Severance with the past. A painful uprooting of accustomed habits, or the elimination of people or things from your life. End of close friendships, associations. Cutting yourself free. "Surgery." Change of consciousness. Entrance into a new state. Assimilation and integration into a new form. Transformation. Liberation. Renewal. New growth possible. You are experiencing such deep emotions that it is like a "little death." An intense sexual experience. Giving up your sense of self to a feeling of merging with another or with the cosmos. Cutting through the superficial surface structure of something to understand what is at the core of it. Cutting things to the bone. Getting down to basics. The transformation of energy from one shape or form into another.

QUESTIONS TO ANSWER:

What do you need to let go of? What is your basic support system (skeletal structure) through this transition? What is being transformed? What new growth is now possible? What are you feeling so deeply and intensely about?

SAMPLE AFFIRMATION:

"I transform and renew myself by letting go of those things no longer necessary to my growth"

14
TEMPERANCE/ART

Sagittarius   Samekh

Fiery enthusiasm. Feelings of confidence and optimism. Being outspoken; frank expression of your thoughts. Being open-minded, free, expansive, independent. Handling volatile situations well. Being healed. Tempering your life and finding the right combinations of things to make you well. Doing physical and spiritual healing work. Circulation of an inner vital current of energy. Working with an inner guide, guardian angel, or benefactor. Cooperation. Accommodation. Compatibility. Applying what you have learned so you can see what is true and how much you have actually mastered. Testing yourself. Trying it out. Management. Recognizing and using resources (time, people, space, materials) available to you. Organization and planning. Combining materials, resources, people or ideas into new forms. Creative activity. Consolidation. Mixing in the right proportion. Bringing together opposite qualities. Tempering. Blending or combining different aspects of your life in a new and different way. Creating harmony. Communicating your ideas to the public.

QUESTIONS TO ANSWER:

What are you feeling optimistic about? How are you combining the resources available to you? What are you testing or trying out? What needs to be healed or brought into balance?

SAMPLE AFFIRMATION:

"I enthusiastically manage my needs and resources to bring about health and harmony."

15
THE DEVIL

Capricorn   Ayin

Judging things only by their surface appearances, thus becoming the slave of fallacy. Living amidst confusion. Believing only what you see. In a state of fear and ignorance. Being in the dark about something, or choosing to ignore the truth. Feelings of doubt and pessimism. Depression. Feeling bound to a situation in which someone else dictates to you. Oppressor/oppressed consciousness. Creating boundaries and limitations in your life; recognizing that they originate from within. Becoming more structured and less flexible, although perhaps with greater focus. Stagnation. Overcome by inertia. This card calls for a sense of humor: being able to laugh at yourself and your own self-importance. Being devilish, mischievous and full of high energy and spirits. Pandemonium. Playing the scapegoat, the gadfly or the devil's advocate to force others to examine their own beliefs. The ability to take incongrous, unrelated things and combine them together in a new, creative way. The ability to synthesize something out of seeming chaos. Creativity, innovation. Overwhelming pride. Personal ambition that leads you to take advantage of others. Manipulating others for personal gain. Acting out your "shadow" self: doing things you would prefer to think you don't do. Using or being used by someone sexually. Being a slave to desires that overpower your judgment. Obsession. Temptation. Evil intentions. Black magic. Jealousy. Trapped in the senses; lacking belief in something beyond the "material world."

QUESTIONS TO ANSWER:

What are the current boundaries and limitations in your life? What or who is obsessing you? How can you channel and structure your energies and desires in creative and nonmanipulative ways? What situation(s) do you need to look at with humor?

SAMPLE AFFIRMATION:

"From darkness and chaos I create opportunities to transcend limitations."

16
THE TOWER

Mars   Peh

The break-up of towering defenses, habits, structures; freedom from ignorance. A spiritual awakening. A bolt of insight from your higher self. A blow to your ego or self-image. Humiliation; thrust down from a high place. Unexpected change or shock. Disruption. Feeling shattered. Anger and frustration. Emotions erupting. Exhaustion or "burn-out," sometimes resulting in illness or accident. Something damaged. Outgrowing your environment. Involvement in a drastic self-improvement program: intensive therapy, exercise, diet, etc. Housecleaning. Fasting. The futility of human structures and technology in the face of Mother Nature. Natural disasters and exodus. Flight from chaos and disaster.

QUESTIONS TO ANSWER:

How are you improving and restructuring yourself and your environment? What are you angry about? What structures in your life are breaking up? What has shattered your complacency? What sudden realization or insight have you had?

SAMPLE AFFIRMATION:

"I liberate myself from the ignorance and limitations of old habits and structures whenever I outgrow their need."

17
THE STAR

Aquarius   Tzaddi

Meditation. Inexhaustible inspiration. Spiritual regeneration. Using active imagination and visualization. Artistic and scientific inspiration. Formulating your ideals and goals. Examining your hopes for the future. Using systems of self-insight such as astrology, Tarot, numerology, etc. Living by your own truth and values rather than those of the outer world. "Freedom is nothing left to lose." Altruism. Nonconformity. Doing the unexpected. The calm after the storm; release after imprisonment. Freedom. Nature worship. Solitary rituals. Peace and serenity. Refreshment, renewal or cleansing. Purification. Baptism. A desire to know the truth, to be open and honest, to communicate with nothing held back. Frankness. Disclosure or discovery of something. Being involved in actions and projects beneficial to your fellow beings. A desire to participate in the enlightenment and con- sciousness-raising of all humankind. Being the "star," the center of at- tention. Public recognition. Being the leader and spokesperson for others. Stubbornly clinging to fixed ideas.

QUESTIONS TO ANSWER:

What aspect of your life is being purified or cleansed? What is being re- newed? What are you inspired to do? For what are you receiving recogni- tion? What are your ideals in the matter?

SAMPLE AFFIRMATION:

"My inner being shines like a star, guiding my actions, renewing and cleans- ing me."

18
MOON

Pisces   Qoph

Self-deception. Illusion. Bewilderment. Confusion. Fluctuation. Waxing and waning of events. Instability. Being swamped by emotions and feelings. Lack of clarity in what you want, as if several parts of you are crying out for dif- ferent things. Facing your subconscious fears. Needing to explore unknown territory. Feeling alone. Your communication with others is filled with mis- understandings. Disillusionment or estrangement from someone or some- thing. Introspection. It is necessary to flow with your feelings. Developing or using your psychic abilities and intuition. Working within the realm of the unconscious, especially with dreams, fantasies and visions to understand what your subconsious is trying to tell you. Something in the past that you have forgotten but which effects your current life through actions inappro- priate to the situation. A karmic relationship from the past that needs to be worked on. A sense of being guided or pulled, or drawn like the tides toward some predetermined purpose. Impelled from within. Evolution. Acting instinctively. Doing something automatically, as in a well-learned skill which you no longer have to "think" about.

QUESTIONS TO ANSWER:

Your fears are symbolized by the dogs, towers and dismal terrain; what do they represent for you? What have you forgotten? What do you instinctively want to do? What kind of cycle or pattern are you repeating? Are your actions appropriate to this particular situation or are you responding to some past situation? What is bewildering or confusing you? What is real and what is illusory?

SAMPLE AFFIRMATION:

"I am impelled to evolve beyond my fears and insecurities. I am willing to walk the path to self-knowledge through the unknown inner realms of myself."

19
THE SUN

Sun   Resh

Enlightenment. Clarity. Understanding. Comprehension. Wisdom. Things previously unclear or hidden have come into the light of day. Overcoming former obstacles. Success. Good luck. Prizes and awards. Fruitfulness. Birth. Wholeness. Freedom and liberation from old forms. Everything and everyone you need is magnetically drawn to you. Ability to visualize what you want and make it reality. A time of creativity and personal growth. Recognition and appreciation of your own accomplishments. Identification with your creative work. Joy. Intense enjoyment and happiness in life. Optimism. Enthusiasm. Commitment to a love relationship with depth of communication and sharing. Good relations with others. Friendship. Good health and vitality. Being active and energized. Altruism, idealism, high hopes. You feel you can achieve anything. Self-importance and vanity.

QUESTIONS TO ANSWER:

What do you now understand? What successes have you achieved? What have you birthed or brought to fruition? What joys are you sharing with others? What commitments have you made?

SAMPLE AFFIRMATION:

"I create warmth and light with my clarity and enthusiasm."

20
JUDGMENT/AEON

Pluto   Shin

An awakening to something you had not seen before. A paradigm shift calling for totally new perceptions. Rebirth. Hearing the "call" of the spirit.

Resurrection. A sense of new life. Development of a new philosophy or sense of purpose. Coming to a crossroads concerning a higher purpose beyond yourself. Researching or examining something in depth. Looking deeply into a matter and determining its worth or value to you. Doing a personal inventory or self-evaluation. A review of past actions; confronting your motives. Accepting personal responsibility for how you have used your opportunities, reacted to initiations and testing. Criticism. Criticizing and judging others, or being criticized by them. Judgments made. Needing to see beyond prejudice and criticism. The voice of conscience. Guilt and forgiveness. Atonement. Repentance. Apology. Synthesizing the different parts of your personality such as the Parent, Adult and Child in transactional analysis. Body, mind and spirit working for one purpose. Regeneration. Transformation. A change from one state or identity to another. A desire to merge with another, sexually or otherwise; or to merge with your own creative works. Realization of parenthood and family; responsibility for others as opposed to selfish self-preservation. Cooperation with other people as a social unit. A Rite of Passage.

QUESTIONS TO ANSWER:

What "call" have you heard? Who or what is being criticized? What judgment is being made? What new realization or epiphany is transforming you? Who or what are you merging with? What or whom are you responsible for?

SAMPLE AFFIRMATION:

"I transform myself daily, awakening yet more to the call of my spirit."

21
THE WORLD/UNIVERSE

Saturn   Tau

Becoming conscious of your limitations and thus freeing yourself to maximize your own potential. Dancing on your limitations. "Squaring the circle": manifesting spirit on earth, or structuring and giving form to spirit. Arrival. Accepting responsibility for yourself and your circumstances. Being involved in a very trying, involved, emotional, all-encompassing experience. A feeling of joy at being alive, rapture in being. Infinite potential. Self-actualization (although not always understood or appreciated by others). Everything is available to you. Living comfortably in the midst of complexity. Or fear of change and complexity is keeping you within a narrow enclosure. Being reminded of your physical nature and the physical laws that bind you. Mother Earth. The Creatrix. She represents that which endures through time. The Source. She is the structure or foundation out of which you came and to which you must return. She reminds you that first you have to take care of your body and the earth you live on, uniting the four elements within you and the four types of people around you in this one endeavor: to heal the four directions of Mother Earth and yourself in the process.

QUESTIONS TO ANSWER:

What are you doing to free yourself from limitations and restrictions in your life? Or what are you doing to work freely within them? What potential do you see in yourself? In the world? What physical needs must you take care of? What is making you dance for joy?

SAMPLE AFFIRMATION:

"The Universe abundantly provides for all my needs."

THE MINOR ARCANA CARDS

Number Cards

(Note: Also refer to Chapter Three, page 53, for interpretations of the suits.)

ACES

MERCURY. Action, ideas, beginnings. Seed. Root. Primary impulse. Possibility. Penetration. Births. Initiation. Opening. Gifts. Potential. Thesis. Starting point. Concentration of will. Attention. Singleness. Mindfulness. Unity. Self-consciousness. Intention. Threshold. Commencement. Focus. Opportunity. (On the Tree of Life—Kether.)

Negatively: You may have difficulty grasping the opportunity offered.

ACE OF WANDS: Consciousness Raising.* Creativity. Desire for self-growth. Inspiration. New idea. Burst of energy.

QUESTIONS TO ANSWER:

What is inspiring you? What has aroused your passions and desires? How do you want to grow? How do you want to express yourself creatively? What do you feel the impulse to do? Into what is your energy and enthusiasm flowing? What new opportunity is being offered to you?

SAMPLE AFFIRMATION:

"I recognize this opportunity for new ideas and creative growth."

ACE OF CUPS: Heart Opening.* The beginning of love, pleasure. The opening of psychic, spiritual or unconscious channels. Receptivity.

QUESTIONS TO ANSWER:

What is making you feel good right now? What would you like to do to indulge yourself? What or who is offering you nurturing or love? What messages are you receiving from dreams and visions? What does your heart feel most open to?

SAMPLE AFFIRMATION:

"I recognize this opportunity to express and accept love."

ACE OF SWORDS: Mind Expanding.* Mental focus. Peeling things away to analyze them; cutting through things. Seeds of truth and justice.

---

*Key concepts from Tarot teacher and counselor Suzanne Judith.

QUESTIONS TO ANSWER:

What new problem are you confronting? What is on your mind? What do you need to analyze? What is the point? Are you being just and fair? What decision do you need to face? Can you determine the truth of the matter? What legal, writing or research opportunities have been presented to you?

SAMPLE AFFIRMATION:

"I recognize this opportunity to discover the truth."

ACE OF PENTACLES: Body Sustaining.* A business or work possibility. Materialization of ideas. Centering or grounding your energy.

QUESTIONS TO ANSWER:

What new opportunities for work, stability, home, money or health do you have? What is making you feel secure and grounded? How can you use a recent gift? What plan are you putting in motion? What kinds of seeds are you planting? How are you being rewarded for your accomplishments?

SAMPLE AFFIRMATION:

"I recognize this opportunity to materialize my ideas."

TWOS

MOON. Personality, mask, feelings. Reflection. Augmentation. Reception. Nurturing. Polarity. Duality. Opposites. Duplication. Balance. Antithesis. Sequence. Memory. Subconsciousness. Femininity. Passivity. Feelings. Striving for balance. Choice. Change. The focus is on the attempt to stay in the middle. Suggests guidance by inner knowing. Oracles. Intuitions. (On the Tree of Life—Chokmah.)

Negatively: Unbalanced. Cold and unfeeling; refusing to see beyond the surface, or overemotional. Refusal to change or fickleness.

TWO OF WANDS: Mars in Aries. Personal power through synthesis of abilities. Ability to make choices. Creative expression. Control over the situation.

QUESTIONS TO ANSWER:

What two ideas are you bringing together in a new and different way? What are you planning to accomplish? What are you competent at? What conflicting desires do you wish to integrate? At what threshold do you stand? What options do you have?

SAMPLE AFFIRMATION:

"I have the power of choice."

TWO OF CUPS: Venus in Cancer. A loving and healing union of opposites.

QUESTIONS TO ANSWER:

To whom are you giving your love and affections? How do you nurture others? What is being healed in your relationship? How are your inner masculine and feminine uniting and working together in your life? What are you lovingly sharing with another?

SAMPLE AFFIRMATION:

"I love others as I love myself."

TWO OF SWORDS: Moon in Libra. Suspending judgment. Blocked emotions. Uncertainty or stalemate. Making peace. Procrastination. Compromise.

QUESTIONS TO ANSWER:

What are you hesitating to do? With whom do you have to make peace or reconcile? What are you struggling to maintain in balance? What decision would you prefer not to make? What would you prefer not to know about?

SAMPLE AFFIRMATION:

"I am diplomatic and nonjudgmental in my dealings with others."

TWO OF PENTACLES: Jupiter in Capricorn. Adaptability. Mobility. Expanding your horizons. Change. Travel. Play.

QUESTIONS TO ANSWER:

What two or more situations are you handling with ease? What are you adapting to? What do you want to change in your home, profession, status, finances, etc.? What are you juggling in order to keep stable (money, weight, lifestyle)? In what ways do you play and use your excess energies? What calls for diplomacy?

SAMPLE AFFIRMATION:

"I handle diverse situations with ease, adapting myself quickly."

THREES

VENUS. Intuitions, affections, beauty. Comings together. Manifestations. Integration. Combination. Sympathy. Fecundity. Understanding. Growth. Multiplication. Synthesis. Harmony. Unfolding. Cooperation. Idealization. All threes deal with the ideal versus the real. They test your ability to handle the mundane and the disappointments of your idealizations. Threes are potential reformers with strong sympathies. (On the Tree of Life—Binah and Saturn.)

Negatively: Cruelty, arrogance and self-indulgence.

THREE OF WANDS: Sun in Aries. Magnetic. Visionary. Established strength. Synthesis of ideas. Foresight. Planning.

QUESTIONS TO ANSWER:

Where do your ambitions lie? Where are you putting your attentions? What and whom are you drawing to yourself through your vitality, power and energy? What are you envisioning for the future? What and with whom do you have to coordinate to achieve your plan?

SAMPLE AFFIRMATION:

"I create my own future by envisioning it clearly."

THREE OF CUPS: Mercury in Cancer. Friendship. Communication. Enjoyment of others. Celebration and joy. Shared ideals.

QUESTIONS TO ANSWER:

How have you been enjoying yourself? How do you relax with others? What is bringing you joy? What talents do you have and how have you been using them? What do you want to communicate or share with others? What cause is there for celebration in your life?

SAMPLE AFFIRMATION:

"I celebrate my joy and happiness."

THREE OF SWORDS: Saturn in Libra. Sorrow. Pain. Alienation. Separation. Jealousy. Creative heartbreak. Feeling hurt.

QUESTIONS TO ANSWER:

In what ways are you suffering? Feeling jealous? Hurt? Has anyone hurt your feelings? What are you feeling sorrowful about? Who would you like to hurt or "get back at"? Can you look at your relationships with truth and honesty? What do you fear most within your relationships?

SAMPLE AFFIRMATION:

"I acknowledge my hurt and pain so that I can face it and work through it."

THREE OF PENTACLES: Mars in Capricorn. Work, especially with others. Creative skills and abilities. Practicality.

QUESTIONS TO ANSWER:

How do you work with others? What are you working on? What is your goal? What skills are you using? Are you willing to persevere? How are you taking or expressing criticism of the work being done?

SAMPLE AFFIRMATION:

"I work well with others, recognizing each person's expertise and value to the job."

FOURS

EARTH/SUN. Grounding. Stability. Order. Completion. Actualization. Law and order. Reason. Consolidation. Focus inward on self. Centering. Assessment of needs. Conventions of society. The material world. Organization. Foundation. Establishment. Perfection. The basic conflict of fours is between desire for law and order and security, and desire for change and expansion from the lethargy, boredom and passivity they engender. Fours mark a passage, turning point or milestone, and thus the establishment of boundaries and limits. (On the Tree of Life—Chesed and Jupiter.)

Negatively: Repression, limitation, narrowness, discomfort, restriction, discontent.

FOUR OF WANDS: Venus in Aries. Celebration and thanksgiving after labor. Optimism. Arrival. Ceremony. Completion of an enterprise.

QUESTIONS TO ANSWER:

What are you bringing to completion, fruition? What role is ritual or ceremony playing in your life? What have you integrated into your life? What Rite of Passage are you experiencing and how are you celebrating it? What are you celebrating?

SAMPLE AFFIRMATION:

"I rejoice in the completion of each stage of my journey and give thanks for the fruits thereof."

FOUR OF CUPS: Moon in Cancer. Lethargy, apathy and discontent. Boredom. Meditation. Withdrawal of the emotions. Loneliness. Passive receptivity.

QUESTIONS TO ANSWER:

How do you feel dissatisfied? Where do you go to find peace and serenity? How is this time of withdrawal and contemplation benefiting you? What are you re-evaluating in your life and relationshps? What are you fantasizing about and what can you do to realize your fantasies?

SAMPLE AFFIRMATION:

"I am receptive to the messages of my dreams and intuition."

FOUR OF SWORDS: Jupiter in Libra. Need for healing. A problem or dilemma being worked on. Illness. Retreat. Rest and recovery. Taking time out.

QUESTIONS TO ANSWER:

From what do you need to rest or retreat? Where do you need to focus your energies in order to recuperate your strength? What do you need to do to gain a better perspective and to be fair and just in the situation? What kind of professional assistance would help most?

SAMPLE AFFIRMATION:

"I give myself time to rest, laying aside plans and turning within for guidance."

FOUR OF PENTACLES: Sun in Capricorn. Centeredness or selfishness. Awareness of personal value and worth. Possessiveness. Power. Giving structure to or establishing order in a situation.

QUESTIONS TO ANSWER:

What is keeping you centered? What are your greatest strengths? How are you powerful? What gives you a sense of security? What do you want to hold on to or possess? Who or what do you need to protect?

SAMPLE AFFIRMATION:

"I hold my power in my own hands; my security lies within."

FIVES

MARS. Reaction. Desire. Challenge. Adaptation. Change. Confusion. Struggle. Conflict. Breakdown. Fate. Guilt. Chaos. Storm and stress. Upset of statically stabilized system of the fours. Humanity. Midway. Bridge. Mediation. Conscience. Temptation. Breaking down force of nature. Tests. Motion coming to the aid of matter. Disturbance. Anger. The fives are indicators of guilt, struggle, conflict. Tests that must be passed for further success or continued achievement. Tearing away all that is useless, undesirable or outdated. The lifegiving drive or force that surmounts obstacles. Revolt against the conventions and traditions of the fours. They represent some kind of loss—of temper, feelings, security or integrity. (On the Tree of Life—Geburah and Mars.)

Negatively: Inertia. Dogma. Repression.

FIVE OF WANDS: Saturn in Leo. Exchange of ideas—sometimes heated. Energetic and competitive games. Confronting obstacles.

QUESTIONS TO ANSWER:

How and with whom are you competing? What obstacles are you confronting? How do you present your ideas to others? With whom are you quarreling or arguing? And over what? What are you so excited about? What games are you playing?

SAMPLE AFFIRMATION:

"I present my ideas clearly and assertively."

FIVE OF CUPS: Mars in Scorpio. Loss and disappointment. Progress hindered. Loss of harmony but the love is still there. Temporary delay. Learning from mistakes and experience.

QUESTIONS TO ANSWER:

What seems lost or down the drain? What do you despair over? What are you disillusioned or disappointed with? What do you feel sorry about? What are some possible alternatives to what you've lost? What awaits your attention? What have you learned from your mistakes?

SAMPLE AFFIRMATION:

"I have felt my loss, yet I continue on my way with the experience I have gained."

FIVE OF SWORDS: Venus in Aquarius. An empty victory using unfair means. Being devisive and unethical. Personal or political strife.

QUESTIONS TO ANSWER:

Do you expect to get "stung" in this situation? What are you afraid of? What is causing division in the solidarity of your group? Why don't you feel good about what you're doing? What do you need in order to feel good? What would be the ethical thing to do? What is so important to you that you have to prove everyone else wrong?

SAMPLE AFFIRMATION:

"I recognize a no-win situation and am willing to withdraw gracefully."

FIVE OF PENTACLES: Mercury in Taurus. Voluntary simplicity and unconventionality. Uncertainty creating anxiety, worry and strain. Loss of job, home, security, Feeling "out in the cold."

QUESTIONS TO ANSWER:

What are your survival concerns? What changes are you having difficulty dealing with? What have you chosen to give up or do without? Why? What are you worried or anxious about? What conventions/traditions are you rebelling against? What inequalities or injustices are you trying to change?

SAMPLE AFFIRMATION:

"I am willing to go through seeming hardships and unconventional life situations to follow my inner values."

SIXES

JUPITER. Exuberance. Reconciliation. A peak experience of some kind. Expressive and expansive. The elements at their practical best (Crowley). Contemplation. Reciprocation. Cooperation. Sharing. Radiating. Choice. Advancement. Harmony. Balance. Sixes indicate the benefits of giving to others, especially reciprocally. Being receptive (sensitive) to people's needs and supplying them. (On the Tree of Life—Tiphareth and the Sun.)

Negatively: Tendency to go to extremes. Self-centeredness. Vanity. Condescension.

SIX OF WANDS: Jupiter in Leo. Self-confidence in your leadership abilities. Advancement toward a goal. Victory and honor. Pride. Teamwork. Journeys.

QUESTIONS TO ANSWER:

What positions of leadership and responsibility have you taken on? What is your relationship with your fellow workers? What has been resolved through your actions? What do you feel confident about? What kind of leadership do others need from you?

SAMPLE AFFIRMATION:

"My confidence in my ability to achieve goals inspires others with whom I work."

SIX OF CUPS: Sun in Scorpio. Memory or renewal of something from the past. Gifts. Friendship. Pleasurable exchange. Ecstasy.

QUESTIONS TO ANSWER:

What memories or relationships from the past have reappeared? What insights or awarenesses have they provided? What is renewing and revitalizing you? What is bringing you pleasure? How are children or childlike enjoyments meaningful in your current situation? What do you give in friendship? What kind of friend are you?

SAMPLE AFFIRMATION:

"My greatest gift is friendship."

SIX OF SWORDS: Mercury in Aquarius. Moving away from danger. Journey in consciousness, or mental travel. Solving problems. Getting distance to see things in perspective.

QUESTIONS TO ANSWER:

What immediate problems are you attempting to solve? Where will you go to solve them? Where in your life right now is mental clarity important? How are you liberating your mind from clutter and false ideas so that you can think clearly? When you step back from your problem to gain a clear perspective, what do you see?

SAMPLE AFFIRMATION:

"I gain perspective on problems and issues by changing my direction and focus."

SIX OF PENTACLES: Moon in Taurus. Sharing your resources. Getting assistance or patronage; drawing to you what you need. Token reforms. Sensitivity to others' needs. An "energy exchange."

QUESTIONS TO ANSWER:

With whom are you sharing your prosperity, resources, or abilities? How and to whom are you mentor, advisor or patron? How are you sharing the wealth (of money, talent, information)? What do you have to give that others need? How are you managing your time? What and from whom do you receive?

SAMPLE AFFIRMATION:

"I give, knowing that I will receive in kind."

SEVENS

SATURN. The maturing process. Inner work. Self-reflection. Struggle. Caution. Tests. Limitation. Discipline. Restraint. Movement. Change. New direction. Equilibrium. Mastery. Rest. Unity within complexity. Self-expression. Independent action. Correction of imbalance. Changing patterns. Awakening. Preparation. Foresight. (On the Tree of Life—Victory and Venus.)

Negatively: Arrogance. Deceit. Manipulation. Unwillingness to face and deal with reality.

SEVEN OF WANDS: Mars in Leo. Facing up to a situation and asserting your point. Character and integrity. Taking a stand. Defending yourself and your needs or beliefs.

QUESTIONS TO ANSWER:

What beliefs or opinions are you holding onto despite criticism and social pressure? Who are you up against? Are you being loyal to yourself? What result would you ideally like if it could be anything you wanted? How can you most effectively take a stand and present your point of view?

SAMPLE AFFIRMATION:

"I stand up for my beliefs."

SEVEN OF CUPS: Venus in Scorpio. Experiencing an altered state of consciousness. Wanting to experience all your fantasies. Caught up in illusions or in the realm of the senses.

QUESTIONS TO ANSWER:

How are you overdoing or indulging yourself? What are your fantasies for the future? List at least seven. What are your current daydreams? How are you deluding yourself? What mystical or religious visions are you experiencing? How are you gratifying your senses?

SAMPLE AFFIRMATION:

"I acknowledge my fantasies, yet ask the universe to provide for my needs."

SEVEN OF SWORDS: Moon in Aquarius. Sneaking around. Lying. Overwhelmed by the odds, avoiding confrontation. Research: collecting the knowledge and ideas of others. Preparation.

QUESTIONS TO ANSWER:

What are you "appropriating"? Who are you deceiving? What is your strategy to achieve your ends? What research are you doing? What ideas are you collecting? How are you maneuvering the outcome? Do you trust the people you are working with? What is confusing you? What can you do to drop your defenses and become more open? What are the weaknesses in your plan, research or work?

SAMPLE AFFIRMATION:

"I research, prepare and gather evidence and resources for my projects."

SEVEN OF PENTACLES: Saturn in Taurus. Fear of failure. Delay. Evaluating the results of your efforts. Assessing mistakes in order to learn from them. Observing the cycles and processes.

QUESTIONS TO ANSWER:

What is growing and maturing that you are concerned about? What do you fear will fail or be spoiled? What mistakes did you make in the past in similar circumstances and what can you do differently now? What investments have you made in time, money or labor that worry you? How have your efforts been worthwhile?

SAMPLE AFFIRMATION:

"I learn from both success and failure by evaluating the process and results."

EIGHTS

URANUS. Giving out, spending, expanding. Order or lack of it. Re-evaluation. Prioritizing. Use of energy. Valuing. Inspiration. Evolution. Balance. Cause and effect. Vibration. Movement. Moving on. (On the Tree of Life—Hod and Mercury.)

Negatively: Up in the air, lack of conclusions, inability to decide. Frustration, jealousy.

EIGHT OF WANDS: Mercury in Sagittarius. Infatuation or falling in love. Activities and energy speeding up. Rapid growth and development. Fast thinking and communication.

QUESTIONS TO ANSWER:

What are you rushing into? A relationship? A new direction for growth? A belief or philosophy? What are you being "carried away" by or overwhelmed with? What do you feel the urge to move on quickly? What do you need to tell others about?

SAMPLE AFFIRMATION:

"I respond quickly when the time is right."

EIGHT OF CUPS: Saturn in Pisces. Energy drain. Self-pity. Retreat. Withdrawal from activites into self. Moving away from old values and beliefs. Sense of aimlessness.

QUESTIONS TO ANSWER:

What do you feel weary of or dissatisfied with? What relationships or values are no longer relevant in your life? What or who is drawing on your energy and leaving you feeling emotionally drained? How can you withdraw or take time off to renew yourself?

SAMPLE AFFIRMATION:

"I take time off to recoup my energy and rediscover my sense of self."

EIGHT OF SWORDS: Jupiter in Gemini. Feeling fenced in. Restrictions. Too many ideas with no direction. Lack of persistence. Paranoia. Blocked energy or creativity. Bound by your own mental obstructions. Waiting to be rescued. Feeling vulnerable and isolated.

QUESTIONS TO ANSWER:

What actions, plans or ideas are being blocked by circumstances beyond your control? What would you like to do if you could get rid of the obstacles and blocks? Who or what could assist you to break free? What benefits do you receive by not acting? What is interfering with your creative expression? Or your ability to communicate?

SAMPLE AFFIRMATION:

"I free myself from my own dilemmas by letting go of the concepts that have bound me."

EIGHT OF PENTACLES: Sun in Scorpio. Self-discipline. Preparation. Attention to detail. Patience. Productivity. Getting your finances and resources in order.

QUESTIONS TO ANSWER:

What are you working on? Or preparing ahead of time? What skill or craft are you learning? What details do you need to examine and take care of? How can you create a regular time and place to work? What preparations do you need to make? What are you doing to take care of your health and well-being?

SAMPLE AFFIRMATION:

"I work patiently and persistently to achieve good results."

NINES

NEPTUNE. Luck, fate. Force. Capability. Obstinacy. Integration. Experience. Solitude. Gestation. Magic. Completion. Initiation. Pure intellect. Conclusion. Fulfillment. Attainment of goal. Change is stability. Self-reliance. Self-awareness. (On the Tree of Life—Yesod and the Moon.)

Negatively: Isolation. Delusion. Denial and rejection. Lack of discipline and self-awareness.

NINE OF WANDS: Moon in Sagittarius. Wisdom and discipline from experience. Independence. Dedication to a cause. Strength and persistence of purpose. Defensiveness.

QUESTIONS TO ANSWER:

What previous knowledge and abilities are you drawing on? What is strengthening you to face opposition? What disciplines are carrying you through? Who or what is demanding a lot from you? What task do you have to handle on your own?

SAMPLE AFFIRMATION:

"From my experiences I have developed the wisdom and experience necessary to act independently."

NINE OF CUPS: Jupiter in Pisces. Satisfaction. Wishes fulfilled. Visualizing what you want. Sensual pleasures. Self-indulgence.

QUESTIONS TO ANSWER:

How have your wishes been fulfilled? What pleasures are being experienced? What do you feel smug about? What do you want to manifest in your life? Can you visualize it in detail?

SAMPLE AFFIRMATION:

"I manifest what I want by visualizing it clearly and precisely."

NINE OF SWORDS: Mars in Gemini. Depression. Suffering. Guilt. Putting yourself down. Nightmares.

How are you putting yourself down? What is the source of your depression? What are you suffering from? How have you been cruel and thoughtless, or who has been cruel and hurt you? What can you do to improve the situation? What thoughts or nightmares are plaguing you?

SAMPLE AFFIRMATION:

"I acknowledge my feelings, then move to release them."

NINE OF PENTACLES: Venus in Virgo. Enjoyment of solitary leisure. Relaxation. Ease. Harvest. Good results from efforts. Material well-being. Reward.

QUESTIONS TO ANSWER:

What are you earning by your endeavors—material wealth, security, status? How are you enjoying what you've earned? How are you spending your leisure time? How do you give thanks for all that you've gained?

SAMPLE AFFIRMATION:

"I use and enjoy the fruits of my labor, allowing nothing to go to waste."

TENS

PLUTO. Regeneration. Release. Responsibility. Consolidation. Sum total of all work done from the beginning. Warnings. Culmination. Ends and beginnings. Results. Karma. Reward and punishment. Concern with the well-being of others. Cycles. New beginning on the social plane of responsibility to the family or community. Recommitment or new direction. Giving meaning or purpose to your experiences. Indicates conditions built up (or existing) over a period of time. Convention. Persistence. Conservatism. Self-will in relation to social conditions. (On the Tree of Life—Malkuth and the Elements.)

Negatively: Overflow or overdose of the element. Rebellion and recklessness.

TEN OF WANDS: Saturn in Sagittarius. Responsibilites. Perseverance in meeting a goal. Burdens. Resentfulness.

QUESTIONS TO ANSWER:

What responsibilities are weighing heavily on your shoulders? What are you feeling burdened with? What is your goal? When will you get there? Who (or what) is restricting you and keeping you from manifesting your full radiant energy? Why have you taken on these responsibilities? How can you best use your powers and energies?

SAMPLE AFFIRMATION:

"I carry out my responsibilities, yet do not deprive others of theirs."

TEN OF CUPS: Mars in Pisces. Being "at home" with yourself and others. Wholeness and completion. Affirming joy in your life. Optimism.

QUESTIONS TO ANSWER:

How are you living in harmony with your environment? What is good in your life? Where are you finding joy? Where is home? What are your hopes for future relationships? What do you want in a family? What needs of family and friends are you serving?

SAMPLE AFFIRMATION:

"I am at home with myself and those I love."

TEN OF SWORDS: Sun in Gemini. Paralysis. The end of a problem, defense, ego hang-up, hostility. Letting go. Acceptance and resignation. Sacrifice.

QUESTIONS TO ANSWER:

In what way are you feeling paralyzed or unable to act? Where do you feel that you have no choice? What are you being forced to accept? What is being sacrificed? What problem can you now let go of? By totally accepting defeat, what are you now free to do?

SAMPLE AFFIRMATION:

"I let go of those things I cannot accomplish to free me to do the things I can."

TEN OF PENTACLES: Mercury in Virgo. Established traditions and conventions. Hierarchies. Inheritance. Endurance and permanence. Prosperity and wealth. Family and home.

QUESTIONS TO ANSWER:

In what ways are you wealthy? What traditions are you carrying on? What are you inheriting—a job, money, an apartment? What do you owe to family influence? What is your status/position in the hierarchy or structure? What will endure beyond this experience or situation? How are you expected to behave under the circumstances?

SAMPLE AFFIRMATION:

"I am rich in family and traditions."

THE MINOR ARCANA CARDS

Court Cards

(Note: Also refer to Chapter 3, page 53, for interpretations of the suits.)

KINGS/SHAMANS

Kings show mastery, ability and authority in the field represented by the suit. They represent experience, power, authority, status. Secure but rigid, limited by the rules they have established. Court Cards often signify both yourself and another in a reading. The King can be a boss, your father or some other authority figure. "He" can also represent the animus in a woman, or a sense of self in a man.

KING OF WANDS: (Fire of Fire) Establishement of self. The ability to be oneself. A benevolent dictator. He takes chances based on flashes of intuition, likes to gamble and is very showy and theatrical. Achievement-oriented. Can be domineering, hot-tempered and arrogant. Creative and self-expressive.

QUESTIONS TO ANSWER:

How are you expressing your sense of self? How are you using your decision-making and leadership abilities? Who is controlling the situation? Who do you admire for their sense of self?

SAMPLE AFFIRMATION:

"I acknowledge my accomplishments and my ability to be self-directed."

KING OF CUPS: (Fire of Water) Established emotions or relationship. The ability to love. A counselor or care-giver. Creative and imaginative. He can either have his feelings under control, keeping a detached awareness, or he can cloud the issue with jealousy and fantasies.

QUESTIONS TO ANSWER:

What feelings are you keeping under firm control? In what ways are you a care-giver or counselor? Who cares for you deeply? How have you established yourself creatively?

SAMPLE AFFIRMATION:

"I acknowledge my inner values, feelings and intuitions."

KING OF SWORDS: (Fire of Air) Established thought. The ability to communicate and be analytical. A writer, lawyer, diplomat or philosopher (professionally or otherwise). Protects and defends. Sharp and quick. He can ruthlessly cut through what he perceives as unnecessary or illogical.

QUESTIONS TO ANSWER:

Who is laying down the law? How are you using your ability to be rational, logical and analytical? Who is judging or criticizing you?

SAMPLE AFFIRMATION:

"I acknowledge my ability to stand up for what I truly believe."

KING OF PENTACLES: (Fire of Earth) Established work. The ability to produce and be practical. A manager, financier or craftsperson. Responsible and trustworthy, yet stubborn and slow to change. A sensualist. Concerned with security and quality.

QUESTIONS TO ANSWER:

How are you using your ability to manage your material affairs? Who is trustworthy yet stubborn? How are you being practical and down-to-earth, or who do you know that is?

SAMPLE AFFIRMATION:

"I acknowledge Mother Earth as the source of my material well-being."

QUEENS/PRIESTESSES

Queens represent inner and personal, rather than worldly, control. They have the ability to nurture and develop things indicated by the suit. They represent mothers and mothering, habits and cultural integration. They administer and channel the power. They rule from the heart. "She" can be the anima in a man, or the sense of self in a woman.

QUEEN OF WANDS: (Water of Fire) Recognizes her personal power. Displays self-confidence, generosity, burning passions and intense desires. Behaves spontaneously and has a quick temper. Utilizes her creative energies and inspires them in others. Love of happiness.

QUESTIONS TO ANSWER:

How are you expressing your creative energies? Who is giving you lots of good ideas and energy? When do you feel powerful and passionate? Who is strong-willed and protective?

SAMPLE AFFIRMATION:

"I recognize my self-potential and my ability to manifest my desires."

QUEEN OF CUPS: (Water of Water) Channels feelings, emotions, dreams, visions. She is the Muse, the Enchantress. She is psychic and deeply emotional, fluctuating like the moon in her emotions. She must be near water and reflects the unconscious in others. She is usually empathetic and understanding, but can be moody and deceitful. Love of love.

QUESTIONS TO ANSWER:

Who wants to protect you and shower you with affection? How are you working with or expressing your unconscious? How are you expressing your emotions? Who is inspiring you with their dreams and openness?

SAMPLE AFFIRMATION:

"I recognize the depth of my emotions and my ability to attract and enchant those around me."

QUEEN OF SWORDS: (Water of Air) Channels thought. Able to speak on the behalf of others. Makes her point well. Sees through deceit and dissembling. A professional woman. Intelligent and self-reliant, with a critical mind and a sharp tongue. Usually fair and just but can be vindictive. Love of ideas.

QUESTIONS TO ANSWER:

How are you utilizing your mental and communicative abilities? Who is helping you see the alternatives by pointing things out to you in a rational, perhaps critical way? How are you being discriminating and analytical?

SAMPLE AFFIRMATION:

"I recognize my inner wisdom and my ability to be fair and just."

QUEEN OF PENTACLES: (Water of Earth) Channels sensory information and practical knowledge. Able to preserve and conserve. Has respect for body, food, land. Is procreative. Has a love of the world, earth, life. Inspires trust and provides security.

QUESTIONS TO ANSWER:

How are you channeling your physical resources? Who inspires your need for practical skills and nurtures your desire for knowledge? Who is reliable and trustworthy? How are you grounded in Mother Earth?

SAMPLE AFFIRMATION:

"I recognize the fertility of my soul and I plant my seeds in prepared soil."

KNIGHTS/PRINCES/SONS

Knights act on, are involved in, and committed to the things indicated by their suit. They represent pure energy and often show where you are putting your energies. Focused but active, they display purpose, courage and a courtly attitude. They are sometimes headstrong, rash, thoughtless and self-centered. For women, knights often represent an animus figure, especially a romantic one. They represent your need to challenge something or go adventuring yourself. They can indicate travel.

KNIGHT OF WANDS: (Air of Fire) Putting energy into self-growth, future prospects, new directions. Willing to take risks. Inspired enthusiasm. Can explode in anger or jealousy. Radiates creative and sexual energy.

QUESTIONS TO ANSWER:

How are you growing and developing? How are you taking risks? Who is radiating creative or sexual energy in your life? Who enthusiastically wants to get going on something?

SAMPLE AFFIRMATION:

"I am willing to act on my inspirations."

KNIGHT OF CUPS: (Air of Water) Following your dreams, visions, ideals, love. Expressing taste and aesthetic sensitivity. Psychic, intuitive sharing of visions and giving love. A romantic dreamer. Can be moody and jealous.

QUESTIONS TO ANSWER:

What dream, vision, ideal or love are you following? Who is inviting you on a journey of emotional significance?

SAMPLE AFFIRMATION:

"I am willing to act on my dreams."

KNIGHT OF SWORDS: (Air of Air) Focused on making a point. Committed to ideas, thoughts, philosophy. Using mentality, communication. Speaking out, telling people off. Assertive and courageous, but headstrong and impatient.

QUESTIONS TO ANSWER:

Where are you charging and why so fast? What point do you feel committed to make? Who has been impatient and careless of your feelings?

SAMPLE AFFIRMATION:

"I defend the right of all to truth and justice."

KNIGHT OF PENTACLES: (Air of Earth) Doing or teaching your accomplishments. Using your knowledge. Committed to security. Stable and reliable but sometimes stubborn. Striving to keep order and uphold standards.

QUESTIONS TO ANSWER:

Who is stable and reliably there for you? Who is committed to security and conventions? How is it going at work or on a project? What needs of your body or of Mother Earth are you sensitive to?

SAMPLE AFFIRMATION:

"I protect and take care of my body and that of Mother Earth."

PAGES/PRINCESSES/DAUGHTERS

Pages signal the need to look into a matter—to study it, to be open to "messages" or new ways and ideas. They act as catalysts for change, indicating an opportunity present. They take risks and are open to new possibilities. They indicate an actual child or your own inner "child"—naive and innocent, learning. Sometimes they come into your life as messengers.

PAGE OF WANDS: (Earth of Fire) Seeks new directions for self-growth and development. Brings messages and telephone calls. Is fiery and daring; takes the tiger by the tail. Hot-tempered. Uninhibited. Frank and forthright in speech.

QUESTIONS TO ANSWER:

What new territories and ideas are you checking out? Who is calling you? Who is enthusiastic about your endeavors or looks up to you as a mature adult? What actions are you risking to take? What are you all fired up about?

SAMPLE AFFIRMATION:

"I am always growing and learning."

PAGE OF CUPS: (Earth of Water) Open to love and new relationships. Willing to take risks with love. Brings messages from your dreams or intuition. Emotionally dependent. In service to others.

QUESTIONS TO ANSWER:

Who depends on you emotionally? What does your intuition say to do? How can you serve others? Who offers unqualified, nonjudgmental love?

SAMPLE AFFIRMATION:

"I am willing to risk loving."

PAGE OF SWORDS: (Earth of Air) Seeks justice and truth. Cuts through depression and heavy, stormy thoughts. Takes risks with communications. Penetrating and cunning. Cuts through cloudy thought to get at the truth of the matter. Sometimes thoughtless, rash and spiteful.

QUESTIONS TO ANSWER:

What do you have to say? What fears must you face? What of significance have you just learned through the media? Who is trying to communicate with you?

SAMPLE AFFIRMATION:

"I face my fears and depressions and risk cutting through them."

PAGE OF PENTACLES: (Earth of Earth) Seeks knowledge, experience and new skills. Vision quest. Seeks guidance from the earth. Examines values. Risks money and security. Takes physical risks.

QUESTIONS TO ANSWER:

What new information are you gathering? What new possibilities do you contain within yourself? Who is bringing you financial information? Are you listening to the earth?

SAMPLE AFFIRMATION:

"I trust in the information my body gives me and am learning to hear how it speaks to me."

THE HISTORY
AND ORIGIN OF
THE TAROT

HISTORY

No one knows for sure where or when the Tarot first appeared. The earliest extant deck we have is the Visconti-Sforza deck, created for a marriage between the Italian Visconti and Sforza families. This was in approximately 1432, and the trumps seem to be already well developed at this time.

Cards were first mentioned in 1367 in legal documents prohibiting them in Bern, Switzerland, then in 1376 in Florence, Italy, where a game called *naibbe* (cards) was forbidden. They were permitted by the Code of Nuremburg in 1380, where they were categorized along with games of chance and gambling.

In 1392 it was recorded that three decks were painted for Charles VI of France by Jacquemin Gringonneur. There are seventeen cards in the Bibliotheque Nationale in Paris that could possibly be from these decks.

By the end of the 15th century, the Tarot de Marseilles had become popular in France and is still used today, both for obtaining answers to questions and for a game called *tarocchi*—a forerunner of bridge.

Playing cards in general seem to have originated in China and Korea in the 10th to 12th centuries A.D., based on the design of paper money. There appears to be no direct relationship between these cards and the Tarot.

In India, playing cards were possibly not used until after cards had first appeared in Europe. Their decks were round and had eight to ten suits of twelve cards each. It is interesting that the four-armed Hindu deity, Ardhanari, carried a cup, a sceptre, a sword and a ring (which was used for money or to indicate wealth), although these symbols are not those appearing on Indian playing cards.

Gypsies (who originated in India as attested by their language, an early form of Sanskrit) did not bring cards to the West, as is often assumed. The gypsies did not move into Europe until the 15th century, whereas cards were available from at least the 14th century. It is true that the gypsies picked up the use of playing cards quickly and perhaps helped spread their use, giving them the reputation of "fortune-telling" devices.

In the late 18th century came the French Revolution and Napoleonic France. Fortune-telling with Tarot cards became popular because of the uncertainty of the times. Etteilla and Madame Lenormand took full advantage, creating their own variations of the Tarot, which are still available. At that time the names of the trumps changed from their former Italian designations to the more common French ones used today.

The early 20th century saw the emergence of a whole new group of Tarot decks from England and America based on western occultism, the Jewish mystical tradition of the Kabbalah and correspondences with astrological symbolism. These included the Waite, Crowley, Case, and Zain decks. Since the 1960s the creation and production of Tarot decks has jumped radically, largely due to the work of Stuart Kaplan of U.S. Games Systems, Inc. His *Encyclopedia of the Tarot* chronicles in pictorial detail the development of Tarot, and his publishing company has made available a vast number of new decks and reproductions of old ones.

There has also been a tradition of self-published decks following personal interests and less widespread philosophies. Among these have been John Cooke's New Tarot for the Aquarian Age; the wiccan Pendragon Tarot; several feminist Tarots: Motherpeace, Amazon and Matriarchal; Bea Nettle's Mountain Dream Tarot; the Dakini Oracle; Oscar Ichazo's Arica Tarot; Morgan's Tarot; and the StarGate System. (Please let me know about other decks which are available.)

ORIGIN

The theories of the origin of the Tarot are much more complex than the history, which is based on substantiated records. Everyone has had their own opinions, none proved in any way, yet each theory has added its impact to the beliefs surrounding the cards, and even the design of them.

Court de Gebelin (1723–1787), a French cleric, linguist and occultist who searched for the "original language," was the first to publish a mystical significance of the Tarot. He believed they were of Egyptian origin, spread by the gypsies, and used in initiation rites into the mysteries of the Egyptian priesthood. This was prior to the discovery of the Rosetta Stone, when Egyptian hieroglyphics had not yet been deciphered. De Gebelin thought that the Tarot contained the story of the history and creation of the world and that the four suits represented the four orders of society: nobles and landholders, clergy, soldiers and commoners (mostly merchants and peasants).

Etteilla, a wig-maker and fortune-teller during the French Revolution and in Napoleonic France, had studied Pythagoras' description of reality in terms of arithmetical relationships. From this he determined that Thoth-Hermes was the originator of the Tarot. The Egyptian god Thoth was counselor to Osiris, scribe of the gods, measurer of time, inventor of numbers and the god of wisdom and magic.

Eliphas Levi (1810–1875) was a French priest who developed the theory of the relationship of the Tarot to the Jewish Kabbalah. He saw the Tarot as the key to the Kabbalah, the Bible and the Key of Solomon. He is best known for his statement, "The practical value of the Tarot is truly and above all marvelous. A prisoner devoid of books, had he only a Tarot of which he knew how to make use, could in a few years acquire a universal science, and converse with an unequalled doctrine and inexhaustible eloquence." He also developed the dialectic principle of numbers based on the Tetragrammaton, the holy name of God—Yod He Vau He—later expanded on by Papus.

Papus (1865–1916), French occult philosopher and physician, and author of *The Tarot of the Bohemians*, felt that the cards originated in Egypt, where they represented initiation tests beneath the pyramids. When the temples of the mysteries were faced with destruction, the hierophant decided that virtue is a fragile thing, and therefore it was best to confide their secrets to vice. Vice would never fail completely. And so the secrets were engraved upon cards and fashioned into a game. "The gypsy . . . has given us the key which enables us to explain all the symbolism of the ages . . . In it, where a man of the people sees only the key to an obscure tradition [are] discovered the mysterious links which unite God, the Universe and Man."

MacGregor Mathers was leader of the Order of the Golden Dawn, founded in 1886 by Dr. Wynn Westcott, Dr. Woodford and Dr. Woodman when they found a text of an ancient Rosicrucian order in a second-hand bookstore. The O.G.D. had a hierarchy which was ascended through elaborate rituals and an emphasis on visualization using the Tarot and the kabbalistic Tree of Life. The order existed only until 1900, yet has been a major influence on contemporary Tarot and western occultism. Among its members and close associates were: W.B. Yeats, Dion Fortune, Sax Rohmer, Florence Farr, Maude Gonne (Irish revolutionary), Arthur Machen, Algernon Blackwood, Charles Williams (author of *The Greater Trumps*), Evelyn Underhill, Israel Regardie, A.E. Waite, Aleister Crowley, A.E., and later, Paul Foster Case.

A.E. Waite (1857–1942) was an English Christian occult philosopher and member of the order of the Golden Dawn. He felt that the symbols of the Tarot were deliberately misleading in order to protect the secrets contained therein. So he set about to correct the misinformation, which included the transposing of the Strength and Justice cards, although he did leave other symbols deliberately misleading. "The true Tarot is symbolism; it speaks no other language and offers no other signs. Given the inward meanings of its emblems, they do become a kind of alphabet which is capable of indefinite combinations and makes true sense in all."

Aleister Crowley (1875–1947) was also a member of the Order of the Golden Dawn but broke away for form his own order, the Ordo Templi Orientis (O.T.O.). Crowley felt that the origin of the Tarot was quite irrelevant. He said we had been given a symbolic map by superiors whose mental processes were, or are, pertaining to a higher dimension. And "in order to understand any card, one must identify oneself with it completely for the moment."

Paul Foster Case (1884–1954) began the Builders of the Adytum in California and developed an excellent Tarot correspondence course. He felt that the Tarot was created by philosophers in the 11th century, in Fez, Morocco, after the burning of the libraries in Alexandria, so that the wisdom of the world could never again be so destroyed. His course involves meditations and visualizations using the correspondences of Tarot with astrology, number, color, sound and the Tree of Life.

Others feel that the Tarot could have been brought to Europe by the Knights Templar, an ascetic military order founded about 1188 A.D. by Hugh de Payens to protect pilgrims and guard the routes to the Holy Land. They, in fact, became quite oriental in their tastes and introduced Europe to other eastern arts and philosophies.

E. S. Taylor, in *The History of Playing Cards* (1865), presents evidence for the Tarot having first arrived in Spain in the early 1300s, which he substantiates by their early name of *naypes* or *naib*, an Arabic term for "deputy." Idries Shah in *The Sufis* says that "the material from which the Tarot cards were copied is still extant. It is 'deputy' or substitute material forming an allegory of the teachings of a Sufi master about certain cosmic influences upon humanity." Thus the cards could have entered Spain or even Italy with the Muslim Moors (Saracens) and there been taught to the Jewish mystics who recognized their source as the same as that of the Kabbalah. Fez, Morocco, whose university was at the time the seat of a blend of Egyptian, Gnostic, Muslim and Hebrew knowledge, is the likely source of such a book.

C.C. Zain (Elbert Benjamine) was originator of the Brotherhood of Light. He felt that the Tarot came from the *Atma Bodha*, or *Book of Soul Knowledge*, known in both India and Egypt. The symbols used in his deck, the Egyptian Tarot, supposedly came from a description by Iamblichus, a Neo-Platonist of the 4th century A.D.

P.D. Ouspensky (1878–1947) said that the possible inventor of the Tarot was Raymond Lully, a 13th-century philosopher and alchemist who wrote about a "philosophical machine" of which one could ask questions and receive answers. Ouspensky felt the Tarot to be a synopsis of all hermetic sciences, which are a system for the psychological study of man in his relationship to the spirit and the physical.

John Cooke, whose New Tarot for the Aquarian Age (or Book of T) was dictated through a Ouija Board in 1962 and 1963, felt that the Tarot were not cards but mighty Egyptian books embodying cosmic principles. He ascribed authorship to Thoth, who by tradition came from Atlantis about 10,000 B.C. and served for half a "Great Year" (approximately 12,000 years—half the 24,000-year cycle of the procession of the equinoxes). His New T is to take us through the next half-cycle. "The Tarot symbols are archetypal symbols of man's unconscious and represent the unfoldment of his unconscious for any given time period." According to Cooke, Madame Blavatsky claimed that the original Tarots were stored in Mesopotamia on cylinder seals of copper and would one day be found.

Vicki Noble, co-designer with Karen Vogel of the Motherpeace Tarot, sees the Tarot as emerging to teach the hidden unwritten mysteries of matriarchal culture. "Just as Noah's Ark [Arca] was a craft for preserving life, so the Arcana in Tarot are a vessel for salvaging spiritual wisdom from the period when the Goddess was worshipped," says Noble in *Motherpeace: A Way to the Goddess through Myth, Art and Tarot.*

Billie Potts, author of *A New Woman's Tarot*, feels that the Tarot "formed a pattern of keys that initiated one into the rites of Goddess worship . . . [it] was devised as an underground book to keep the faith alive, namely the persecuted faith of the Old Religion of the Goddess rite."

Barbara Walker, in *The Women's Encyclopedia of Myths and Secrets*, argues for there being a connection between the Aryan earth goddess Tara (a manifestation of Kali) and the Tarot. She is possibly the source of the Latin Terra Mater and the Celtic Tara. In Tibet a painted dice board called "the twenty-one Taras" was used for divining. This board is similar to that used by Tantric Buddhists for a spiritual teaching aid called the Game of Rebirth. Walker feels that the Tarot could picture symbolic death and reunion with the Goddess Kali herself.

And Pietropaulo de San Chirico said, "I am of the opinion that none of these found the cards, but that the cards found them."

There have also been several attempts to determine the origin of the Tarot through an examination of its name. Some of the clues we have are:

*Tarotee—the name of the classic pattern on the reverse side of the cards.

*Tares—a small dot border on old cards.

*River Taro—in Northern Italy. Merchants could have gotten the ideas for cards in India and developed them when they returned to this area of Italy.

*Tar—Road; Ro—King or Royal. From the Egyptian, meaning "Royal Road."

*Taru—Hindu word for cards.

*Torah—first five books of the Old Testament, meaning "divine law."

*Rota—Sanskrit root meaning "wheel," as in "Wheel of Life."

*Ator—a form of the name of the Goddess Hathor, one of the oldest of the Egyptian deities—often synonomous with Isis and Nuit.

*Turuq—Arabic, meaning "four ways" and possibly referring to the four elements and the four suits.

*Tao (Chinese) and Tariqa (Arabic)—both meaning "The Way."

The Grail legends point up interesting parallels to the structure of the Tarot, having four important symbols which are similar to the four suits:

CUPS—The Grail itself, the cup used at the Last Supper.
SWORDS—The "sword of spirit" that belongs to King David, which some say was also the sword Excalibur.
WANDS—The Lance of Longinus, which pierced Christ's side.
PENTACLES—The stone platter used at the Last Supper.

A case has also been made by Jessie Weston in *From Ritual to Romance* for the similarity between the Grail objects and the treasures of the *Tuatha de Danan* (People of the Goddess Danu of ancient Ireland). Their treasures were: The Cauldron of Regeneration which could never be empty, the Sword of Nuada, the Spear of Lug, the Stone of Sovereignty belonging to Fal.

And these symbols are again very similar to those held by the Hindu God Ardhanari: a cup, a sword, a scepter, a ring.

Barbara Walker notes in *The Women's Encyclopedia of Myths and Secrets* that the Greek Goddess "Nemesis" (Fate) carried a cup, an apple wand, a wheel and a sword.

The very mystery of the origin of the Tarot adds to its power. A good case can be made that it was simply a medieval invention used to describe life during the middle ages. The four suits described the four classes: aristocracy (Swords), clergy (Cups), merchants (Pentacles) and common folk (Wands).

Yet, with the wealth of study that can be made of the cards, the surprises and discoveries that can be made through that study, and the correspondences with so many other mystical traditions and hidden beliefs, I choose to believe that the Tarot didn't just happen by accident. The Tarot is a map, deliberately drawn to aid each of us who stumbles upon this path. Who first drew this map, and when and where, is another story, for another day.

ADDITIONAL READING:

The Encyclopedia of Tarot. Stuart Kaplan. New York: U.S. Games Systems, 1978.

The Devil's Picturebook. Paul Huson. New York: Putnam, 1971.

The Tarot. Richard Cavendish. New York: Harper & Row, 1975.

TABLES OF CORRESPONDENCES

The most completely thought-out system of metaphysical correspondences I have found is that of the Order of the Golden Dawn, developed by Mathers and further evolved by Aleister Crowley, A.E. Waite, Dion Fortune, Paul Foster Case and the B.O.T.A. It is followed by the majority of Tarot commentators such as Eden Gray and Rachel Pollack.

The Golden Dawn correspondence give us a Tarot capable of being related (synchronized) to astrological signs and planets, sound, color scales, gems, perfumes, incenses, herbs and drugs, Hebrew letters, the kabbalistic Tree of Life, mythologies, angels and numbers. In meditating on a card it is possible to involve all your senses through these means. Therefore, whenever correspondences are appropriate I will refer to those of the Golden Dawn, which are given, along with some variations, in this appendix. It should be noted that these correspondences are works in progress or working theories that Crowley, Case, Waite and others continued to experiment with themselves. Therefore, you should consider these correspondences only as starting points for your own work. The areas that I feel are in the most need of work are those of herbs and perfumes. Each geographic locale has its own native herbs and plants that probably can be placed on the Tree of Life and associated with the Major Arcana. Also many of the perfumes are those coming from endangered species, such as ambergris from whales. It is up to us to find substitutes that will not further endanger the lives of any beings.

If you have been working with another system with which you feel comfortable, simply adapt and write in your own correspondences. Always go with what feels right to you.

TABLE OF CORRESPONDENCES

NO	CARD	HEBREW LETTER	LETTER MEANING	ASTRO-LOGICAL	MUSICAL NOTE	COLOR
0	FOOL	Aleph	Ox	Uranus	E	Pale Yellow
1	MAGICIAN	Beth	House	Mercury	E	Yellow
2	HIGH PRIESTESS	Gimel	Camel	Moon	G#	Blue
3	EMPRESS	Daleth	Door	Venus	F#	Emerald Green
4	EMPEROR	Heh	Window	Aries	C	Scarlet Red
5	HIEROPHANT	Vau	Nail or Hook	Taurus	C#	Red Orange
6	LOVERS	Zain	Sword	Gemini	D	Orange
7	CHARIOT	Cheth	Fench	Cancer	D	Orange-Yellow
8	STRENGTH	Teth	Serpent	Leo	E	Yellow
9	HERMIT	Yod	Hand (open)	Virgo	F	Yellow-Green
10	WHEEL OF FORTUNE	Kaph	Hand (closed)	Jupiter	A#	Royal Violet
11	JUSTICE	Lamed	Ox Goad	Libra	F#	Emerald Green
12	HANGED MAN	Mem	Water	Neptune	G#	Deep Blue
13	DEATH	Nun	Fish	Scorpio	G	Blue-Green
14	TEMPERANCE	Samekh	Prop	Sagittarius	G#	Blue
15	DEVIL	Ayin	Eye	Capricorn	A	Indigo
16	TOWER	Peh	Mouth	Mars	C	Scarlet Red
17	STAR	Tzaddi	Fish-hook	Aquarius	A#	Violet
18	MOON	Qoph	Back of Head	Pisces	B	Violet-Red
19	SUN	Resh	Head	Sun	D	Orange
20	JUDGMENT	Shin	Tooth	Pluto	C	Red
21	WORLD	Tau	Mark	Saturn	A	Blue-Violet

EM	ANIMAL	PLANT	MAGICAL WEAPON	PERFUME
ourmaline, Turquoise	Eagle, Man, Butterfly	Aspen, Grapes Peppermint	Dagger & Fan	Galbanum
Tiger Eye, Citrine, Fire Opal, Agate	Ibis, Ape, Swallow	Marjoram, Palm, Vervain (Cerebral Excitants)	Wand, Caduceus	Mastic, Mace, Storax
Moonstone Pearl	Dog	Almond, Pomegranate, Hazel, Moonwort (Emmendgogues)	Bow & Arrow	Camphor, Aloes, Menstrual Blood
Emerald, Rose Quartz	Sparrow, Dove, Swan	Corn, Myrtle, Rose, Clover, Cypress (Aphrodisiacs)	Girdle or Belt	Sandalwood, Myrtle, Rose, Sage
Ruby	Ram, Owl	Oak, Tiger Lily, Geranium	Horns, the Burin	Dragon's Blood
Topaz Carnelian, Lapis Lazuli	Bull	Mallow, Sugar Cane	Labor of Preparation	Storax
Alexandrite, Agate	Magpie	Orchid, Rush, LSD	Tripod	Wormwood
Amber, Chalcedony	Sphinx, Crab, Turtle	Lotus, Olive, Watercress	Fiery Furnace	Onycha
Cat's Eye, Topaz, Chrysolite	Lion	Sunflower (Carminatives)	Discipline	Olibanum
Peridot, Bloodstone	Rhinoceros, Dog	Snowdrop, Aspen, Narcissus (Anaphrodisiacs)	Wand & Lamp	Narcissus, Mace
Sapphire, Amethyst, Lapis	Eagle, Sphinx	Hyssop, Oak, Poplar, Coca	Scepter	Saffron, Cedar
Emerald, Coral, Jade	Elephant, Crane	Aloe, Tobacco	Cross of Equilibrium	Olibanum, Galbanum
Beryl, Aquamarine	Snake, Eagle, Scorpion	Lotus, Ash, Water Plants, Fermented Grapes (Purges)	Cup & Cross	Myrrh, Onycha
Snakestone, Bloodstone	Wolf, Beetle, Crayfish	Cactus, Yew, Aspen, Myrtle	Evil Eye, Pain of Obligation	Benzoin, Opoponax, Assafoetida
Jacinth, Amethyst	Horse, Dog, Centaur	Rush	Arrows	Aloes
Black Diamond, Jet, Obsidian	Goat, Ass	Hemp & Marijuana Thistle, Fig, Orchis Root	Evil Eye, Lamp	Civet, Musk, Nutmeg
Ruby, Garnet	Bear, Wolf, Horse	Absinthe, Rue, Tobacco	Two-edged Sword	Dragon's Blood, Pepper
Turquoise, Rock Crystal	Peacock, Man, Eagle	Silver Fir, Olive, Coconut (Diuretics)	Censer	Galbanum
Milk Opal, Moonstone, Pearl	Dolphin, Fish, Scarab	Poppy, Hazel, Opium, Nettle (Narcotics)	Magic Mirror	Ambergris
Diamond, Heliotrope	Sparrowhawk, Lion	Laurel, Sunflower, Heliotrope	Bow & Arrow, Spear	Olibanum, Cinnamon, Cinnabar
Fire Opal, Malachite	Lion	Hibiscus, Red Poppy (Nitrates)	Wand, Lamp	Olibanum
Onyx, Jet, Lapis Lazuli, Black Pearl	Crocodile, Dragon	Cypress, Hellebore, Yew, Nightshade	Sickle	Frankincense, Assafoetida, Sulphur

SELECTED BIBLIOGRAPHY

Since there exist several extensive bibliograhies of the Tarot, I will not duplicate those efforts. Some of the following books are recommended in the text; others influenced the development of this book.

INTERPRETATIONS AND SPREADS

Arrien, Angeles. *The Tarot Workbook*. Sonoma, CA: Arcus Publishing Co., 1984.

Butler, Bill. *Dictionary of the Tarot*. New York: Schocken Books, 1975.

Douglas, Alfred. *The Tarot: The Origins, Meaning and Uses of the Cards*. Baltimore: Penguin Books, 1973.

Fairfield, Gail. *Choice-Centered Tarot*. Self-Published, 1982. Available from Choice-Centered Astrology and Tarot, P.O. Box 31816, Seattle, WA 98103.

Gearhart, Sally. *A Feminist Tarot: A Guide To Intrapersonal Communication*. Persephone Press, 1977. P.O. Box 7222, Watertown, MA 02172.

Gray, Eden. *Mastering the Tarot: Basic Lessons in an Ancient Mystic Art*. New York: New American Library, 1971.

Noble, Vicki. *Motherpeace: A Way to the Goddess through Myth, Art and Tarot*. San Francisco: Harper and Row, 1983.

Pollack, Rachel. *Seventy-Eight Degrees of Wisdom: A Book of Tarot*. Wellingborough, Northamptonshire: The Aquarian Press. Part 1: *The Major Arcana*, 1980. Part 2: *The Minor Arcana and Readings*, 1983.

Potts, Billie. *A New Women's Tarot*. Elf and Dragons Press, 1978. P.O. Box 609, Woodstock, NY 12498.

HISTORY AND ORIGIN OF THE TAROT

Cavendish, Richard. *The Tarot*. New York: Harper and Row, 1975.

Huson, Paul. *The Devil's Picturebook: The Compleat Guide to Tarot Cards*. New York: Putnam, 1971.

Kaplan, Stuart. *The Encyclopedia of Tarot*. New York: U.S. Games Systems, 1978.

Walker, Barbara G. *The Women's Encyclopedia of Myths and Secrets*. San Francisco: Harper and Row, 1983.

See also: Douglas, above.

KABBALA, ALCHEMY, MEDITATION AND TAROT

Case, Paul Foster. *The Tarot: A Key to the Wisdom of the Ages*. Richmond, VA: Macoy Publishing, 1947.

_____. *The Book of Tokens: 22 Meditations on The Ageless Wisdom*. Builders of the Adytum, 1934. 5105 North Figueroa St., Los Angeles, CA 90042.

Crowley, Aleister (The Master Therion). *The Book of Thoth: An Interpretation of the Tarot*. New York: Samuel Weiser, 1974.

Fortune, Dion. *The Mystical Qabalah*. London: Ernest Benn, 1957.

Gray, William G. *Magical Ritual Methods*. New York: Samuel Weiser, 1969.

Hoeller, Stephan A. *The Royal Road: A Manual of Kabalistic Meditations on the Tarot*. Wheaton, IL: The Theosophical Publishing House, 1975.

Knight, Gareth. *A Practical Guide to Qabalistic Symbolism*. (Volumes 1 and 2 in one edition) New York: Samuel Weiser, 1978.

Roberts, Richard and Joseph Campbell. *Tarot Revelations*. San Francisco: Richard Roberts, 1979.

Steinbrecher, Edwin C. *The Inner Guide Meditation*. Santa Fe, NM: Blue Feather Press, 1978.

Wang, Robert. *An Introduction to the Golden Dawn Tarot*. New York: Samuel Weiser, 1978.

_____, *The Qabalistic Tarot: A Textbook of Mystical Philosophy*. York Beach, ME: Samuel Weiser, 1983.

NUMEROLOGY AND TAROT

Hasbrouck, Muriel Bruce. *The Pursuit of Destiny*. New York: Destiny Books, 1976.

Javane, Faith and Dusty Bunker. *Numerology and the Divine Triangle*. Rockport, MA: Para Research, 1979.

MYTHOLOGY, SYMBOLISM AND TAROT

Cooper, J. C. *Symbolism: The Universal Language*. Wellingborough, Northamptonshire: The Aquarian Press, 1982.

Cirlot, J. E. *A Dictionary of Symbols*. Trans. by Jack Sage. New York: Philosophical Library, 1962.

Graves, Robert. *The White Goddess*. New York: Farrar, Straus and Giroux, 1966.

Harding, M. Esther. *Woman's Mysteries, Ancient and Modern: A Psychological Interpretation of the Feminine Principle as Portrayed in Myth, Story and Dreams*. New York: Harper and Row, 1980.

Nichols, Sallie. *Jung and Tarot: An Archetypal Journey*. New York: Samuel Weiser, 1980.

Weston, Jessie. *From Ritual to Romance*. New York: Anchor Books, 1957.

See also: Walker, under History.

ADDITIONAL KEYS TO TAROT

Arrien, Angeles and Jim Wanless. *The Wheel of Tarot: A New Revolution*. Sonoma, CA: Arcus Publishing, forthcoming.

Balin, Peter. *The Flight of the Feathered Serpent*. Venice, CA: Wisdom Garden Books, 1978.

Blakely, John D., *The Mystical Tower of the Tarot*. London: Robinson and Watkins, 1974.

Denning, Melita and Osborne Phillips. *The Magick of the Tarot*. St. Paul, MN: Llewellyn, 1983.

Papus. *The Tarot of the Bohemians: The Most Ancient Book in the World: For the Use of Initiates*. Trans. by A. P. Morton. No. Hollywood: Wilshire Book Co., 1973.

Raine, Kathleen. *Yeats, the Tarot and the Golden Dawn*. Dublin, Ireland: Dolmen Press, 1976.

Williams, Charles. *The Greater Trumps*. New York: Farrar, Straus and Giroux, 1950.

JOURNAL WRITING

Field, Joanna. *A Life of One's Own*. Los Angeles: J. P. Tarcher, 1981.

Rainer, Tristine. *The New Diary: How to Use a Journal for Self-Guidance and Expanded Creativity*. Los Angeles: J. P. Tarcher, 1978.

PENDULUMS AND CRYSTALS

Crow, W. B. *Precious Stones: Their Occult Power and Hidden Significance*. London: The Aquarian Press, 1968.

Harner, Michael. *The Way of the Shaman: A Guide to Power and Healing*. New York: Harper and Row, 1980.

Hoffman, Enid. *Huna: A Beginner's Guide*. Rockport, MA: Para Research, 1976.

Lorusso, Julia and Joel Glick. *Healing Stoned: The Therapeutic Use of Gems and Minerals*. Brotherhood of Life, 1981. 110 Dartmouth, SE, Albuquerque, NM 87106.

Morris, Freda. *Self-Hypnosis in Two Days*. New York: E. P. Dutton, 1974.

ASTROLOGY

Greene, Liz. *Saturn: A New Look at an Old Devil*. New York: Samuel Weiser, 1976.

Hickey, Isabel M. *Astrology: A Cosmic Science*. Self-Published, 1970. 35 Maple Street, Watertown, MA 02172.

Jocelyn, John. *Meditations on the Signs of the Zodiac*. Blauvelt, NY: Multimedia Publishing Corp., 1970.

ACTIVE IMAGINATION AND CREATIVE VISUALIZATION

Gawain, Shakti. *Creative Visualization*. Mill Valley, CA: Whatever Publishing, 1978.

Mariechild, Diane. *Mother Wit: A Feminist Guide to Psychic Development: Exercises for Healing, Growth and Spiritual Awareness*. Trumansburg, New York: The Crossing Press, 1981.

Masters, Robert and Jean Houston. *Mind Games*. New York: Dell Publishing, 1972.

Samuels, Mike and Hal Bennett. *Spirit Guides: Access to Inner Worlds*. New York/Berkeley: Random House/Bookworks, 1974.

Starhawk. *The Spiral Dance: A Rebirth of the Ancient Religion of the Great Goddess*. New York: Harper and Row, 1979.

Vaughan, Frances E. *Awakening Intuition*. Garden City, NY: Anchor Press/Doubleday, 1979.

ON JUNG'S THEORY OF SYNCHRONICITY

Bolen, Jean Shinoda. *The Tao of Psychology: Synchronicity and the Self*. New York: Harper and Row, 1982.

Jung, Carl G. "Foreword" in *The I Ching or Book of Changes*. Trans. by Richard Wilhelm. London: Routledge and Kegan Paul, 1950.

Progoff, Ira. *Jung, Synchronicity and Human Destiny: Noncausal Dimensions of Human Experience*. New York: Dell/Delta, 1973.

PROSPERITY, PLANNING AND DESIGN

Hanks, Kurt, et al. *Design Yourself!* Los Altos, CA: William Kaufmann, 1977.

Koberg, Don and Jim Bagnall. *The Universal Traveler: A Soft-Systems Guide to: Creativity, Problem-Solving and the Process of Reaching Goals*. Los Altos, CA: William Kaufmann, 1973.

Ross, Ruth. *Prospering Woman: A Complete Guide to Achieving the Full, Abundant Life*. Mill Valley, CA; Whatever Publishing, 1982.

Sher, Barbara. *Wishcraft: How to Get What You Really Want*. New York, NY: Ballantine Books, 1979.

ADDITIONAL RESOURCES

Astrological Charts: Send birthdate, exact time of birth, and birthplace to Astro Computing Service, P.O. Box 16297, San Diego, CA 92116. (Approximately $3.00)

Music for guided visualizations, relaxation and meditation: *Halpern Sounds*. 1775 Old Country Road #9, Belmont, CA 94002.

Tarot Cards: The most extensive listing, carrying most of the cards mentioned in this book and many European cards, is *The Best of Cards Catalog*, U. S. Games Systems, Inc., 38 East 32nd Street, New York, NY 10016. (Send $2.00)

Tarot Correspondence Course: Builders of the Adytum, founded by Paul Foster Case, a California non-profit corporation, teaching the Western Mystery School tradition, "whose Tarot Keys are used for meditation, self-transmutation and spiritual growth." Write for more information to: Builders of the Adytum, 5101 North Figueroa Street, Los Angeles, CA 90042.

Choice-Centered Tarot Correspondence Course: Consists of six one-hour lectures on cassette tapes and a workbook which contains illustrations for the taped lectures and homework questions, taught by Gail Fairfield. Write for more information to: Gail Fairfield, P. O. Box 31816, Seattle, WA 98103.

Tarot News: Up-to-date information on new Tarot decks, book reviews, the Annual Tarot Symposium, Tarot and education, articles, Tarot-inspired art and poetry, new spreads and layouts and much more. Contributions of articles, artwork and news welcome. Write for information to: Gary Ross, editor, *The Tarot Network News*, 2860 California Street, San Francisco, CA 94115.

The Annual Tarot Symposium: Held every year for the last five years in San Francisco. One or two days of lectures, slide presentations, workshops, ritual, artwork and crafts. For more information write: Gary Ross, 2860 California Street, San Francisco, CA 94115.

CRITICAL RAVES FOR MARY K. GREER'S *TAROT FOR YOUR SELF*

"Undoubtedly the best book on Tarot that has appeared in 25 years—possibly forever."
SHE TOTEM

"The most thorough tarot book that I have ever read."
BEEF
(Quarterly of Art, Music and Culture)

"Exceptional."
PSYCHIC GUIDE MAGAZINE

"A book not meant to be read in the traditional sense. It is meant to be experienced."
NEW REALITIES MAGAZINE

"Tarot is carefully probed, explained, and unfolded in this amazing workbook."
MAGICAL BLEND MAGAZINE

"One of the most holistic and in-depth books on the tarot I've seen."
HARVEST

"A very different book and very powerful. I can't do this book justice. This book is positive and powerful."
THESMOPHORIA

Thoroughness seems to be the watermark of this book."
THE WISE WOMAN

"Lots of new ideas to work with and ways of using the tarot for thinking, meditation, reading, and as a general study."
PEGASUS

"Absolutely lovely, a wonderful idea. I'm very impressed and think it's just what has been needed."
VICKI NOBLE,
co-creator of *Motherpeace Tarot*

"A delight and a treasure. A MUST for every Tarot student and professional. I wish I'd written it!"
GAIL FAIRFIELD,
author of *Choice-Centered Tarot*

"Your book is wonderful and I plan on using it in my teaching."
FFIONA MORGAN,
creator of *Daughters of the Moon Tarot*

"One of the best Tarot self-teach books I have seen."
RUTH WEST, creator of *Thea Tarot*

"So useful, playful, thorough, and exactly what I've wanted."
GINA COVINA,
author of *City of Hermits*

"I'm writing to say how much I like TAROT FOR YOUR SELF!"
DIANE WAKOSKI, Poet